Violence and the World's Religious Traditions

Violence and the World's Religious Traditions

An Introduction

Edited by

MARK JUERGENSMEYER,

MARGO KITTS, AND

MICHAEL JERRYSON

OXFORD
UNIVERSITY PRESS

OXFORD
UNIVERSITY PRESS

Oxford University Press is a department of the University of Oxford.
It furthers the University's objective of excellence in research, scholarship,
and education by publishing worldwide. Oxford is a registered trade mark of
Oxford University Press in the UK and certain other countries.

Published in the United States of America by Oxford University Press
198 Madison Avenue, New York, NY 10016, United States of America.

© Oxford University Press 2017

The essays in this volume were originally published in *The Oxford Handbook of Religion and* Violence (2013).

Library of Congress Cataloging-in-Publication Data
Names: Juergensmeyer, Mark. editor. | Kitts, Margo, date. editor. |
Jerryson, Michael K., editor.
Title: Violence and the world's religious traditions : an introduction /
edited by Mark Juergensmeyer, Margo Kitts, and Michael Jerryson.
Description: New York : Oxford University Press, 2017. |
Includes bibliographical references and index.
Identifiers: LCCN 2016033664 (print) | LCCN 2016035675 (ebook) |
ISBN 9780190649661 (paperback) | ISBN 9780190649654 (cloth) |
. ISBN 9780190649678 (updf) | ISBN 9780190649685 (epub)
Subjects: LCSH: Violence—Religious aspects. | BISAC: RELIGION / Comparative
Religion. | RELIGION / Religion, Politics & State. | SOCIAL SCIENCE /
Violence in Society.
Classification: LCC BL65.V55 .V57 2017 (print) | LCC BL65.V55 (ebook) |
DDC 201/.76332—dc23
LC record available at https://lccn.loc.gov/2016033664

1 3 5 7 9 8 6 4 2
Paperback printed by WebCom, Inc., Canada
Hardback printed by Bridgeport National Bindery, Inc., United States of America

Contents

*Violence and the World's
Religious Traditions*

Introduction

THE ENDURING RELATIONSHIP
OF RELIGION AND VIOLENCE

Mark Juergensmeyer, Margo Kitts, and Michael Jerryson

THE DARK ATTRACTION between religion and violence is endemic to religious traditions. It pervades their images and practices, from sacred swords to mythic conquests, from acts of sacrifice to holy wars. Though much has been written about particular forms of violence related to religion, such as sacrificial rites and militant martyrdom, there have been few efforts to survey the phenomena in all of the world's major religious traditions, historically and in the present, viewing the subject from personal as well as social dimensions, and covering both literary themes and political conflicts.

This compact one-volume collection of essays provides such an overview. Each of the essays explores the ways in which violence is justified in the literary and theological foundation of the tradition, how it is used symbolically and in ritual practice, and how social acts of vengeance and warfare have been justified by religious ideas. The essays show how acts of destruction in the name of God or the gods of religion have been rooted in historical and literary contexts from early times to the present.

Contemporary acts of violence related to religion are profuse. Since the end of the Cold War, violence in the name of religion has erupted on nearly every continent, and many of its perpetrators have claimed divine justification for their actions. Although no longer novel, such violence and the adulation of its prophets continue to confound scholars, journalists, policy-makers, and members of the general public. Some of them have argued that these forms of violence are not really religious—they are symptomatic of something else and thus constitute an anomaly, a perversion of foundational religious teachings. Yet it is precisely the foundational religious teachings that many of its perpetrators claim sanctify violence. Others cite bloody legends of martyrs and heroes and argue that religions, or some of them, are violent at the core, their leaders masterminds of criminal behavior. Yet the essays here show that there are more nuanced interpretations of the presence of violence in so many different traditions.

Is violence, then, the rare exception in religious traditions or is it one of the rules? Adherents to most religious traditions almost universally regard their own faith as pacific, as one that abhors violence and proclaims reconciliation among foes. Perhaps they are right, since the overwhelming message of scriptural writings and prophetic voices is that of love, peace, and harmony. And yet both historians and keen observers also see another side. They point to the legends of war, sacrifice, and martyrdom that cling to the histories of all the great religious traditions. The disconnection between these two points of view raises some profound questions: Is violence peripheral to the religious imagination or at its core? Is it religion that promotes violence, or some other social or natural factor? Is religion even distinguishable from those factors? Some argue that the great global religious traditions, because of their long histories of intertwining clerical authority with political powers, are more inclined to violence than are local ones. Yet sources for local religions, collected often at the crossroads between tradition and modernity, also report many forms of ritualized violence, such as assault sorceries, martial initiations, and prebattle sacrifices. Thus, for scholars of the global and the local, the question looms: what, why, and how deep is the link between religion and violence?

As the scholars included here explore the answers to this question, they have to deal with semantic complications. *Religion* and *violence* are both ambiguous terms. The search for a suitable definition of religion has exercised the scholarly imagination for centuries, luring psychologists, sociologists, anthropologists, theologians, philosophers, ethologists, and others into debates over its meaning. Must a religion be centered on supernatural beings? Does the term refer to social behavior or private? Is dogma or praxis the key to its essence? Is it a philosophical system or a poetic structure, a matter of art? Violence, too, is not an easy thing to identify. Immediate bodily harm, verbal assault, social manipulations, cultural destruction, injurious magic, political oppression—the range of ways of thinking about violence is enormous. From whose perspective and at what point is an act to be deemed violent? What act cannot be construed as violent in some way? For instance, are we talking only about war and genocide or about psychological coercion, social restrictions, and binding categorizations as well?

The scholars represented here have wrestled with these issues and many more. Their collective work reflects the complex and contested meanings of both *religion* and *violence*. While the contributors do not operate with a single definition for either term, they use these words in a manner that illuminates relationships and deepens the understanding of particular phenomena. In this book we have tried to avoid the phrase "religious violence," since it can be interpreted as saying that religion causes violence. Instead, we discuss "religion and violence," the relationship between the two that is often more frequent than the peaceful upholders of the traditions would like.

These essays are one part of a larger publication project, *The Oxford Handbook of Religion and Violence,* which addresses major dimensions of the topic: overviews of major *religious traditions*, which are included here; *patterns and themes* relating to religious violence, such as sacrifice and martyrdom, which are explored in crossdisciplinary or regional analyses; major *analytic approaches*, from literary analyses to social scientific studies, which are surveyed with an eye toward showing the diversity of analytic perspectives; and *new directions* in theory and analysis related to religion and violence, which provide novel insights into the understanding of this important field of studies.[1] In its entirety, the *Handbook* forges new paths in the analysis of religion and violence, anticipating the way this field of studies will continue to evolve. The essays here, taken from the first part of the *Handbook*, provide the groundwork for understanding the many dimensions of religion and violence that scholars explore.

This book provides overviews of Hindu, Buddhist, Chinese, Sikh, Jewish, Christian, Islamic, African, and Pacific Island religious traditions as they have engaged with violence. While the ideas and adherents of most of these traditions are spread out throughout the globe, they are anchored in distinctive histories and cultures that set them apart from one another. For instance, Jewish, Hindu, Chinese, and Buddhist traditions draw from respective sets of sources that are thousands of years old. Christianity and Islam are more recent, and the Sikh tradition emerged in the 1600s as one of the youngest of the global religions. Some traditions, such as Christianity, Buddhism, and Islam, are united by core beliefs and ideological frameworks; others, such as Hindu, Jewish, Chinese, African, and Pacific Island traditions, tend to be rooted in particular places and are linked with specific communities and social systems. The traditional religious communities differ also in size; Islamic, Hindu, Christian, and Buddhist traditions have over one billion adherents each, while the numbers of Jewish, Sikh, and Pacific Islander followers are only in the millions. Together, however, these traditions influence over six and a half billion people around the world. The histories of their relationship to violence are a part of the fabric of global history.

Each of the essays in this book introduces readers to the diversity within the religious tradition under consideration. Within Christianity, for instance, the Protestant and Catholic histories of violence distinctively differ. In the Hindu traditions, devotees of Vishnu (Vaishnavites) have one theology and history, devotees of Shiva (Shaivites) another, and the communities related to the earlier Brahmanical and Vedic traditions in India yet another. Differences also emerge between theological pronouncements in scripture and the actual instances of violence in society. In some cases, sacred texts do not just pronounce but describe forms of violence such as sacrifice and warfare; these accounts are found in the Jewish Torah, the Qur'anic surahs, the Buddhist sutras, the Christian gospels, and the Hindu epics. Violence is also embedded in religious symbols. The sword of the Buddhist bodhisattva Manjushri, for instance, symbolizes the cutting away of illusion; the cross that represents Jesus's persecution and death signifies the atonement of Christians from sin; the warlike tattoos of the Chinese martial gods are believed by adherents to invigorate warriors. The essays here review these theological and symbolic connections to violence and their historical and social manifestations, including warfare, torture, ritual, and suicide. Through a historical lens, the contributors, intimate with the religious traditions, provide intricate perspectives on the various ways each religious tradition is linked with violence.

The essay on Hindu traditions, by Veena Das, sets out the complex dynamic of religious attitude and violent practice as represented in the history of Indian ideology and poetics, focusing on ambivalent nuances in reports of animal (and human) sacrifice and in gendered violence. The essay on Buddhism, by Michael Jerryson, explores the paradox of irenic abstractions about Buddhist nonviolence versus culturally embedded customs prescribing acts of coercion and self-immolation; both are represented in Buddhist texts and social realities. By looking at the exception to the rule, Jerryson isolates key doctrinal passages that allow for violence and their historical physical manifestations. Regarding religion in China, Meir Shahar points out that the category of religion eludes traditional

Chinese thinking; yet, despite the periods of harmony among official Buddhism, Daoism, and Confucianism, Shahar observes the historical reverence for martial gods and practices of religiously sanctioned human sacrifice and self-mortification. Cynthia Keppley Mahmood places the Sikh tradition in the context of the shifting sands of India's religious history; she describes the reverence for certain Sikh gurus as being associated with martyrdom and violence and relates the Sikh history of violence to the militant drive for a Sikh homeland—Khalistan—in recent decades. Ron E. Hassner and Gideon Aran begin with divergences among ethnic Jews regarding identity and scriptural adherence and then explore the way violence is portrayed in biblical prescriptions and stories as well as post-biblical history and interpretation; they also discuss the extracanonical books and Talmud and the legacy of violence in Jewish mysticism and messianism. In covering the diversity in the Christian tradition, Lloyd Steffen probes the multilayered Christian imagination regarding violence, from the inception of Christianity in political executions and apocalyptic dreams through its intertwining with political empires, wars, and crusades to its internal struggles regarding heresy, slavery, missionary zeal, just war, and social justice. Bruce B. Lawrence contrasts Islam in 611 with the Islam associated with terrorism on 9/11. He summarizes a complex trajectory of defiant moralism as well as ethical compromise, from Islam's revolutionary roots in human rights through its early rules for how to and when to wage war, the eventual (post-Mohammed) establishment of jihad as an instrument of state, the crystallization of rules in response to the Crusades, the founding of "gunpowder empires" such as the Ottoman, and finally to Muslim responses to European colonization.

Nathalie Wlodarczyk, examining a wide range of African customs and legends, shows among other things that African traditional religion provides notions of a thriving spirit world that offers "sacred warriors" ritualized protections and martial enhancements when defense of community is urgent. Among the variety of Pacific Island religious cultures that Andrew Strathern and Pamela J. Stewart describe, notions of violence vary hugely—from physical harm to slights of honor to mystical assault—but hierarchical societies in the Pacific have tended to be supported by ritual and cosmological structures that may be harnessed for revenge and war.

The images and acts of destruction described in the essays in this book can be collectively described as "religiously related violence," though it is clear that there are many ways of interpreting that phrase. In some cases the ideas related to violence are rooted in the basic beliefs of the tradition;

in other cases they and the practices associated with them are not narrowly theological. Aside from ritual sacrifice, real acts of violence are seldom intrinsic to any specific religious experience—wars are often justified in the name of religion, for instance, when the primary purpose is to extend political power. Because violence in both real and symbolic forms is found in all religious traditions, it can be regarded as a feature of the religious imagination. Almost every major tradition, for example, has some notion of sacrifice and some notion of cosmic war, a grand moral struggle that underlies all reality and can be used to justify acts of real warfare.

Thus the study of violence in religion and the religious dimensions of violent situations do much to shed light on the nature of religion itself. The essays in this book are intended to provide a window into this complex topic and illuminate the way violence has been a part of each of the world's major religious traditions. We hope that in addition to being an overview of this topic it will also be useful for understanding religion in all of its complexity, its myriad historical, literary, social, and personal forms.

Notes

1. Mark Juergensmeyer, Margo Kitts, and Michael Jerryson, eds., *The Oxford Handbook of Religion and Violence* (New York: Oxford University Press, 2013).

Chapter 1

Violence and Nonviolence at the Heart of Hindu Ethics

Veena Das

A STARTING PREMISE on any reflection on violence is the acknowledgment that violence is not a self-evident transparent category.[1] While the application of physical force on an unwilling person in order to injure might seem to be the most obvious and manifest sign of violence, even this minimal definition confronts such issues as who counts as a person, what counts as consent, and is intentionality to injure necessary for an act to count as violence? In this overview, I take an engagement with these questions at the very heart of my project, which is to examine how we might render a certain anxiety around violence as integral to the imagination of an ethical life in Hindu texts and practices. But how is one to define what would count as a Hindu (versus, say, Vedic) text? As many scholars have argued, the term *Hindu* cannot be projected back into time for it is a product of a long history in which it becomes a word at hand for a dispersal of names, places, objects, gestures, and schemes for living a good life (Llewellyn 2005).

It is important to state that problems of definition are not unique to Hinduism. The philosopher of religion Hent de Vries offers us the following provocation: "Nothing allows us to determine in advance, let alone on the basis of some philosophically or transcendentally construed a priori, what, precisely religion in its very 'concept'—may still (or yet again) make possible or necessary, visible and readable, audible and palpable" (de Vries 2010: 1). The texts coming from the Hindu tradition (however retrospectively defined) face the additional problem that there have been powerful forms of repudiation of these texts' claims to philosophical or theoretical intervention made by philosophers of great repute. Despite attempts to reclaim Hindu texts for a philosophically informed ethics (Billimoria,

Prabhu and Sharma 2007; Paranjpe 1998) the difficulties of treating them as more than exotic traditions have been formidable.[2] Then how should one read these archives so that we neither romanticize them as bearers of some superior mystical traditions nor assume that they already belong to a past that has little to contribute to our lives now?

Given the enormity and range of the sources (from textual sources to ethnographies) that can come under the rubric of the term *Hindu*, it is not possible to give a chronological account of debates on violence and non-violence within the confines of a chapter. I have, therefore, chosen to pres-ent two domains of discussion on which I track the reflections on violence and nonviolence and ask, especially, What is the imagination of how human societies can find a way out of cycles of violence? These two domains are defined by (a) the relation to animals as sacrificial offerings and as food in the language of ritual and (b) gendered violence in the imagination of sovereignty in the mythic register. I follow this discussion with some contemporary examples of violence and nonviolence and ask how new forms of collective life such as the imaginary of the nation shape the expression and experience of violence. However, I also claim that in the figure of Mahatma Gandhi we have some important experiments with these questions, and I signal these moments at various points in the text. My attempt here is not to give a history of these concepts but to construct an archive in which different temporalities are embedded. As Cavell puts the argument for inheritance so well: "It is not for the text to answer the questions you put to it, but for you to respond to the questions you dis-cover it asks (of itself, of you)" (2003: 248). Toward the end of the chapter, I reflect on the question of whether the forms that contemporary Hinduism has taken are able to respond at all to the questions the texts ask of us—or if the place where the archive lives is in ordinary actions that turn away from the nationalist imaginings of Hinduism today? Is the task of scholar-ship, then, to patiently establish if texts and practices of Hinduism can offer a view of the moral life that can bring to the fore a different con-ceptual furniture than that which privileges the relation of philosophy, antiphilosophy, and political theology to essentially Greek, Judaic, and Christian traditions?[3]

The Claims of the Animal

In a text written in the thirteenth century of the Common Era, titled *Dharmaranya Purana* to depict the "history" of the Modh Brahmins and

Baniyas of Gujarat,[4] we get an interesting glimpse of an argument between the Brahmins, who are depicted as those who perform sacrifice, and the Jains, who are shown as upholders of *ahimsa* (nonviolence). The debate is staged in the court of a Jain king. Jain monks accuse the Brahmins of indulging in violence and urge the king to withdraw patronage from the Brahmins. The Brahmins retort that it is hypocritical to assume that anyone can live without violence for, in order to live, it is necessary to eat, and that act means that we are bound to inflict violence, whether on animals or plants. They argue further that violence is much more expansive than physical harm and who, they ask, is free of harboring anger and jealousy, which are also forms of violence (see Das 1977). This debate, despite its local character, resonates with an important cultural theme enacted at various levels of Hindu texts and practices—that is, can the killing of animals in sacrifice be regarded as a dramatization of everyday acts of violence that we commit simply in order to live? Instead of thinking of sacrifice as primarily an act of communication between humans and gods with the animal offering as the object that mediates the two, as dominant theories of sacrifice in anthropology are inclined to do (Hubert and Mauss 1964),[5] I point to a different cultural logic in which the eating and killing of animals in sacrifice are integrally linked with the violent preconditions of our life. From this perspective, sacrifice provides a dramatic expression of the ambivalence that surrounds the topic of violence and nonviolence—one might regard ritual violence as enacting puzzles about the costs we pay in order to live. Let us first consider the logic of sacrifice in the Vedic texts and in the Brahmanas (texts that provide explanations of Vedic injunctions of sacrifice), composed roughly from 1500 to 500 BCE. The Vedic texts distinguish between domestic animals (*pashu*) and wild animals (*mriga*)—killing of animals could take the form of either sacrifice, in which the offerings are domestic animals (including humans), or hunting that was oriented to wild animals. Here I choose to amplify three different strands that speak to the problem of converting the facts of violence into nonviolence—or at least into violence that we can live with. These three strands are (a) the ritual words and acts that convert the animal from a victim to a willing participant and, hence, the euphemistic expressions that redefine violence as a kind of pacification, (b) ritual substitution that keeps the symbolic presence of violence very much in the picture without actually committing the acts of killing, and (c) shifting the weight of ritual action from the act of killing to that of regeneration.

Killing as Pacification: Euphemistic Character of Ritual Vocabulary

In his classic work on the religion of the Vedas, Oldenburg (1988) describes the moment of the killing of the animal by strangulation as follows:

> The sacrificial animal was killed with the expressions, common also to other people, of efforts to free oneself from the sin of a bloody deed and from impending revenge. It was told 'You are not dying, you are not harmed, you are going to the gods along beautiful paths'...the killing was called euphemistically 'to get the consent of the animal.'
>
> (Oldenburg 1988: 292)

The exact ritual term for this process was *sangyapan* which literally meant "taking the consent." As Émile Benveniste has shown in a short essay on euphemisms, this region of linguistic expressions hinges on the paradox that one wishes to bring to mind an idea while avoiding naming it specifically (1971: 266). Euphemisms are distinct from taboos on speaking certain words. In the latter case the issue is that of avoidance—in the former case, different words are substituted for those words that must not be uttered, thus concealing the nature of the act and yet bringing it to mind. Benveniste concludes his essay with this stunning observation: "Just as in the Vedic ritual of sacrifice, the victim is 'appeased' (*samayati*) or 'made to consent' when in actual fact it is 'strangled,' so the fire that is extinguished is 'appeased'" (1971: 270). Thus, language transforms the killing the animal into the creation of a beatific path for it to reach the gods. The sacrificer's (yajaman's) desire for heaven is made to merge with the animal's desire to reach heaven through this ritual. By becoming the sacrificial victim voluntarily the animal is seen to reach heaven directly without going through endless cysles of rebirth.

Now what is the nature of the idea that is brought to mind while avoiding its naming in the ritual characterization of strangulation as "consent"? I suggest that what is at stake in the euphemistic sacred vocabulary is the question of death—not the death of the animal that is being ritually strangled but the sacrificer's death that is being warded off. Thus the violence being done to the animal in the public (*srauta*) ritual is an anticipation or prefiguration of the violence that will be done to the sacrificer in a final sacrifice that he will perform—the sacrifice of the self as an offering to the gods in the final death rituals.

Mariasusai Dhavamony (1973) noted that it is through sacrifice that man ransoms his being from the gods in Vedic sacrifice, and scholars such as Anand Coomaraswamy (2000) explicitly drew attention to the offering of squeezed soma plant in sacrifice, saying that when soma and *agni* ("fire") are united in sacrifice they jointly overcome the force of death and redeem man since man is born in debt to death. Anthropologists have shown that the structure of the cremation rituals is best understood through the vocabulary as well as the spatial and temporal organization of sacrificial rituals (see Das 1977; Parry 1994). In his brilliant analysis of the cremation rituals, Charles Malamoud (1996) uses a culinary vocabulary to think of the transformation of the corpse through the cremation fire that "cooks" it to make it into an oblation fit to be offered to the gods, similar to other fires such as the cooking hearth and the digestive fire in the body.

The implications of the euphemisms used in the sacred vocabulary pertaining to killing as well as the strict analogy between cremation and sacrifice, or rather cremation as sacrifice, has an important bearing on our argument on the close braiding of violence and nonviolence. The ritual words and acts do not so much expel violence as make it the general condition of our lives in which we share with animals the common condition of being ransomed to death. It is understandable that the Jains (and Buddhists) with whom the Brahmins debate about whether violence committed in sacrifice is violence at all accused the Brahmins of ritual trickery. It is also a fact that for the Brahmin sacrificer as well the interpreters from the hermeneutic school of Mimamsa, there is no respite from the reality that all violence mimes the ultimate violence of death. As Wendy Doniger summarizes this melancholy sense, the texts are saying that "human beings are, like all other animals, fit to be sacrificed to the gods, they are, as it were, the livestock of the gods" (Doniger 2009: 152).

Ritual Substitution

The logic of substitution is widely acknowledged to be at the heart of sacrifice by social theorists (Girard 1997; Lévi-Strauss 1963, 1969). However, how to interpret the fact of substitution is the subject of considerable debate. Among these theorists, Lévi-Strauss is famous for his distrust of sacrificial logic. In his words:

(Totemism) is a quantified system while (sacrifice) permits a continuous passage between its terms; a cucumber is worth an egg as a sacrificial victim, an egg a fish, a fish a hen, a hen a goat, a goat an ox. And this gradation is oriented; a cucumber is sacrificed if there is no ox but the sacrifice of an ox for want of a cucumber would be an absurdity.

(Lévi-Strauss 1969: 224)

Lévi-Strauss founded his theoretical observations on the ethnography of sacrifice among the Nuer. Matters are much more complicated when it comes to understanding Vedic sacrifice, for, as noted in the last section, there is a different temporal horizon to these matters. Animals fit for sacrifice (pashu) are defined in a series of five, and man is included in the series as among those who can be sacrificed. One of the Brahamanic texts notes that the gods first used man as a sacrificial beast—as the sacrificial quality went out of him it entered the next in the series—thus the bull, then the stallion, then the billy goat, and so on. It is interesting that, after the enumerated animals are exhausted, the sacrificial quality then goes to rice and barley, which become complete sacrificial oblations. One text draws attention to the silent screaming of the rice and barley as they are offered in sacrifice (see Doniger 2009). The series is an oriented one, as Lévi-Strauss saw, but this is not a matter of mere contingency (for want of an ox, an egg, etc.); rather, even if each substitution leads to a lesser degree of violence and even if we cannot hear the silent screams of rice and barley, we cannot escape violence altogether, for, in the final sense not only human, but all existence entails violence. In the later devotional cults, vegetarian offerings are substituted for the sacrificial victim for many of the gods and goddesses who required sacrifice, but the memory of the original sacrifice is retained by such acts as the forceful smashing of the coconut and the red color put on the coconut; an origin myth in which a goddess explicitly states that she will accept the offering of a coconut in lieu of a head is often evoked to explain this change (Doniger 2009: 561). Unlike the idea of a scapegoat that is from outside the community and can carry away the sins of the community (see Girard 1977), the substitution here only points to temporal dislocations—either a past is evoked in the form of a myth in which the coconut represents the original violent event of sacrifice, or the animal sacrifice points to the future in which the sacrificer will be the victim. In either case, the horizon of thought is that of death and its intimacy with violence.

Sacrifice as Regeneration

The third strand that I mentioned is that of converting the violence of sacrifice into regeneration. Consider the *purusha sūkta*, hymn 10.90 of the Rigveda, which describes the original sacrifice of *purusha* or the primeval man. It is from his dismembered body that both the natural and the social order are created, as different parts of the sacrificed body become the furniture of the universe. The *varna* (caste) hierarchy, as is well known, is created at this sacrificial moment with the mouth becoming the Brahmin, the arms the Kshatriya, the stomach the Vaishya, and the feet the Shudra. In a repetition of the original sacrifice, death rituals re-create death as an act of sacrificial offering and regeneration (Das 1977, Parry 1994). However, not everyone buys into the story of sacrifice as beatific regeneration and, as persistent critiques from not only the Buddhists and the Jains but also from the later devotional cults show, a shift of perspective from man to that of animal and from the future to that of the present moment has the potential of stripping the story of its comforting moment to make visible the utter devastation that sacrifice might bring to the world.

One such thought is present in the epic Mahabharata that will be analyzed in the next section when King Janmajeya performs the infamous snake sacrifice in which, instead of the prescribed horse, the king vows to burn every snake in the sacrificial pyre to avenge the death of his father by snakebite. In an act reminiscent of this terrible sacrifice, the Mahabharata details the *abhichara* (magical, clandestine) sacrifice performed by Drupad who wanted to generate a son who would be so powerful as to wipe out his enemies, the Kshatriyas or warrior kings, from the earth. Thus the texts recognize that not all sacrifice can achieve the aim of regeneration and that sacrifice contains in itself the dark energies fueled by such passions as anger and vengeance that can lead to massive destruction. As Doniger (2009) observes, "The Mahabharata sees a vice behind every virtue, a snake behind a horse, and a doomsday behind every victory" (Doniger 2009: 276).[6]

On the positive side, the Vedic sacrificial ritual contains many other acts than killing. In the interpretations of the Mimamsa scholars, the theme of gift, renunciation, and transfer of properties plays an important role in interpretation as does the question of how a reorganization of desire (from objects to heaven, not as a place but as an empty signifier), might take place (see Das 1983).

The Eating of Animals

The debates on violence and nonviolence that we tracked in the case of sacrifice find an interesting resonance in the dilemmas on the eating of animals. I focus on three specific issues and then consider how we might connect these with the question of what Cora Diamond (2008) called the difficulty of reality and the difficulty of philosophy. Here are the questions I want to discuss.

First, how are rules of interpretation in sacrifice applied to other domains of life and especially to the question of the consumption of meat? Second, in what manner does the notion of *ahimsa* (nonviolence) join the eating of animals conceptually to other forms of cruelty? Davis (2010) has convincingly argued that the scholastic tradition of the Dharmashastras relied on Mimamsa principles of interpretation, but it also translated its core elements into the mundane world of human society. The focus of theological reflection then became the everyday world of *varna* and *ashrama* (caste and life stages). For our purposes, it is interesting to reflect on the application of the principles of Mimamsa on the eating of meat. Davis gives the example from the fifth chapter in *The Laws of Manu*, in which there seem to be contradictory injunctions on this issue. Thus, one of the rules states that one can never obtain meat without causing injury, and therefore one should abstain from eating meat (5.48); while another rule says that there is no fault in eating meat, drinking liquor, or having sex for these are the natural activities of creatures, though abstaining from such activities carries great rewards (5.56). Davis shows how, applying the notion of what is a rule in the Mimamsa, the tenth-century commentator Medhatithi argues that not all rules carry the same force since explanations and exhortations are not at the same level as the rules with injunctive force. More interestingly, the text makes a distinction between what is primary and what is secondary in any act—concluding that killing the animal is secondary and eating the meat is primary (Davis 2010: 58). This is an interesting commentary precisely because it brings intentionality into the question of what constitutes violence. Was the pleasure of the act centered on the killing or on the eating? Further, I suggest that this reflection on the everydayness of ethical acts brings into view the more profound issue of whether our motives are transparent to us—a point that has relevance to how we might understand what is a violent act.

Let us suppose for a moment that our theoretical stakes are not centered on *what* we can learn about the Hindu notions of violence and nonviolence but *how* such notions might provide an archive for reflecting on contemporary dilemmas. Then, one of the most interesting figures we might turn to is Mohandas Gandhi. Gandhi is widely recognized as having brought the principles of nonviolence or *ahimsa* to the political arena in the struggle against colonial rule. However, scholars have wrestled with the question of influences behind the depth and range of Gandhi's ideas on *ahimsa*. We should note that *ahimsa* for Gandhi is not limited to the eating or killing of animals—his ideas of both violence and nonviolence are more expansive. Thus, for instance, he stated that not hurting a living thing is a part of *ahimsa*, but it is its least expression—it was hatred of any kind that Gandhi defined as violence (Gandhi, M. K. 1938). We might refer back to the debate between the Brahmins and the Jains in which Brahmins offered this expanded notion of violence. However, for Gandhi, the matter does not stop there for he also shows in his life and his politics that resisting injustice is also part of his definition of *ahimsa*. This is why his expanded idea of nonviolence includes for him *satyagraha* (truth force or tenacity in the pursuit of truth) and *brahmacharya* or celibacy (Gandhi, R 1982). Among his recent interpreters, Akeel Bilgrami (2002), Leela Gandhi (2006), and Bhrigupati Singh (2010a) offer some fascinating insights into this range of Gandhi's thought. For Leela Gandhi (2006), Gandhi's early interactions with the various late Victorian animal welfare societies in London and their hospitality to him decisively influenced the affectivity and anti-constitutionalism behind his ideas of *ahimsa*. What was at stake in human-animal relations for both the proponents of vegetarianism in London and for the later Gandhi was a vision of how nongovernmental sociality might be imagined. Thus, Leela Gandhi draws attention to Gandhi's essay on enlightened anarchy, written in 1939, in which he argued that true *ahimsa* could only be achieved in independent India if it agreed to an experiment with statelessness. The structure of governance, he argued, whether British or Indian, becomes contaminated by violence or *himsa*. The claim that Gandhian politics owed some of its inheritance to the radicals who lived and worked on the margins of late Victorian culture is unexceptionable—the difficulty is that the other parts of Gandhi's inheritance are left unexamined. For instance, while it is true that Gandhi rejected the governmentality of the biopolitical state, surely he did not reject the government of the self. It is in this rift that the inheritance of an expanded notion of *himsa* and *ahimsa* in varied Hindu traditions found expression in Gandhi's politics.

Akeel Bilgrami (2002) disregards the practice of dietetics and concentrates instead on asking: How did Gandhi reconcile the idea of *satyagraha* as moral resistance with the exhortation that his satyagrahis must abstain from any moral judgment against the British rulers, which he saw as a sign of violence? The result is a highly original reading in which Gandhi's differences from, for example, Mill's idea of tolerance or from the Western philosophical traditions in which moral action and moral judgment are integrally linked are brought out with great finesse. The question that Bilgrami does not ask, however, is this: In what regard might we consider Gandhi's thought as anchored on the expanded notions of violence and nonviolence that were the subjects of much debate between Indic traditions—Brahmanism versus Buddhism and Jainism and later debates among Hindus sects elaborated in discursive forms as well as ritual practices? Alternately, to what extent, might we see Gandhi as a critic of the apologetics offered by Hindu scholars and practitioners? Singh (2010a) takes an important step toward the direction of linking dietetics with control over sexuality through the contrast between eroticism and asceticism in the government of the self (both at national and individual level), but his essay veers toward comparisons with Thoreau and Nietzsche rather than in the direction of engaging the archive from Hinduism. It seems to me that after some early leads in Ramachandra Gandhi (1982), the attempts to grapple with these difficult issues have remained sporadic.

Why Animals?

In his famous formulation on animal symbolism in totemism, Lévi-Strauss (1963) formulated his famous proposition that "animals are good to think with." In privileging the question of the animal as a concrete other to the human for articulating how we might think of the braiding of violence and nonviolence in texts and practices of Hindus, I am trying to tap into a different region of thought. In considering what death is to an animal, we might find that we are not able to inhabit its body in our imagination. I have suggested that in thinking of what it is to kill an animal in sacrifice and for food, the Vedic texts on sacrifice are struggling to find a language for depicting the cost of living that we pay—the violence of sacrifice is the way in which they imagine that one could ransom oneself from death. Ironically, we find that when the figure of the cow appears in the nationalist mobilization during the late nineteenth and early twentieth centuries, it now appears as an animal that condenses a Hindu cosmology and that also signifies the inability to imagine what it is for the other (as in the figure of the Muslim) to die as witnessed in brutal riots in which Muslims could be freely killed as revenge for the killing of the cow (see Freitag 1989; Pinney 2004; Yang 1980). Simultaneously it signals to a profound issue—the incapacity to imagine one's own death—to have a genuinely embodied sense of being extinguished. Cora Diamond (2010) in her profound reflections on J. M. Coetzee's (1999) Tanner Lectures on the lives of animals, articulated through the literary figure of Mrs Costello, in the novel *Elizabeth Costello*, says the following:

> I want to describe Coetzee's lectures, then, as presenting a kind of woundedness or hauntedness, a terrible rawness of nerves. What wounds this woman, what haunts her mind, is what we do to animals. This, in all its horror, is there in our world. How is it possible to live in the face of it? And, in the face of the fact, that for nearly everyone, it is as nothing, as the mere accepted background of life?
>
> (Diamond 2008: 47)

I suggest that the figure of the animal is important in understanding violence, precisely because in the contemplation of the killing of animals in sacrifice, it brings to the fore that accepted background of life that Diamond finds to be so wounding. If there is a glimmer of a hope here, it is that we learn to live with the awareness of the way our lives are entangled with other lives and forms of suffering entailed in our living, to which we might not normally give another thought. I am not suggesting that the texts resolve these issues—just that they make us think of the violence we routinely commit. My deep disappointment with the way that these issues are made to disappear in the new guises in which Hinduism seems to tackle the issue of violence and nonviolence in the period we might name as that of the modern, and especially the deflection of the problem of what it is to imagine doing violence to another can hardly be overstated. So I will let a different voice, that of Gandhi on the issue of the cow protection movement that had led to riots in 1893 and subsequent episodes of violence between Hindus and Muslims, have the last word on this.

> But just as I respect the cow, so do I respect my fellowmen....Am I, then, to fight with or kill a Mahomedan in order to save a cow? In doing so, I would become an enemy of the Mahomedan as well as of the cow. Therefore, the only method I know of protecting the cow is that I should approach my Mohemadan brother and urge him for the sake of the country to join me in protecting her. If he would not listen to me I should let the cow go for the simple reason that the matter is beyond my ability. If I were overfull of pity for the cow,

I should sacrifice my life to save her but not take my brother's. This,
I hold, is the law of our religion.

(Gandhi in Hind Swaraj, 1938)

Women, Warfare, and Sovereignty

With this section we shift the scene of violence from that of sacrifice to
that of warfare especially as it pertains to the way in which kingship is
imagined within what I have elsewhere called an alternate founding story
of sovereignty (Das 2010a). While the connection between sovereignty
and the subjugation of violence is the dominant theme of any story of
sovereignty, we can treat the epic war of Mahabharata as educating us in a
different kind of story in which one mode through which men seek their
way out of cycles of violence is to join their own destiny to that of creatures
lower than the human. The scene of sovereign violence then turns out to
be one of vulnerability in which to be in the grip of violence is also to be in
danger of losing the self. The voice of the woman appears as the voice of
interrogation so that one might read the epics Ramayana and Mahabharata
as an argument with the gods (Das 1998).

Sheldon Pollock (2007), among other scholars, has noted the complementary relationship between the two great epics, Ramayana and Mahabharata. Most important to the texts is the agon—the Ramayana, as Pollock
says, is a tale of othering, the enemy is nonhuman, even demonic and the
war takes place far away; the Mahabharata is a tale of "brothering," the enemy
are kinsmen and the war takes place at home. It is also well known that
both epics have spawned many versions in Sanskrit as well as in the vernacular languages and that stories from the epics provide a staple diet for oral
epics as well as traditions of recitation, performance, and image making.

For reasons of space, I limit myself to the Mahabharata and refer to
only one episode from Rama's story. The question remains similar to the
earlier question asked—how is society to imagine a way out of cycles of
violence? Out of the scenes of intense sexual violence depicted in the
Mahabharata, we come to a different way of thinking about sovereignty
and sexuality, not through concepts of contract and obligation as in
European theories of sovereignty but through the intense debates on violence and nonviolence, cruelty and noncruelty. I suggest that it is not in
the kinship with gods but in kinship with animals that the epic sees a way
out of the cycles of violence in which the agonistic kingly lineages get
implicated. And nature is not the scene of unmitigated violence for which

social contract provides a way out, as in a Hobbesian view of the world[7]—rather it is the earth that is tired of the endless violence that men perpetrate on one another, and it is from within the scene of intimacy that a way out of violence is found.

Striving for Noncruelty

The epic tells us on many occasions that *anrishansya* or noncruelty is the highest *dharma*. Why noncruelty and not nonviolence? Doniger (2009) suggests that the text offers a "compromise." In her words, "The issue of non-cruelty to animals is a minor variant on the heavier theme of non-violence *(ahimsa)*...in an age when violence toward both humans and animals in inevitable" (Doniger 2009: 270). But the issue is not that of a particular age or a society mired in violence but rather that the accepted background of our lives as humans is put into question. The epic mode dramatizes the question of violence and asks: What does it mean to relate to the other if the self is lost—an inevitable risk of violence as the epic sees it. Instead of thinking of non cruelty as a compromise, what is being suggested is a new modality of relationships even when, and especially when, the self of the male subject is lost as it comes into the grip of the violence of warfare (see Hiltebeitel 2001).

I begin with two observations fundamental to this story. First, a strong theme of the Mahabharata is to show how even the tragedy of great events and decisions is contained in the every day. Second, the epic dramatizes the moral as the point when we are put in the grip of an uncertainty—in the text this uncertainty hangs over the every day as the female voice emerges in the interrogation of various male characters and even of Krishna, the god who is present in every scene of violence.

The Scene of Violence and the Loss of Self

The argument in this section will be developed neither through plot and narration nor in terms of characters since the text uses multiple frames, embedding stories within stories and using techniques of side-shadowing to suggest other lives that the characters might lead (Hiltebeitel 2001). Further, we can regard the epic as a living tradition and will, indeed, make reference to literary creations that contribute to the story (see Sharma 2009). Doniger (2009: 263) summarizes the bare bones of the central story in the following terms:

The five sons of King Pandu, called the Pandavas, were fathered by gods…all five of them married Draupadi. When Yudhishthira lost the kingdom to his cousins in a game of dice, the Pandavas and Draupadi went into exile for twelve years, at the end of which, with the help of their cousin the incarnate god Krishna, who befriended the Pandavas and whose counsel to Arjuna in the battlefield of Kurukshetra is the Bhagvad Gita, they regained their kingdom through a cataclysmic battle in which almost everyone on both sides was killed.

The bare bones of the story of course tell us nothing, (as Doniger's ironic condensation shows) about the texture of the text or its place in moral argumentation in the making of Indian sensibilities. I will therefore turn to two kinds of scenes[8]—the first I call the scene of the loss of self as one comes within the force field of violence, and the second I call the scene of instruction, in which the virtue of noncruelty is offered as a way out of violence enunciated sometimes through animal stories. It is of the utmost importance that the value of noncruelty is advocated precisely at some juncture in which violence or some form of violent death has taken place. It is as if noncruelty, defined simply as a desire not to injure others, is seen as a realistic starting point for imagining how humans make their way out of cycles of violence. Otherwise said, one might define anrishansya or noncruelty as a mode of being that re-creates the theme of nonviolence but on a minor key humanizing the impersonal force of both violence and blind adherence to dharma.

The Dice Game

Let us place ourselves in the public assembly of the Kaurava King. Here the dice game is in progress. Having lost everything else, Yudhishthira has waged Draupadi, the wife he shares with his brothers, and has lost the wager. An usher is sent to bring her to the public assembly. But she presents him with a cascade of questions of which the most important is "Go to the game. Having gone, ask Yudhishthira in the *sabha* (assembly), what did you lose first, yourself or me?" As Hiltebeitel interprets this question, the term *atmanam* in the question could be translated as "yourself" but also as "the self." Behind the legal question then, as to whether one who has already lost himself can wager another or whether the wife is the property of the husband, lurks the philosophical question, were you in possession of your self when you entered the contract? In the sabha the question will snowball reducing the most learned to utter silence.

Draupadi, having been dragged to the assembly stands now in a completely dishevelled condition in public before all the assembled kings, which include her elders. Here she is insulted, called a whore for having five husbands; invited to sit on the bare thigh of Dushasana, a younger brother of Duryodhana; and yet, the elders assembled do nothing. When Draupadi again asks if Yudhishthira had lost himself before he put the wager on her, she gets no response. Challenged by the questions of Draupadi, Bhishma, the eldest patriarch, can only say that the course of dharma is subtle and that only Yudhishthira, the most learned in the ways of dharma, would be able to answer her question. As readers, we are astonished that the same Yudhishthira who is able to answer the subtlest of questions on dharma is now reduced to silence. The crisis is temporarily resolved by the intervention of the blind king Dhritrashtra but not before terrible oaths of revenge have been uttered and the destruction of the entire Kuru race is predicted on the inexorable logic of insult and vengeance.

The most important lesson we learn from this episode is that dharma, on which the stability of the earth rests, becomes mute in the face of a question asked by a woman. Draupadi's question hovers on the text and, though she is saved from the ignominy of standing naked in the full court of men by the miraculous intervention of Krishna, a cycle of violence has been let loose. A public debating forum on the righteousness or otherwise of moral conduct fails in the presence of violence that is simultaneously public and intimate. Even if the war will be won, the self and all forms of relatedness will become frayed, if not lost.

The Hesitation of Arjuna

The second scene I consider is the famous battle scene in which Arjuna is standing in the battlefield and refusing to go into a battle that will result in the death of his kin. Krishna advises him that the violence is not only necessary but that, in the broader scheme of things, it is no violence. I cannot go into the literature on the philosophy of action to which notions of violence and war in the Bhagvad Gita have contributed, but I note that the text shows in full light how nonviolence, which Krishna propagates as the highest dharma, is enmeshed in violence.[9] There is also a difference between how Arjuna is to be consoled for he is facing future actions as he is about to wage violence and how Yudhishthira is to be consoled as he faces the old king Dhritarashtra and his wife, Gandhari, who have lost all their sons *after* the battle. In the latter event, even though the scene is that of reconciliation, dark residues of anger remain, for even as Yudhishthira touches Gandhari's feet, his nails go black from the anger that is transmitted from Gandhari's body to his. Further, it is not Krishna, the god, who can speak of noncruelty to either Arjuna or Yudhishthira, since he stands accused of encouraging the war. Even contemporary Indian literature retains this sense of the unjustness that was committed by not only the Kauravas but also the Pandavas. If Draupadi's voice showed dharma to have been silenced in the scene of sexual violence witnessed earlier, it is Gandhari, the mother of the Kauravas, who has lived her married life in voluntary blindness, whose grief leads to her cursing of Krishna. In Alok Bhalla's lovely translation of the Hindi play *Andha Yug* (Bharati 2010), we can hear her rage against Krishna:

> What have you done Krishna! What have you done!
> If you wanted...You could have stopped the war...
> You may be a god...You may be omnipotent
> Whoever you are...
> I curse you and I curse all your kinsmen.

Krishna accepts the curse, which then leads to the complete extinction of his lineage, while he is killed like a wild animal in his old age. What is haunting, though, is Bharati's depiction of what Krishna has taken on himself in this terrible war. He says:

> *In this terrible war of eighteen days,*
> *I am the only one who died a million times.*
> *Every time a soldier was struck down,*
> *Every time a soldier fell on the ground.*
> *It was I who was struck down,*
> *It was I who was wounded,*
> *It was I who fell to the ground.*

It seems that in order to get out of the cycle of violence, it is not the divine voice but the human voice, or one on a scale even lower than the human that will have to be recovered. The text of the Mahabharata goes in that direction, but Bharati of the Andha Yuga tried to capture the terrible violence done to women during the Partition riots of 1947 through the analogical rendering of the epic, and this had no such consolation. The question of how to break this cycle of violence was simply set aside in nationalist imageries as the question of violence between Hindus and Muslims, especially through the enactment of violence against women, became a recurring feature of independent India. But let us return to the epic.

Noncruelty or the Humanization of Dharma

Explaining the concept of noncruelty Mukund Lath asks us to look for its meaning in the actions of various characters of the Mahabharata, since the word does not seem to carry much importance outside the epic. In Lath's words,

> Literally the word *anrhamsya* means the state, the attitude, of not being *nrhamsa*. The word *nrhamsa* is common enough in Sanskrit literature; it literally means one who injures man....But the word (*anrshmsya*) has more than a negative connotation; it signifies good-will, a fellow feeling, a deep sense of the other. A word that occurs often with *anrhsamsya*, therefore, is *anukrosha*, to cry with another, to feel another's pain. All these meanings are brought out in the stories. (2009: 84)

I do not have the space to visit all the stories that would be relevant here. Let me briefly allude to the moment when in answer to a question posed by a divine being (Yaksha, who turns out to be the Dharma himself), Yudhishthira answers that noncruelty is the highest dharma. As we saw, it was the same Yudhishthira whose actions in the dice game had led to the unleashing of a cycle of violence, but more importantly his actions have shown that any learned public discourse on right and wrong becomes impossible for the one whose self is lost. So, is the modality of noncruelty as a way of being in the world what Yudhishthira *arrives* at, learning this virtue only after his silence in the assembly? Would it be possible to say that noncruelty lowers the sights from Dharma with a capital *D* to dharma in the lower key, as a way by which he might recover his lost self?

Humanizing Dharma

The different stories through which a human scale or at any rate a scale lower than that of the gods might be found to speak about noncruelty do not parse out the concept into different parts. Rather they allow us to circle around the concept so that a swarm of ideas is generated around it. The first such idea is that of breaking the rigid lawlike regularity of the relation between karma or action and its fruits, its consequences for humanizing the force of dharma. The second is the exploration of the meaning of togetherness, and the third is that of the obligation of a writer toward his (by extension her) character—thus not simply how one *is* in the world but also how one *imagines* others might live in the world. A common thread uniting these ideas is that noncruelty is generated from within the scene of intimacy and is hence perhaps to be distinguished from compassion as an impersonal virtue that is to be extended to all beings.

Since I do not have the space to tell the corresponding stories in any detail, I will simply summarize how each dimension of noncruelty is summarized in a particular story. The point about the humanization of dharma is related through the story of the sage Mandava and Vidura, the youngest uncle of the Kauravas born through a Shudra woman. Mandava curses Yama, the god of Dharma to be born as a human through a Shudra woman as punishment for the fact that he (Mandava) was cruelly punished for a childhood prank on the logic that every action has its consequences. Mandava decries that henceforth no one will be held responsible for childhood pranks, thus loosening the severe and impersonal logic of action and consequences through the modality of noncruelty. The second point, that noncruelty is to be learnt from mutual intimacy, comes out in various animal stories of which the most famous story is that of the parrot and the tree. A tree withered and died because a fowler mistakenly pierced it with a poisoned arrow. All the birds left the tree, but a parrot stayed on and slowly began to wither away for lack of nourishment. When asked to explain why he did not leave the withered tree for another with foliage and fruits, the parrot replied that since he was born there, had grown up, and received protection from the tree, out of noncruelty and sympathy, he would not leave the withered tree.

Contrasting the qualities of nonviolence and noncruelty, Hiltebeitel (2001: 213) interprets this story to say, "While ahimsa tightens the great chain of beings, anrishamsya softens it with a cry for a *human* creature-feeling across the great divides." Dalmiya, interpreting the same story sees it as a parable of the relational (Dalmiya 2001: 297). In both Hilte-beitel and Dalmiya, the force of a concept such as noncruelty comes from the fact that a disposition is generated through the experience of togetherness—if the parrot had gone to a different tree no one would have termed it as betrayal. The second animal story is the iconic one of Yudhishthira refusing to abandon a dog that had attached itself to him even though Lord Indra, who ruled the heavens, threatens that this act will mean a loss of the promised heaven to the king. Yudhishthira, too, explains that, out of a feeling of noncruelty, he could not abandon the dog even though it was pure contingency that the dog had attached itself to him.

Two features stand out in these animal stories. First, the quality of non-cruelty is demonstrated across species and at moments when it is not through language or through appeals to such distant moral concepts as obligation or rule-following but through a sense of togetherness that has developed by the sheer contingency of having been brought together—the fated circumstances of togetherness. Second, it is from within a scene of intimacy that dispositions toward noncruelty develop.

At this point, we might recall the two women, Draupadi and Gandhari, who became the causes for the destruction of the Kshatriyas and of Krishna's dynasty, respectively, thus ending the cruelty of the warrior clans. From the ashes of the heroic project of warrior castes emerges the possibility that there is another kind of intimacy between men and women, humans and animals that can offer a noncruel way of inhabiting the earth. The Mahabharata names it noncruelty. We could name the epic as an argument with gods rather than a resolution about the connection of sov-ereignty, violence, and sexuality. In showing that the most powerful are also the most vulnerable, especially to the ever-present threat of the loss of self, the Mahabharata enacts this argument through a proliferation of fig-ures, both minor and major. It reminds us that the stirring message about the necessity of war given by Krishna on the battlefield must one day come full circle when war ends, in the grieving prince, Yudhishthira, who seeks not incentives to wage war but consolation—for when all have been destroyed, what is left for the prince to take pleasure in?

IN SELECTING HOW problems of violence and nonviolence are voiced in relation to sacrifice and warfare, I hope to have shown that the tradi-tions harbor a deep ambivalence about even the most revered myths and rituals. There is no doubt that the same religious archive that can justify killing in sacrifice and remain silent in the face of the sexual humiliation of a woman can, and has been used to legitimate violence against lower castes or against women in other contexts. However, scholars have often been content to take explicitly formulated rules (as in Manu or, in particular, episodes of violence against lower castes or forest tribes in epics) to be sufficient for understanding Hinduism without paying attention to how divided these traditions could be in confronting profound questions about violence and nonviolence. Even Rama, a king regarded as the most righteous of all, has been faulted for following his kingly dharma in killing a Shudra ascetic whose pursuit of Vedic knowledge was said to have violated the correct order of caste. However, in the hands of a poet such as Bhavabhuti (eighth century), when Rama performs the hateful task of killing the Shudra, he experiences a repetition of the violence he had inflicted on his beloved Sita in exiling her to the forest, also in fulfilment of his kingly duty. In verse 2.70 of the *Uttararamacharita* (Rama's Last Act), translated by Pollock (2007), Rama says:

> O my right hand,
> bring down this sword
> upon the Shudra monk
> And bring the dead son of the Brahman
> back to life. You are a limb of Rama's—
> who had it in him to drive
> his Sita into exile,
> weary and heavy with child.
> Why start with pity now?
> (somehow striking a blow) There, you have done
> a deed worthy of Rama. Let the
> Brahman's son live again.

One might say that such laments and the utter contempt with which Rama utters his own name do not console the Shudra who has been killed, but they do show that there is room for critique here. It is in the conflict of voices, both in the social order and within the self, that the possibility of reclaiming a religious archive becomes attractive, not in opposition to other traditions but in company with them. One final question one might ask is whether modernity completely alters the nature of the questions that Hinduism can ask of itself? I have indicated in various places in the essay that the braiding of violence and nonviolence and the profound ambivalence toward violence finds expression in contemporary India in the figure of Gandhi, but one might ask if the question identified as central to the archive on sacrifice and on sovereignty in Hindu texts and practices, namely, how can human societies find a way out of cycles of violence, find any resonance in contemporary India?

Hinduism's Modernity or Modernity's Hinduism?

The transformation of Hinduism in contemporary India is a vast subject in its own right. My aim here is a limited one. I ask, has the religious archive become irrelevant under conditions of modernity and postmodernity? For some scholars there is an inherent discordance between Hinduism and modernity. Thus, for instance, David Smith writes, "Hinduism is threatened by modernity, and modernity is threatened by Hinduism.... Hinduism is the best or at least the largest single instance of a traditional culture. As such it can stand as the type, the very image of tradition, as modernity's opposite" (Smith 2003: 6). For several other scholars, modernity and its institutions, such as the nation form, have distorted the nature of Hinduism to the extent that its contemporary forms have become unrecognizable as forms of faith (Nandy 1983) and become new forms of identity politics. Striking a somewhat different note, Dilip Gaonkar suggests the idea of creative adaptation as the site where "people 'make' themselves modern as opposed to being 'made' modern by alien and impersonal forces, and where they give themselves an identity and distinction" (Gaonkar 1999: 2).

In this spirit, I take three regions of thought to consider how questions of violence and nonviolence fold into practices of self-making in relation to contemporary challenges. First, I ask, how does the notion of *satyagraha* (soul force) as developed in Gandhian thought and practice draw on the languages of sacrifice we discussed earlier? Second, I take the emergence of Dalit writings as recasting the relation between sovereignty and violence, from the perspective of the Shudras—the lowest caste in the varna hierarchy. Finally, I examine the frequent claim that alignment between nationalism and Hinduism has led to the casting of the Muslim in India as the figure of the absolute other. For reasons of space, I will not be able to offer a comprehensive analysis of these issues but will confine myself to a few examples of the complex ways in which the ideas embedded in the religious archive appear to find life but not in places where one would expect them to be.

In her comparative study of sacrifice, Kathryn McClymond asks what the study of traditional sacrifice has to do with life today? Her answer is that "...[t]raditional forms of sacrifice are continually being transformed into metaphoric sacrifice through new configurations of the various sacrificial procedures...[and that]...sacrificial imagery and rhetoric carry tremendous weight beyond religious arenas" (McClymond 2008: 160). She also asserts that national imageries of sacrifice carry as much weight as traditional sacrifice. The idea of sacrifice in the commentarial literature on Vedic sacrifice is not that of simply killing but of making visible and dramatizing one's own inevitable death. In Gandhi's hands, this idea gets transformed into several notions—*satyagraha* that goes straight to offering oneself as the object of violence and thus overcoming the fear of death, fasting as the ability to heal the body politic through the purification of one's own body and cultivation of the ascetic self as *tapas* (penance) to relate to the others who are affirmed in their difference by an identification with their suffering (Skaria 2009, 2010). Ajay Skaria has made sustained attempts to show how Gandhi's ideas of tolerance and political friendship challenge secular and liberal notions of what it is to inhabit the world with the other. A specific concept that he draws on in Gandhi's writings is that of *tapasya* (practices of asceticism). During the Khalifat movement, Skaria says, Gandhi insisted that the only way to create friendship between Hindus and Muslims was to create bonds through unconditional suffering on behalf of the Muslims by the Hindus. Consider his statement, "The test of friendship is a spirit of love and sacrifice independent of expectation of any return" (Gandhi as cited in Skaria 2009: 224). As Skaria rightly concludes the tapasya or suffering one undergoes on behalf of another is to create a bond between two people who consider themselves apart, not joined by shared history or syncretism as in liberal ideas of what would be the conditions of possibility for building tolerance. While Gandhian techniques of the body—fasting, nonviolent protests, sitting in silence—have become part of the repertoire of political action in India, there is further scope for thinking the form and content of political theology that can stand as an alternative (for better or for worse) to the strongly Christianized political theologies on offer now.

It is precisely this issue that is taken up by Debjani Ganguly (2002 2005) in a compelling and original understanding of Dalit discursive forms, especially the works of B. R. Ambedkar. Ganguly argues that life-forms within which caste is embedded are not available to the "rational, systemic, disembodied public self of the modern social scientist" or even to the Dalit activists because they are all implicated in the social scientific representations of caste that are invested in a normative modernity that can only render caste in a retrogressive light. Ganguly gestures to a hetero-temporality and argues that appreciating the multifarious ways in which caste comes to be written on the body politic needs a nonpedagogical sensibility that could decipher how the various kinds of pasts among which the history of caste oppression is but one such past are layered on each other. She shows how the mythic register operates in Ambedkar's writings to make parallel claims over a past from a Shudra perspective. Ganguly calls such appropriations principled forgetting—others might call these wilful forgetting. The point, however, is that various Indian archives (Hindu and Buddhist) speak in Ambedkar's writings as they do in other oral mythologies of Dalit castes. When Ambedkar pronounced that he was in some genealogical continuity with Vyasa, the author of Mahabharata, and Valmiki, the author of Ramayana, who were both outcasts, since he, too, though an outcast, was called on to write the Constitution of Independent India, we come to appreciate the complex ways in which he saw himself in relation to Indian (including Buddhist) archives. It is surely not accidental that the texts he evokes are the authoritative texts on sovereignty.

As my last example of the transformation of Hinduism in the contemporary era, I consider the question of the presence of the Muslim as an other within Indian polity. Several authors have argued that the most decisive transformation of Hinduism was its conversion into a political identity, announced in V. D. Savarkar's (1942) notion of "Hindutva" to distinguish it from matters of faith, belief, or ritual (van der Veer 1994). For Sarvarkar, a Hindu is any person who considers the land from Indus to Sindhu as his fatherland (*pitribhu*) and regards it as *punyabhu*—sacred or pure land. By this definition, Muslims, who simultaneously define themselves as Indian as well as members of a transnational *umma* or religious community, are disqualified from being Indians. The political aspirations for Sarvarkar is to make India a Hindu nation. Many scholars who have argued that for a militant Hindu Right the Muslim is wholly other see the roots of Hindu rage against Muslims in a variety of conditions, but a loss of "masculinity" as a result of colonization is identified as a major concern. The position of the Hindu Right has been vigorously opposed by proponents of secularism, who nevertheless avoid the issue of how communities within a national polity could learn to inherit a divided and contentious past (but see Amin 2015).

As an illustration of this issue, let us discuss the possibilities of multiple and conflicting pasts with regard to the destruction of the Babri mosque in a prolonged dispute over sacred spaces that many see as emblematic of the politics of religious nationalism. Van der Veer (1994), in his analysis of Hindu nationalism, has argued that it is not Sarvarkar's ideas per se but their deployment for bringing together Hindus across sectarian, regional, or caste divides that makes them politically relevant. The discourse on Hinduism as a political entity seems to rely primarily on the idea of historical hurts and traumas caused the Hindus through Muslim invasions and the destruction of Hindu temples (Cohen 2010). Yet Muslims and Hindus have a long history of both intimacy and conflict—I have elsewhere called this agonistic belonging—the conflicts assuming a shared symbolic space (Das 2010b). Second, there are many levels at which such conflicts are mediated, and the technologies of mediation are sufficiently different for us to give far more careful thought to what is at stake for understanding the nature of these conflicts. First, it is important that law courts have been involved in addressing disputes such as those over sacred spaces (as well as many others), showing that parties to the dispute find vocabularies to convert what would be purely theological or historical questions into questions for the law that allow for a deferral if not a resolution. Second, we have evidence from both historical and ethnographic writing that, while involved in different kinds of conflicts, Hindus and Muslims living in proximity engage in the commerce of life in which they are able to evoke different kinds of pasts making the identities Hindu and Muslim unstable (Gilmartin and Lawrence 2000).

In the case of the Ram Janambhumi and Babri Masjid dispute, which has been lingering in courts since 1885, Deepak Mehta (2011) shows that over a period of time legal questions altered as new parties were added to the dispute. Thus the courts have had to deal with such issues as the nature of religious property; whether a deity is a juristic personality; and also whether parties to the dispute are consolidated groups of Hindus and Muslims or if there are different legal personalities involved—for example, Sunni Waqf Board versus Shia Waqf Board as well as different Hindu sects; and finally, what did right to worship mean in legal terms? Mehta shows that the category of "status quo" is used by judges to get over the impasse these questions create, because no resolution of the questions seems possible without endangering what the courts call "public order." There is the fascinating question here as to whether any principles of interpretation derived from the hermeneutic traditions of Hindus or

Muslims can be deployed by judges who must speak in secular languages, but answering that question would require an investigation into the thousands of pages generated by the case in the forms of legal briefs, judgements, and so on with an analytical eye rather than one that transports current political concerns into reading this archive. Perhaps a new way of addressing the question of conflicted pasts is being crafted, though we do not yet have the vocabulary to render this explicit.

A long route has been traversed in this chapter. To address the question how do human societies find a way out of cycles of violence, I first took the case of sacrifice and argued that the defence of killing is not so much an indifference to the suffering of animals as an occasion to dramatize and make visible the fact of one's own inevitable death. Yet, as we saw, the animal might not consent, and the earth might get tired of the wanton destruction of the beings that reside on it. In the case of the fraternal wars described in the epic Mahabharata, stories of sexual humiliation, wrongful killing, vengeance, and deceit blow up the cover of honorable exchange of violence among equals. We saw that the voice of the woman becomes the voice that interrogates the conceits of Dharma. In each case, the texts are not satisfied with offering prescriptive rules but rather, they zone in on a problem that cannot be resolved and is thus carried on, taking new forms into the future.

In the case of contemporary Hinduism, I do not find much engagement by the prominent political actors (such as Vishwa Hindu Parishad or RSS) with an archive, at least in the public domain. However, I do find that hints of ways of inheriting multiple pasts are present in the register of everyday life, such as when a Hindu healer in a low-income neighborhood begins to dream of ayats in the Quran as a way of healing those afflicted with malignant spirits or a Hindu mother makes room for her Muslim daughter-in-law to be able to say her prayers. Or for that matter, when a Jain finds that he can make an alliance with an animal rights activists and find a language for saying how much the suffering of animals wounds him, thus bridging the divide between religious and secular languages (Laidlaw 2010). These moments are easily suppressed in official discourses of both Hindus and Muslims now. So I will conclude with two moments of resonance with the thoughts on violence and nonviolence traced from the texts. The first resonant moment is in Gandhi's words when he says that, if he cannot persuade a Muslim to relinquish the killing of a cow as a gesture of friendship with the Hindus and for the good of the country, then he will let the cow go on the grounds that the matter is "beyond my capability." In other words, if I am a beaver, I should not carry the guilt of not being able to build a dam. When does one simply accept and endure the fact that the world has a say in the projects through which we carve our moral selves? However disappointed in each other we might be, we are not allowed to carry that fact to the point where we end up cursing the world and unleashing our own violence on it.

The second resonant moment for me is of women who had witnessed their husbands and sons burnt to death in the violence against Sikhs in Delhi in 1984 sitting in the streets in a stonelike posture—dirty, disheveled, refusing to bathe, until the government publicly acknowledged the violence done to their community (Das 2007). The moment is etched forever in my memory as if it were the story of Draupadi who lived in the gestures through which dirt and pollution were made to speak. Out of such gestures—as those of Gandhi turning away from the violence against Muslims or the slum-dwelling women in Delhi refusing to consent to keeping silent about violence—I know that the archive has a life. Can contemporary social science recover such gestures from everyday life, recognize the waxing and waning of religious conflicts rather than letting them imprison her in a fascination with the horror of our present condition, and still recognize itself as "social science"?

Notes

1. I am grateful to the editors and, especially, to Michael Jerryson for their insightful comments on earlier versions of the paper that helped me to knit the main arguments together.
2. I am not suggesting that such repudiations go uncontested but rather that it is not easy to move from the position in which the task of students of Indian texts is to simply render their content, to the position where they would be taken as texts to be developed, repudiated, accepted within the normal give and take of theoretical discussions.
3. The centrality of these traditions is taken for granted in the long history of theorizing on the political-theological where terms such as *philosophy* and even *antiphilosophy* are assumed to be about the tensions between the Greek, Judaic, and Christian inheritance of scholarly traditions. Yet the difficulties of overcoming such restriction of vision cannot be laid simply on the doors of European hegemony which becomes nothing more than a lament.
4. This text is to be distinguished from the Dharmaranya Purana in the Pauranic canon (see Das 1977).
5. For a detailed critique of this model for a general theory of sacrifice see Das (1983) where I argue that the sacrificer is not defined in Vedic sacrifice as a bearer of sin

but rather as a desiring being. Sacrifice then is about reordering of desire and not about expiation of sin.

6. I have not specifically taken up the issue of horse sacrifice that referred to the display of kingly power, but it is worth noting that the substitution of the horse by the snake also shows the dark side of kingship.

7. Such a view of nature in which sheer force is the operative principle of life is not unknown to the Hindu imaginary—*matsya nyaya*—or the law of the fishes in which the bigger fish eat the smaller fish is used to describe the direction of violence in nature. However, in the Mahabharata, there is layering of another thought in which it is the violence perpetrated by men that makes the earth as a living entity, tired of the burden she has to bear.

8. This is a very small selection of the scenes—a fuller description would take a monograph but see, especially, Hiltebeitel (2001).

9. See, for instance, Bilwakesh (2009) on this point. The concepts of the Bhagvad Gita might have gone important transformations, as it was translated into Persian on Dara Shikoh's behest as *Sirr ol Asrar*, then into Latin by Anquetil-Dupperon, followed by A. W. Schlegel's annotated translation into Latin. Although recent scholarship notes the importance of the German debate on the Bhagvad Gita in the critical engagement with the text and especially its theory of inaction in action, the issue of translation of concepts across philosophical traditions has not received much attention.

Bibiliography

Amin, Shahid. *Conquest and Community: The Afterlife of Warrior Saint Ghazi Miyan*. Delhi: Orient Black Swan, 2015.

Benveniste, Émile. "Euphemisms Ancient and Modern." In *Problems in General Linguistics*. Trans. Mary E. Meek, 265–271. Coral Gables, FL: University of Miami Press, 1971.

Bharati, Dharamvir. *Andha Yug: The Age of Darkness*. Trans. Alok Bhalla. Manoa: Hawaii University Press, 2010.

Bilgrami, Akeel. "Gandhi's Integrity: The Philosophy behind the Politics." *Postcolonial Studies* 5.1 (2002): 79–93.

Billimoria, Purhottam, Joseph Prabhu, and Renuka M. Sharma eds. *Indian Ethics: Classical Traditions and Contemporary Challenges*. Burlington: Ashgate Publications, 2007.

Bilwakesh, Nikhilesh. "Emerson, John Brown and Arjuna: Translating the Bhagvad Gita in a Time of War." *ESQ: A Journal of the American Renaissance* 55.1 (2009): 27–58.

Cavell, Stanley. *Emerson's Transcendental Etudes*. Palo Alto, CA: Stanford University Press, 2003.

Coetzee, J. M. *The Lives of Animals*. Ed. and introduced by Amy Gutmann. Princeton, NJ: Princeton University Press, 1999.

Cohen, Lawrence. "Ethical Publicity: On Transplant Victims, Wounded Communities and the Moral Demands of Dreaming." In *Ethical Life in South Asia*. Eds. Anand Pandian and Daud Ali, 253–275. Bloomington: Indiana University Press, 2010.

Coomaraswamy, Anand. *Perception of the Vedas*. Ed. Vidyanivas Misra. Delhi: Indira Gandhi National Center for the Arts, 2000.

Das, Veena. *Structure and Cognition: Aspects of Hindu Caste and Ritual*. Delhi: Oxford University Press, 1977.

Das, Veena. "The Language of Sacrifice." *Man*, new series 18.3 (1983): 445–462.

Das, Veena. "Narrativizing the Male and the Ffemale in Tulasidas's Ramach-aritamanasa." In *Social Structure and Change: Religion and Kinship*. Eds. A. M. Shah, B. S. Baviskar, and E. A. Ramaswamy, 65–92. Delhi: Sage Publications, 1998.

Das, Veena. *Life and Words: Violence and the Descent into the Ordinary*. Berkeley: University of California Press, 2007.

Das, Veena. "Sexuality, Vulnerability and the Oddness of the Human: Lessons from the Mahabharata." *Borderlands* 9.3 (2010). www.borderlands.net.au/vol9no3/html.

Das, Veena. "Moral and Spiritual Striving in the Everyday: To be a Muslim in Contemporary India." In *Ethical Life in South Asia*. Eds. Anand Pandian and Daud Ali, 232–253. Bloomington: Indiana University Press, 2010.

Davis, Donald R. *The Spirit of Hindu Law*. Cambridge, UK: Cambridge University Press, 2010.

de Vreis, Hent. "Introduction: Why Still Religion?" In *Religion Beyond a Concept*. Ed. Hent de Vries, 1–100. New York: Fordham University Press, 2008.

Dhavamony, Mariasusai. *Phenomenology of Religion*. Rome: Universitá Gregoriana Editrice, 1973.

Diamond, Cora. "The Difficulty of Reality and the Difficulty of Philosophy." In *Philosophy and Animal Life*. Eds. Stanley Cavell, Cora Diamond, John McDowell et al., 43–91. New York: Columbia University Press, 2008.

Doniger, Wendy. *The Hindus: An Alternate History*. New York: Penguin Press, 2009.

Flood, Gavin. *An Introduction to Hinduism*. Cambridge, UK: Cambridge University Press, 1996.

Freitag, Sandra B. *Collective Action and Community: Public Arenas and the Emergence of Communalism in North India*. Berkeley: University of California Press, 1989.

Gandhi, Leela. *Affective Communities: Anticolonial Thought, Fin De Siecle Radicalism and the Politics of Friendship*. Durham, NC: Duke University Press, 2006.

Gandhi, Mohandas K. *Indian Home Rule or Hind Swaraj*. Ahmadabad: Navjivan Publications, 1938.

Gandhi, Mohandas K. *The Collected Works of Mahatma Gandhi*. New Delhi: Ministry of Information and Broadcasting, 1958–1990.

Gandhi, Ramchandra. "Brahmacharya." In *Way of Life: King, Householder, Renouncer*. Ed. T. N. Madan, 205–223. Delhi: Vikas Publications, 1982.

Ganguly, Debjani. "History's Implosion: A Benjaminian Reading of Ambedkar." *Journal of Narrative Theory* 37.3 (2002): 326–347.

Ganguly, Debjani. *Caste, Colonialism, and Counter-Modernity: Notes on a Postcolonial Hermeneutics of Caste*. London: Routledge, 2005.

Gaonkar Dilip. "On Alternative Modernities." *Public Culture* 1.1 (1999): 1–18.

Gilmartin, David, and Bruce A. Lawrence, eds. *Beyond Turk and Hindu: Rethinking Religious Identities in Islamicate South Asia*. Gainesville: University of Florida Press, 2000.

Girard, René. *Violence and the Sacred*. Trans. Patrick Gregory. Baltimore: Johns Hopkins University Press, 1977.

Hiltebeitel, Alf. *Rethinking the Mahabharata: A Reader's Guide to the Education of the Dharma King*. Chicago: University of Chicago Press, 2001.

Hubert, Henri and Marcel Mauss. *Sacrifice: Its Nature and Functions*. Trans. W. D. Halls. Chicago: University of Chicago Press, 1964.

Laidlaw, James. "Ethical Traditions in Question: Diaspora Jainism and the Environmental and Animal Liberation Movements." In *Ethical Life in South Asia*. Eds. Anand Pandian and Daud Ali, 61–83. Bloomington: Indiana University Press, 2010.

Lath, Mukund. "The Concept of Anrshamsya in the Mahabharata." In *Reflections and Variations on the Mahabharata*. Ed. T. R. S. Sharma, 82–89. Delhi: Sahitya Academy, 2009.

Lévi-Strauss, Claude. *Totemism*. New York: Beacon Press, 1963.

Lévi-Strauss, Claude. *The Savage Mind*. Chicago: University of Chicago Press, 1969.

Llewellyn, J. E. ed. *Defining Hinduism: A Reader*. London: Routledge, 2005.

Malamoud, Charles. *Cooking the World: Ritual and Thought in Ancient India*. New York: Oxford University Press, 1996.

McClymond, Kathryn. *Beyond Sacred Violence: A Comparative Study of Sacrifice*. Baltimore: Johns Hopkins University Press, 2008.

Mehta, J. L. "Problems of Understanding." *Philosophy East and West* 39.1 (1989): 3–12.

Oldenburg, Hermann. 1894. *Religion of the Vedas*. Delhi: Motilal Banarisidas, 1988.

Paranjpe, Anand C. *Self and Identity in Modern Psychology and Indian Thought*. New York: Plenum Press, 1998.

Parry, Jonathan P. *Death in Banaras*. London: Cambridge University Press, 1994.

Pinney, Christopher. *Photos of the Gods: The Printed Image and Political Struggle in India*. London: Reaktion Books, 2004.

Pollock, Sheldon trans. *Rama's Last Act by Bhava-bhuti*. New York: New York University Press, 2007.

Savarkar, Vinayak Damodar. 1922. *Hindutva*. Poona: S. R. Date, 1942.

Sen, Chitrabhanu. *A Dictionary of the Vedic Rituals: Based on the Sratua and the Grihya*. Delhi: Concept Publishing, 1978.

Sharma, T. R. S. "Introduction: Many Makers Many Texts/Contexts." In *Reflections and Variations on the Mahabharata*. Ed. T. R. S. Sharma, 1–37. Delhi: Sahitya Academy, 2009.

Singh, Bhrigupati. 2011. "Agonistic Intimacy and Moral Aspirations in Popular Hinduism. A Study in the Political Theology of the Neighbor." *American Ethnologist* 38.3 (2011): 430–450.

Skaria, Ajay. "Gandhi's Politics: Liberalism and the Question of the Ashram." In *Enchantments of Modernity: Empire, Nation, Globalization.* Ed. Saurabh Dube, 119–234. New Delhi: Routledge 2009.

Skaria, Ajay. "Living by Dying: Gandhi, Satyagraha and the Warrior." In *Ethical Life in South Asia.* Eds. Anand Pandian and Daud Ali, 211–232. Indiana University Press, 2010.

Smith, David. *Hinduism and Modernity.* Oxford, UK: Blackwell Publishing, 2003.

Veer, Peter Van der. *Religious Nationalism: Hindus and Muslims in India.* Berkeley: University of California Press, 1994.

Yang, Anand A. 1980 "Sacred Symbol and Sacred Space in Rural India: Community Mobilization in the 'Anti-Cow Killing' Riots of 1893." *Comparative Studies in Society and History,* Vol. 22.4 (1980): 576–596.

Chapter 2

Buddhist Traditions and Violence

Michael Jerryson

IN RECENT STUDIES, psychologists have found that the color orange releases more serotonin into our brain, which calms and relaxes us. It simply might be a coincidence that this hue is most frequently used for Buddhist monks' robes in Asia; however, the sensation of calm is also associated with Buddhism itself. The saffron robes have become a trademark of Buddhism around the world. Their colors usually range from bright orange to dark brown to black (Japanese *unsui*), depending on the ordination lineage of the school (*nikaya*). Corresponding to the neurological associations is the general conception that Buddhist traditions are irenic, encapsulated in the practice of meditation and complete withdrawal from worldly affairs (*lokiya*).

It is thus unusual to encounter such militant nomenclatures as Saffron Army or Saffron Revolution in the discussions of contemporary Buddhist monastic movements. Although some saffron armies, such as those of the Sri Lankan Janatha Vimukthi Peramuna (People's Liberation Front) are armed, others are not (Abeysekara 2002: 222–229). In September 2007, Burmese Buddhist monks employed Gandhi's nonviolent methods of protest against their government and were met with violence (Skidmore & Wilson 2010; Schober 2010). Whether violent or peaceful, these militant characterizations illustrate the Buddhist ambivalence toward violence.

Violence is a social phenomenon that pervades every religious tradition. In regard to physical acts of violence, there is a robust history of Buddhists who commit suicide and engage in conflicts and wars. Buddhist monasteries have served as military outposts, monks have led revolts, and Buddhist principles have served as war rhetoric for heads of state. Some of these acts of violence draw on Buddhist scriptures; others invoke Buddhist symbols. In addition to Buddhism's history of violence, Buddhist traditions globally influence religious acts of violence. Contemporary attacks of suicide martyrdom can be traced back to Japanese kamikazes during

World War II, which influenced the communist-leaning Japanese Red Army. On May 30, 1972, Red Army gunmen Tsuyoshi Okudaira, Yasuyuki Yasuda, and Kozo Okamoto committed the first contemporary suicide attack in the Middle East during the Lod Airport Massacre in Israel (Reuter 2004: 136–137).

Perhaps the core element that draws Buddhist traditions into the social realm of violence is their identification: "I am a Buddhist," which often is coterminous with a number of ethnic and national markers, (e.g., Tibetan Buddhist, Thai Buddhist, etc.). The construction of an identity requires the distinction between those within and outside the imagined community. This politicized element has been the genesis for many structural forms of violence over the centuries. In early South Asian societies, Buddhist traditions were aniconic and without strict identity markers, but as early as the first century CE, this changed. The crystallization of a Buddhist identity introduced adherents of the *Buddhadharma* (Buddhist teaching) to a new arena of politics and forms of alterity.

Since the third century BCE, Buddhists have clashed with opponents of different faiths, Buddhists from different countries, and even Buddhists of different ordination lineages within the same country. On most occasions, the mixture of Buddhist authority and political power has provided a recipe for violence. Early scriptures were ambiguous as to the relationship between Buddhist principles and sovereignty, due in part to the crucial patronage of the Buddha by the north Indian monarchs of Magadha and Kosala in the fifth century BCE. As states developed, Buddhist authority served to legitimize kings and rulers by granting them religiopolitical titles such as *chakravartin* (universal rule; literally, "one who turns the wheel"), *dhammaraja* ("ruler of the Buddhist doctrine"), or *dalai lama* ("ocean of wisdom"). Buddhist states have used violence externally as well as internally. Early South Asian religious literature charged rulers with protecting their subjects from external forces (which involves warfare) and with upholding the law by inflicting physical punishments.

In the era of nation-states and nation building, Buddhists such as Tibetan, Thai, Cambodian, and Burmese consider their nationality intimately connected with Buddhism. Due to this collusion of identities, an attack on the nation becomes an attack on Buddhism (and vice versa). The issue of multiple interrelated identities raises a larger and more problematic question: What is Buddhism?

Similar to other religions, the Buddhist system is a theoretical construct that becomes tradition through the imputation of culture. Officially there are more than 350 million Buddhists in the world; however, if we include unofficial estimates from China and other countries, there are over 1.3 billion adherents. There are Buddhist communities in more than 135 countries, and each community possesses unique characteristics endemic to its school and location. In such a way, Buddhism is a global religious system that encompasses a canopy of people, rituals, scriptures, and beliefs. But what is the theoretical construct that binds these communities together?

The Buddhist theoretical construct is predicated on the teachings of the Buddha. Buddhists worldwide take refuge in the Buddha, whether he is conceived as historical or cosmological (Jerryson 2010: 5). Although the teachings vary among Buddhist communities, all acknowledge the Four Noble Truths (Sanskrit: *catvari aryasatyani;* Pali: *cattari ariyasaccani*): Life is suffering, there is a cause to this suffering, there is a cessation to this suffering, and there is a path to cessation. There is no uniform initiation into Buddhism as in the case of a Christian baptism or the Islamic declaration of faith (*shahadah*), although some Buddhist traditions have initiation rites. Perhaps the closest to a lay profession of faith in Buddhist traditions is to seek refuge in the three jewels (Sanskrit: *triratna;* Pali: *tiratana*): the Buddha, the Dhamma (the doctrine), and the Sangha (community that upholds the teachings). That said, Tantric practitioners take refuge in a fourth jewel: their guru.

In drawing the parameters for Buddhist traditions, it is clear that there is a high variance of cultural practices and beliefs. This chapter will cover the history of Buddhist traditions and violence with special attention to the scriptural justifications, symbols, and actual manifestations of violence.

Ethical and Scriptural Justifications for Violence

Every global religion contains scriptural interdictions on violence; Buddhist traditions are no exception. There are numerous passages within Buddhist scriptures that uphold the notion of *ahimsa* (nonviolence) and equanimity. Nonetheless, like every other global religion, Buddhist traditions have adherents that commit violence and justify their acts with scriptures. These Buddhist scriptures either condone the use of violence or are hermeneutically ambiguous.

Most canonical sources lack a specified author because an indication of an author would impose a sense of temporality and reduce a scripture's sacrality. Thankfully, the nature of these scriptures is not germane to this overview; rather, what the scriptures say and the influence they carry are. Buddhist scriptures are organized into three baskets of texts (Sanskrit: *Tripitaka*; Pali: *Tipitaka*): the scriptures on monastics (*Vinaya*), the scriptures of discourses (Sanskrit: *Sutras*; Pali: *Suttas*), and the scriptures of higher knowledge (Sanskrit: *Abhidharma*; Pali: *Abhidhamma*). The orthodox language in Theravada is Pali; the orthodox language in Mahayana and Vajrayana is Sanskrit. In addition, many important Buddhist scriptures are in the local or regional vernacular.

Because Buddhist traditions began in South Asia in the fifth century BCE, early Buddhist thought was largely influenced by South Asian worldviews that include Brahmanism and Jainism. Each religious tradition that emerged from the subcontinent before the Christian era (or even the Buddhist era), was heavily influenced by the laws of action (Sanskrit: *karma*; Pali: *kamma*). Buddhism was no exception to this. According to Buddhist scriptures, a person accrues demerit through violent actions or even intentions to commit violence. The most severe of these actions is murder.

The esteemed Buddhist scholar Paul Demiéville argues that no other precept is so strictly followed by all Buddhists and goes so far as to say that not killing is a characteristic "so anchored in Buddhism that it is practically considered a custom" (Demiéville 2010: 18). This custom is perhaps best understood as one of five moral precepts (Sanskrit: *panchashila*; Pali: *panchasilani*), which are to abstain from killing sentient beings, stealing, lying, partaking of intoxicants that cloud the mind, and sexual misconduct. This practice is analogous to the five restraints (*yama*) in Hindu traditions, and underscores the social ethics of South Asian traditions. In addition to lay practices, there are canonical and commentarial sources throughout the different Buddhist schools that contain severe interdictions on violence. They also contain the exception to the rule. Analogous to Carl Schmitt's notions of *Ausnahmezustand* (state of exception), Buddhist exceptions empower or legitimate kings and rulers.

These exceptions are not generated in a vacuum and did not remain simply "exceptions." The scriptures that condone or justify violence are connected to physical acts of violence. Either Buddhist authors try to rationalize the previous violence of Buddhist rulers—such as the early Magadha king Ajatashatru who killed his father, Bimbisara—or condone the current acts of a Buddhist state (often in defense of the religion), such as the Japanese imperial violence from the start of the Meiji period (1868) and onward.

In most cases, the state of exception depends on three variables: the intention of the person who commits the violence (e.g, is it accidental or deliberate, and if deliberate, is the mind clear of hatred and avarice?), the nature of the victim (e.g., human, animal, or supernatural), and the stature of the one who commits the violence (e.g., is the person a king, soldier, or a butcher?). Buddhists have applied these variables to condone or, at times, even to advocate murder. Although there are some texts (Sanskrit: *sutra*; Pali: *sutta*) that traverse doctrinal boundaries, in order to preserve the distinctions between schools I will treat these exceptions within their doctrinal categories of Theravada (Path of the Elders), Mahayana (Great Vehicle) and Vajrayana (Diamond Vehicle) and, when necessary, indicate, regional specificities.

Theravada Scriptures

The teachings of Theravada are predominantly practiced in Sri Lankan, Thai, Burmese, Cambodian, Lao and early Indian traditions. Within the Theravada doctrine (*dhamma*), violence is categorically condemned as an unwholesome act (*akusala*); however, there are degrees of condemnation, especially in regard to the state.

Theravada doctrine on violence derives from the Three Baskets (Tipitaka), which is commonly referred to as the Pali Canon and its commentaries. Since ordained men and women model behavior as bearers of the dhamma, one of the ethical cornerstones in the Pali Canon is the *Vinaya*, the monastic codes. Interestingly, within the monastic tradition murder is ranked third out of four defeats (*parajika*) and results in permanent expulsion from the Sangha (the four defeats are sex, stealing, murder, and false claims of enlightenment). Although ranked third out of the four, murder is among the greatest sins (*adhamma*) a person can commit.

The *Vinaya* is replete with examples of violent scenarios. In most occasions, the prominent factors in the monk's penalty are whether the act was successful or not, and (2) her/his intentionality. The nature of one's kamma (literally, one's action) is predicated on the outcome of the action; failed attempts to commit violence are penalized because of the intention but do not carry the full penalty of a successful action. Correspondingly, accidents are generally critiqued in Buddhist scriptures as a result of a lack of mindfulness, and the penalties are not as severe as deliberate acts of violence. The Buddhist emphasis on intention distinguishes the tradition from other regionally prominent religious traditions, such as Jainism.

Intention

The first book of the *Vinaya* is the "Suttavibhanga," or "The Analysis of the Rules." It distinguishes the acts of manslaughter and attempted murder from the act of murder in numerous accounts. In one particular instance, an accidental death caused by pushing one's father yields no offense; the failed attempt to kill one's father by pushing him results in a grave offense. However, a death caused by the deliberate intention to kill results in expulsion (Horner 1938: 139). The same rationale is applied to issues of euthanasia and abortion. If a monk or nun advocated a quick death or techniques to abort a pregnancy and the advice led to a death, the person was expelled from the Sangha. Advice that was not heeded carries lesser penalties. Insanity also plays a role in assessing the act of murder. In a previous life as the Brahman Lomakassapa, the Buddha killed hundreds of creatures but was not in the correct state of mind. Lomakassapa was "unhinged" with desire, and the text explains that a madman's crimes are pardonable (Horner 1963–1964: 14–17).

Nature of the Victim

Regardless of intention, a monk's murder of a nonhuman does not result in expulsion. Monks who kill fearsome dryads (*yakkha*) and other nonhuman beings commit grave offenses (*thullaccaya*), which requires confessions (Horner 1938: 146–147). The monk Udayin's killing of crows (or of any other animal) also only merits a confession (Horner 1942: 1).

The commentaries offer similar interpretations of offenses related to murder. The famous Indian scholar monk Buddhaghosa (fifth c. CE) analyzed the monastic laws on murder in his *Sumagala-vilasini* and claimed:

> In the case of living creatures without [moral] virtues, such as animals, [the act of killing] is less blameworthy when the creature has a small body, and more blameworthy when the being has a large body. Why? Because the greater effort [required] in killing a being with a large body; and even when the effort is the same, [the act of killing a large-bodied creature is still more blameworthy] because of its greater physical substance. In the case of beings that possess [moral] virtues, such as human beings, the act of killing is less blameworthy when the being is of little virtue and more blameworthy when the being is of great virtue. But when the body and virtue [of creatures] are equal, [the act of killing] is less blameworthy when

the defilements and force of the effort are mild, more blameworthy
when they are powerful.

(Gethin 2004: 171–172)

The *Vinaya* rules and Buddhaghosa's accounts explain, among other things,
Theravada dietary habits. Thai, Lao, Burmese, and Sri Lankan lay Buddhists
will generally eat chicken and pork and avoid beef, because the cow is a
much larger animal. They also provide an area of ambiguity with regard to
humanity and virtue. This distinction between human/nonhuman and
virtuous/nonvirtuous humans has been raised in other Buddhist sources.

One of the more popular accounts comes from the Sinhalese mythohistorical chronicle, the *Mahavamsa*. The Buddhist king Dutthagamani
wages a just war against the Damil invaders led by King Elara. After a
bloody and victorious battle, Dutthagamani laments for causing the
slaughter of millions. Eight enlightened monks (*arahant*) comfort him
with the explanation:

> From this deed arises no hindrance in thy way to heaven. Only one
> and a half human beings have been slain here by thee, O lord of
> men. The one had come unto the (three) refuges, the other had
> taken on himself the five precepts. Unbelievers and men of evil life
> were the rest, not more to be esteemed than beasts. But as for thee,
> thou wilt bring glory to the doctrine of the Buddha in manifold
> ways; therefore cast away from thy heart, O ruler of men!

(Geiger 1993 [1912]: 178)

The monks' explanation includes the prerequisites discussed earlier for
being a Buddhist, in this context the taking of the three refuges, and following the five moral precepts. By distinguishing Buddhists from non-
Buddhists, the murders in this narrative are dismissed, since the
non-Buddhists possess such little virtue they are on par with animals.
Furthermore, the king has pure intentions with the desire to support and
defend the Buddhist doctrine. The *Mahavamsa*'s rationale and context were
not overlooked by Sri Lankan Buddhists centuries later in their twenty-six
year civil war against the Liberation Tamil Tigers of Eelam (LTTE, 1983–
2009) and has permeated Southeast Asia as a form of rhetoric, such as
during the Cambodia anticommunist campaign in the 1970s.

A similar rationale was used by the prominent Thai Buddhist monk
Kittiwuttho in the 1970s during the Thai campaign against communism.

For Kittiwuttho, a communist was a bestial type of a person and not a complete person at that. More importantly, her or his death served to support
the Buddhist doctrine (Keyes 1978: 153). Kittiwuttho drew on the *Anguttara
Nikaya*, "To Kesi, the Horse Trainer," to justify his stance on killing communists. Not widely used for this purpose, "To Kesi the Horse Trainer" is
about the Buddha's conversation with a horse trainer on the similarities
between training people and horses. At one point, the Buddha explains
that if a tamable person does not submit to any training, the untamable
person is killed. However, shortly after this statement the Buddha explains
that death is meant as the Buddha's abandonment of that person's needs,
thus meaning the death of the person's ultimate potentiality (Thanissaro
2010). While Kittiwuttho's use of this text is problematic, it is demonstra-
tive of how Buddhist exceptions have been applied to justify violence.

Stature of Those Who Kill

Monastic ethics serve as exemplary rules for others to model, but the 227
rules for Theravada monks are not required for the laity. Different roles
merit different ethics; the ethics for a monk is not the same as it is for a
butcher or a soldier (although butchers were noted for having to spend
many anguishing lifetimes to redress their negative karma). As for soldiers, Buddhist scriptures remain ambiguous in certain places as to the
ramifications of their occupations. Some impose restrictions on monastic
interactions with soldiers or declare that soldiers may not ordain while
serving the state, but most do not directly condemn a soldier for following
her or his duty. Instead, what is repeatedly emphasized in the ethics of
this position is the soldier's state of mind.

One example of this comes from the fourth book and eighth chapter of
the *Samyutta Nikaya*, "Gamanisamyutta" or the "Connected Discourses to
Headmen." The Buddha counsels a headman Yodhajiva, who is a mercenary under the assumption that mercenaries who strive and exert themselves in battles will be reborn in the heavens. The Buddha explains that,
when a mercenary dies with the debased thoughts of slaughtering and
killing other people, he is reborn in either the hell or animal realms
(Bhikkhu Bodhi 2000: 1334–1335). In this scenario, Yodhajiva is cautioned
to avoid debased thoughts at the time of death but not to avoid the act of
killing. This warning against ill thoughts is relevant whether a person
commits an act of aggression or even an act of self-defense. However, the
ambiguity about the act itself is present and is found in contemporary

contexts as well. In the recent civil war with the LTTE, Sri Lankan Buddhist monks preached to soldiers in order to suffuse their minds with mercy and compassion. Buddhist soldiers with "cool heads" are less apt to make mistakes on the battlefield and harm civilians (Kent 2010: 172).

A unique set of ethical parameters is for kings and just rule, which in the contemporary context apply to nation-states. According to the commentaries (*atthakatha*), Theravada's earliest model of a just ruler was the Mauryan emperor Ashoka. After a successful and bloody campaign against the Kalinga in which more than 100,000 died and 150,000 were enslaved, Ashoka repented and turned to the Buddhist doctrine. Typically, Ashoka's reign is praised after his turn to the Buddhist doctrine (and thus, after his conquests). However, Ashoka never disbanded his army after his Buddhist epiphany. He maintained the state policy of capital punishment and, according to literary records, killed more than 18,000 Jains and committed other atrocities well after his turn to righteous Buddhist kingship (Jenkins 2010: 63).

Early Buddhist scriptures tacitly support states, which may be due partly to the fact that the Buddha received most of his principle support in his early years from the kingdoms of Magadha and Kosala. The Buddha's relationship to the two kingdoms was stressed at times by their internecine conflict. As a moral and ethical liaison for both kingdoms, the Buddha responded on these occasions by condoning wars of defense over wars of aggression. This endorsement of defensive violence employs one of two modes on the ethics of state violence. According to Steven Collins, Theravada scriptures present on occasion a categorical imperative to avoid violence. On other occasions, the doctrine offers an ethics of just war through reciprocity; the Buddha counsels kings to administer judgments and punishments, but with a clear and calm mind (Collins 1998: 420).

This latter mode is best evident in the 239th rebirth story of the Buddha, the "Harita-Mata-Jataka," or the "Blue-Green Frog Birth Story," in which the Buddha addresses a recent attack by the kingdom of Kosala on the kingdom of Magadha. As in other rebirth stories, the narrative serves as a didactic for the particular context as well as general readership. The story tells of a water snake that falls into a trap and is attacked by a throng of fish. Appealing to a blue-green frog for help, the frog, which is the Buddha-to-be, replies to the entrapped snake, "[i]f you eat fish that get into your demesne, the fish eat you when you get into theirs. In his own place, and district, and feeding ground, no one is weak." Following the frog's explanation, the fish seize and kill the snake (Cowell 1895: 165).

Ethics of state violence are mentioned several times in the *The Questions of King Milinda*. Throughout the text, the Indo-Greek king Menander I questions the Buddhist monk Nagasena about Buddhist principles. In the fourth book, called "The Solving of Dilemmas," the king lists eight classes of men who kill living beings: lustful men, cruel men, dull men, proud men, avaricious men, needy men, foolish men, and kings in the way of punishment (Davids 1894: 17). As in the case of the other seven types of men, a king by his nature adjudicates punishments and kills living beings.

This aspect of rule is further described in a later conversation, when the king explains that, if a man has committed a crime, the people would request that the criminal be deprived of goods, bound, tortured, put to death, or beheaded (Davids 1894: 239). In neither conversation does Nagasena dispute the king's views on murder, and the presence of these duties in a book on Buddhist ethics is unmistakably notable. This approach to just rule is found in other canonical sources such as the twenty-sixth and twenty-seventh books of the *Digha Nikaya*, "The Sermon on the Knowledge of Beginnings," and "The Lion's Roar at the Turning of the Wheel." In both books, the king is entrusted with the moral responsibility to uphold the law and mete out punishments. Balkrishna Gokhale argues that early Buddhist thinkers had a Weberian conception of the state: "For them the state is an organization of force or violence the possession of which is largely restricted to the king and his instruments" (251).

While this concept of the state was taken for granted by early Buddhist thinkers, it became emboldened by modern Buddhist advocates and rulers, such as the Sri Lankan government in its indiscriminate use of force against the LTTE and the Thai state and its use of *lèse majesté* to impose corporal punishment on those who disrespect the Buddhist monarchy.

Mahayana Scriptures

The Mahayana doctrine can be found primarily among Indian, Chinese, Korean, Japanese, and Vietnamese traditions, and its scriptures cover a vast array of sub-schools and corresponding soteriologies. Mahayana's doctrinal stances on violence are similar to those found in Theravada in many respects. Its scriptures condemn violence and hold murder as an unwholesome act (*akushala*). In some Mahayana traditions, this abhorrence of violence requires that practitioners maintain a strict vegan diet. Yet ethical exceptions also exist in Mahayana doctrine. Most of the exceptions in regard to these variables derive from two principal ideas within Mahayana: skill in means (*upaya*) and emptiness (*shunyata*).

Mahayana ethics on violence are found primarily within the second of the three baskets (*Tripitaka*), the *Sutras*, and the commentaries. Some traditions refer to multiple sources in their ethical discussions, while other traditions base their ethics solely on one text, such as the *Perfection of Wisdom* texts (*Prajnaparamita*) or the *Lotus Sutra*. Although there are some commentators, such as Asanga and Vasubandhu, who address violence within their treatment of ethics, most of the scriptures on violence are in a narrative style.

Intention

Even though Mahayana notions of skill in means and emptiness provide justifications for violence, or in these instances murder, the actors must not have ill thoughts or intentions when they perform the violence. Rather, their intentions should be compassionate and imbued with skill in means. In this vein, most exceptions require that the actor be a bodhisattva—an enlightened being. However, this is not always the case; in some cases the absence of any ill intent is sufficient to pardon an act of violence. In Chan Buddhism, the *Treatise of Absolute Contemplation* explains that murderous acts are analogous to brush fires. "The man who renders his mind similar [to the forces of nature] is entitled to do equally as much" (Demiéville 2010: 56). Likewise, Japanese Zen interpretations of killing stress the vacuity of the act. Killing puts an end to the passions of a person's mind and fosters the Buddha-nature within (ibid., 44). Intentionality is a critical component in Mahayana ethics of violence. It is not simply whether a person engages in an accidental or deliberate action, but there are also exceptions that allow for intentional violence.

At times, violence by lay practitioners is permitted; of particular note is the act of suicide in the Chinese traditions. Within the Chinese traditions, the *Lotus Sutra* provides a literary blueprint for self-immolation practices. The chapter "The Original Acts of the Medicine King," tells of a bodhisattva who covers himself with oil and fragrance, wraps his body in oil-soaked clothes, and burns himself (the self-immolation lasts for 1,200 years). The Buddha explains to the reader that the bodhisattva's act is one that anyone meritorious may do:

> Gifts of his own body, such as this one, number in the incalculable hundreds of thousands of myriads of millions of *nayutas*. O Beflowered by the King of Constellations! If there is one who, opening up his thought, wishes to attain *anuttarasamyaksambodhi* [consummation of incomparable wisdom], if he can burn a finger or

even a toe as an offering to a *Buddhastūpa* [Buddhist relic shrine],
he shall exceed one who uses realm or walled, wife or children,
or even all the lands, mountains, forests, rivers, ponds, and sun-
dry precious objects in the whole thousand-millionfold world as
offerings.

(Benn 2007: 61)

Here, the exception to intended violence is the conscious sacrifice of one's
body. Suicide is also noted in other sources such as the "Hungry Tigress
Jataka," in which the Buddha-to-be offers his body to a starving tigress so
that she may feed her cubs. Sources like "The Hungry Tigress Jataka,"
have been cited as rationalizations for the contemporary Tibetan practice
of self-immolation.

Skill in means is a method employed by awakened beings to help others awaken. Perhaps the most famous example of this comes from a section in chapter 3 of the *Lotus Sutra*, "The Burning House." The *Lotus Sutra*
is one of the core scriptures in the Chinese Tiantai and the Japanese
Tendai and Nichiren schools and is considered sacred. In the text, the
Buddha tells a parable to his disciple Sariputra about an old man and his
children. The man attempts to rescue his children from a burning building, but they are enthralled by their games and do not heed his warnings.
In order to get them to leave, he promises them three gifts; when they
escape the building, they receive the greatest of these gifts. Sariputra
praises the Buddha and correctly interprets that the man should not be
condemned for lying, even if he had not given the children any gifts. His
action was just because he was trying to liberate the children from a very
painful experience.

The *Lotus Sutra* provides not only the strategy of skill in means but also
ambiguous excerpts on violence. In 1279 CE, Nichiren writes to his devoted
samurai follower, Shijo Kingo, and explains that Shijo's faith in the *Lotus
Sutra* helped saved him from a recent ambush. He enjoins Shijo to employ
the strategy of the *Lotus Sutra* in his future work and quotes a section from
chapter 23 of the *Lotus Sutra*:

"'All others who bear you enmity or malice will likewise be wiped
out.' These golden words will never prove false. The heart of strategy and swordsmanship derives from the Mystic Law. Have profound faith. A coward cannot have any of his prayers answered."

(Nichiren 2009: 1001)

The sentence quoted from the *Lotus Sutra* is generally regarded as metaphorical, but in this context Nichiren applies it literally in his address to a samurai about past and future acts of violence.

Another seemingly metaphorical use of violence is found in the Chinese text *The Sutra of the Forty-two Sections*. In one of the aphorisms by the Buddha, the text compares fighting in battle with attaining the Way:

> A man practicing the Way is like a lone man in combat against ten thousand. Bearing armor and brandishing weapons, he charges through the gate eager to do battle, but if he is weakhearted and cowardly he will withdraw and flee.... If a man is able to keep a firm grip on his wits and advance resolutely, without becoming deluded by worldly or deranged talk, then desire will disappear and evil will vanish, and he is certain to attain the Way.
>
> (Sharf 1996: 370)

The use of war as a metaphor was also used by the Indian Buddhist monk Shantideva in his commentary, *Engaging in Bodhisattva Behavior*. However, in neither the *Lotus Sutra* nor the *Sutra of the Forty-Two Sections* (or even in *Engaging in Bodhisattva Behavior*) do we find direct advocacy of violence; instead we encounter ambiguous passages for such an interpretation.

Perhaps the most extreme measure of skill in means to justify violence is found in the chapter "Murder with Skill in Means: The Story of the Compassionate Ship's Captain" from the *Upayakaushalya Sutra*, or the *Skill-in-Means Sutra*. In one of his many previous births, the Buddha is the captain of a ship at sea and is told by water deities that a robber onboard the ship intends to kill the five hundred passengers and the captain. Within a dream, the deities implore the captain to use skill in means to prevent this, since all five hundred men are future bodhisattvas and the murder of them would invoke on the robber immeasurable lifetimes in the darkest hells. The captain, who in this text is named Great Compassionate (Mahakarunika), wakes and contemplates the predicament for seven days. He eventually rationalizes:

> "There is no means to prevent this man from slaying the merchants and going to the great hells but to kill him." And he thought, "If I were to report this to the merchants, they would kill and slay him with angry thoughts and all go to great hells themselves." And he thought, "If I were to kill this person, I would likewise burn in the

great hells for one hundred-thousand eons because of it. Yet I can bear to experience the pains of the great hells, that this person not slay these five hundred merchants and develop so much evil *karma*. I will kill this person myself."

(Tatz 1994: 74)

The captain subsequently murders the robber, and the Buddha explains, "For me, *samsāra* was curtailed for one hundred-thousand eons because of that skill in means and great compassion. And the robber died to be reborn in world of paradise" (ibid.). Here, the skill in means is motivated by compassion, which ameliorated the karmic results of murder.

Nature of the Victim

The School of Emptiness (*shunyavada*) derives its teachings in part from the pan-Buddhist positions of no-self (Sanskrit: *anatman;* Pali: *anatta*) and of the two-truths model: conventional truth and ultimate truth. Buddhists recognize that there is no eternal self (or, no-soul) and that everything we perceive in this world is impermanent and thus constitutes conventional truth. The philosopher Nagarjuna is the most prominent and respected advocate of this principle and extends the idea of no-self to reality in its entirety, claiming that all phenomena are empty of essence. While emptiness serves to explain reality ontologically and epistemologically, it also provides a lens for valuing human life. This line of reasoning raises the query: If human life is empty of any true nature, what is destroyed in a murder?

One element that is commonly presented when justifying murder is the dehumanization of the intended victim(s). This dehumanization is present in Theravada when monks consider communists or the followers of the Tamil king Elara less than human and thus meritoriously expendable. Within Mahayana doctrine, some humans are designated as *icchantikas*, those who are those barred from enlightenment.

Mahayana doctrine typically advocates proselytizing, with people undertaking the bodhisattva vows to work toward liberating all sentient beings (*bodhicitta*). This all-encompassing ethos has an exception with the *icchantika*. Considered the most vile and debased creatures, they have either committed the worst of deeds or repudiated the basic tenets of the doctrine; they are classified at a lower level than animals. Some texts, such as the Chinese version of the Mahayana *Mahaparinirvana Sutra*, consider it more harmful to kill an ant than an *icchantika*. Within this text, the Buddha explains that no negative karma accrues from killing them:

"Just as no sinful *karma* [will be engendered] when one digs the ground, mows grass, fells trees, cuts corpses into pieces and scolds and whips them, the same is true when one kills an *icchantika*, for which deed [also] no sinful karma [will arise]."

(Ming-Wood 1984: 68)

Perhaps the most extreme religious rhetoric of dehumanization occurs within Mahayana doctrine: If a person is empty of substance, what is being murdered? One scripture that offers an answer is the Chinese text called the *Susthitamati-Paripriccha*, which is often referred to as *How to Kill with the Sword of Wisdom*.

Within the text, the fully enlightened being Manjushri explains to the Buddha that, if one were to conceive of sentient beings as only names and thoughts, she or he should kill those names and thoughts. However, as long as a person clears the mind of holding a knife or killing, to kill the "thoughts of a self and a sentient being is to kill sentient beings truly. [If you can do that,] I will give you permission to cultivate pure conduct [with me]." (Chang 1983: 65). Later in the text, Manjushri attempts to assuage bodhisattvas of their guilt from committing violence and advances to kill the Buddha with his sword. The Buddha explains that there is neither kill-ing nor killer. Hence, Manjushri does not suffer any negative repercus-sions for attempting to kill the Buddha, since ultimately "there is no sword and no karma and no retribution, who performs that karma and who will undergo the karmic retribution?" (Chang 1983: 69). The acts in this real-ity are empty of true existence; therefore violence is empty of any true repercussion. Another Chinese text, *The Catharsis of Ajatashatru's Remorse*, justifies an act of matricide in a similar fashion. Manjushri defends the criminal and explains that since the actor's thoughts were empty at the time of the deed, he should be exonerated (Demiéville 2010: 42).

Stature of Those Who Kill

In some texts, killing or war is justified so long as it is done to defend the religion. In the Tibetan version of the Mahayana *Mahaparinirvana Sutra*, Buddhists, especially kings, are expected to take up weapons and fight to defend their religion (Schmithausen 1999: 57–58). Similar to Theravada doctrine, Mahayana doctrine contains different ethics for rulers than for lay practitioners. The Mongolian text *White History of the Tenfold Virtuous Dharma* instructs rulers to destroy those against the Buddhist teachings and to implement harsh measures when necessary (Wallace 2010: 93).

The South Asian *Arya-Bodhisattva-gocara-upayavishaya-vikurvana-nirdesha Sutra (Satyakaparivarta)*, which is loosely translated at *The Noble Teachings through Manifestations on the Subject of Skill-in-Means within the Bodhisattva's Field of Activity*, also provides instructions for rulers, which includes ways to administer Buddhist-sanctioned torture, capital punishment, and other forms of violence. In the text, the king is warned to avoid the exercise of *excessive* compassion and to imprison, terrorize, beat, bind, or harm "uncivilized people" (Jenkins 2010: 64).

Mahayana doctrine provides a similar structure of exceptions for violence as Theravada. However, the principles of emptiness and skill in means create a distinctive set of ethical considerations. These principles are shared in Vajrayana doctrine, which is often said to have evolved out of Mahayana doctrine.

Vajrayana Scriptures

Vajrayana is a contested term, and scholars are not in agreement as to the traditions that fall under its canopy. Some scholars argue that it is principally an offshoot of Mahayana doctrine that is specifically Tibetan and Mongolian, while others identify the term with similar appellations such as Tantrayana or Mantrayana and consider the term to include Indian, Nepali, Tibetan, Mongolian, and Japanese traditions. Whether one considers Vajrayana a Tibetan nomenclature or a descriptor of various traditions, it inevitably involves tantras. Tantra is another term that is highly contested, and a replete discussion of it would stretch beyond the parameters of this chapter.

Tantra texts often prescribe transgressive actions. For the *tantrika*, if one is bound by conventional taboos, then s/he is not truly free of the world and its fetters. Often acts of transgression are sexual or violent in nature. In addition to its transgressive inclinations, Tantra texts are intended to be esoteric. Most traditions require special ordinations for their initiates and gurus to explain the doctrine. This complexity adds several lays to the texts and often leads to the Buddhist hermeneutics of provisional meanings (*neyartha*) and definitive meanings (*nitartha*). With the help of one's guru, provisional meaning can be discarded for the highest truth of the scripture. Some texts, such as the Indian and Tibetan *Kalachakra Tantra (Wheel of Time Tantra)*, may prescribe violence, but this is argued to be a provisional interpretation. When the text encourages readers to kill, lie, steal, and commit adultery, commentators explain the metaphorical nature of it (Broido 1988: 100). In this vein, a venture into an ethics of violence is fraught with distinct hermeneutical challenges.

Vajrayana doctrine is suffused with texts and commentaries that reject the use of violence. Many of the Tantra texts criticize Hindu texts and their position on animal sacrifices, or their contextual advocacy of justified violence in the *Bhagavad Gita* and other sources. However, Vajrayana texts offer arguments that are quite similar in nature to those that they critique. For instance, the Tibetologist Jacob Dalton locates in the *Kalika Purana* detailed instructions for human sacrifices to Kali or to the *heruka* Buddha and his mandala assembly. In such cases, the position in which the severed head comes to rest reveals signs of a kingdom's success (Dalton 2011: 90).

The seemingly contradictory status of Vajrayana texts serves as a poignant reminder that texts are not ahistorical and bereft of contexts; rather, they were born at different times, from people with various schools of thought. The texts display various accounts for justified violence. Of particular distinctive prominence among the texts are those pertaining to intentionality, such as defensive violence and liberation killing, and the stature of those who kills, which is primarily found in the bodhisattva.

Intention

Many of Vajrayana's ethical foundations for justified violence are coterminous with those in Mahayana doctrine. A motif that justifies violence in Vajrayana scriptures is defense; one of the most ubiquitous of reasons to commit violence. The questions arise though: What are the determinations of the aggression that necessitates the defense, and what does that defense entail? Within Vajrayana scriptures, defense is mounted through rituals of sacrifice and cosmic battles.

Tantra texts range from ritual to practical and yogic purposes. Most germane to our discussion is the tantric ritual goals, which involve the pacification of diseases, enemies, and emotions; augmentation of money, power, and merit; control of opponents, gods, and passions; and the killing of enemies, gods, sense of self, and so on (Davidson 2005: 35). Among the defensive rituals is the rite of fire sacrifice (*abhichara-homa*), which in the Indian *Mahavairochana-abhisambodhi Tantra* subdues hated foes. There are disparate but concerted commentaries on the fire sacrifice that expand on its transgressive and violent nature. The Indian Buddhist scholar-monk Bhavyakirti writes on the *Chakrasamvara Tantra:*

Then the destruction of all, arising from the vajra, is held [to be accomplished] with the great meat. It is the dreadful destroyer of all the cruel ones. Should one thus perform without hesitation the rites of eating, fire sacrifice (homa), and sacrificial offerings (bali) with the meats of dogs and pigs, and also [the meat of] those [chickens] that have copper [colored] crests, everything without exception will be achieved, and all kingdoms will be subdued.

(Gray 2007: 252)

Whereas Bhavyakirti's commentary invokes the violent sacrifice of animals for defensive purposes, other texts have more inclusive and aggressive positions. Vajrayana doctrine differs considerably from Theravada doctrine on the killing of animals, especially for dietary purposes. In Mongolian and Tibetan traditions, adherents are encouraged to eat larger animals instead of smaller ones. The death of one large animal such as a cow could feed many, whereas the death of one shrimp would not satisfy a person.

Defense does not pertain to simply threats of the state but also include preemptive attacks due to an imminent cosmic war. The most notable of these is found in the Indian and Tibetan Kalachakra Tantra, referred to as the Wheel of Time Tantra. As mentioned by the Buddhologist Lambert Schmithausen, the text describes an eschatological war in which the army of the bodhisattva king of Shambhala finally conquers and annihilates the Muslim forces in order to destroy their barbarian religion and to reestablish Buddhism. We should not overlook the historical context of this text; it is estimated by scholars that it was composed during the Muslim invasions of northern Indian in the eleventh century.

In some texts, the Mahayana principle of skill in means is applied to show violence as a redemptive act, which is often referred to as liberation killing. Such is the case of the bodhisattva Vajrapani, who kills the Hindu god Mahesvara and revives him as an enlightened follower of the Buddha. Tibetan Buddhists from the Nyingma school have killing rituals that are meant to liberate their enemies (Mayer 1996: 108). The Sarvadurgatiparishodhana Tantra, translated as The Purification of All Misfortunes, advocates the killing of those "who hate the Three Jewels, those who have a wrong attitude with regards to the Buddha's teachings or disparage the [Vajrayana] masters" (Schmithausen 1999: 58). This position is partly justified through the notion of compassion, where killing an evil person prevents that person from committing further negative actions (karma).

One of the most famous of these examples comes from the Tibetan *Chos 'byung me tog snying po*, which details the Buddhist assassination of the Tibetan ruler Lang Darma in 841. At the time, the Tibetan king Lang Darma oversaw policies that reduced the power and control of monasteries and was viewed as anti-Buddhist. The author Nyang Nyi ma 'od relates that the Buddhist monk received a vision from a protective Buddhist deity, who directed him to kill the ruler. This killing both liberated the country from an anti-Buddhist ruler and also liberated the ruler—through his murder. The narrative of this liberation killing is part of the Tibetan collective memory, and the murder is recalled in ritual yearly in Tibetan monasteries in their dance—the *cham* (Meinert 2006: 100–101). This violent practice of liberation did not end in the ninth century, nor was it restricted to ignoble kings. The presence of Tibetan Buddhist Tantric ritual killings and blood sacrifice was widespread enough for King Yeshe O (942–1024 CE) to publicly oppose them and to argue hermeneutically for a distinction between the tantric practices of liberation rites and sacrifice (Dalton 2011: 106–108).

Stature of Those Who Kill

Among the Vajrayana foundational principles is the Mahayana conception of the bodhisattva, a being who is either enlightened or on the path to enlightenment. In some texts, these individuals, who are endowed with perfected compassion and wisdom, gain the benefits from an ethical double standard. As seen in the scriptures about the bodhisattva Manjushri, ordinary people are bound by the provisional ethics; however, bodhisattvas may do anything, even commit murder. Fully enlightened beings are not hindered by the attachments of ill thoughts, so their actions are different from others. In addition, they use skill in means to liberate people and protect the religion. Within the Mergen Gegen tradition, Tibetan lamas identify the Mongol emperor Chinggis (Ghengis Khan) as an incarnation of the bodhisattva Vajrapani. As Vajrapani, his function is to protect Buddhism and destroy heretics. This rationale applies to Tantric masters: Buddhist yogis. In the Tibetan *Song of the Queen Spring*, the Fifth Dalai Lama explains that advanced Buddhist yogis can commit just acts of violence because of their command over mental states and emotions (Maher 2010: 85). It is in this context that the Fifth Dalai Lama justifies violence committed by his school's protector, the Mongol ruler Gushri Khan. In addition to the fact that Gushri Khan was defending the dharma, the Fifth Dalai Lama explains that the ruler was a bodhisattva (ibid., 88).

Symbolic Representations of Violence

The Four Noble Truths focus on suffering (Sanskrit: *dukkha*; Pali: *duh-kha*), a painful theme that serves as the bedrock for Buddhist worldviews. Although the Four Noble Truths discuss the suffering of the world (and the need to liberate oneself from it), there is violent rhetoric, imagery, and legends in Buddhist traditions as well. Some of these are global, whereas others are culturally specific to their locality. Whether global or locally relevant, symbolic representations of violence are generally found in eschatological accounts, legends about nemeses, or tantric imagery.

Military metaphors and similes abound in Buddhist scriptures. We find examples in places such as the *Dhammapada*, where the "conqueror of the battlefield" is compared to the "conqueror of the self," or in the *Lotus Sutra* with references to bodhisattvas who conquer the evil one, Mara. One of the most the more popular parables, the "Chulamalunkya Sutta" in the *Majjhima Nikaya*, uses the example of a soldier to illustrate the distinction between beneficial and unbeneficial questions. The Buddha discusses the problems of a soldier wounded by a poisoned arrow. The soldier is more intent on learning who shot the arrow and why than on addressing the imminent issue of the poison and dying. Often times, military metaphors and similes are related to kingship in Theravada scriptures (Bartholomeusz 2002: 41).

The Buddhist system presents time as cyclical in nature but linear in its progression. In this manner there is no ultimate end time, rather a beginning and an end to every cycle. Throughout Buddhist and Hindu societies there is the general consensus that we are living in the fourth era: the age of destruction (*kali yuga*). According to Buddhist scriptures, the end of a cycle is signaled by the disappearance of the teachings and the marking of a new cycle. At times, Buddhist relics symbolically mark the new cycle, such as the reconstitution of the Buddha's bones (*sarira*), the coming of the next Buddha (Sanskrit: *Maitreya*; Pali: *Metteya*), or the reappearance of his begging bowl and robes (in some cases, the destruction of the Buddha's begging bowl signals the end). Millenarian movements are not necessarily violent, but the ones that are violent use these and other signs to justify their actions.

Often, violent millenarian movements invoke the imagery and rhetoric of Mara, the maker of death and desire. In the narrative of the Buddha's enlightenment, Mara is his principal adversary, who tries to prevent the Buddha from reaching enlightenment. Violent millenarian movements view Mara as their adversary, such as the one led by the Chinese Buddhist monk Faqing in 515. Faqing announced the coming of the new Buddha, Maitreya, and commanded 50,000 men to battle against the forces of Mara. The more people a soldier killed, the more he advanced in the prescribed bodhisattva paradigm (Demiéville 2010: 25).

Mara is one of the elite among Buddhist literary adversaries. Another nemesis in Buddhist lore is the Buddha's cousin Devadatta, who vied for control of the Sangha and has become a literary scapegoat. In many scriptures, he tries to repudiate the Buddha's authority and to kill him. In one famous encounter present in children's books, Devadatta sends a crazed and furious elephant named Nalagiri at the Buddha. The elephant comes close to crushing a baby in its path, but the Buddha intervenes and calms the wild elephant. Of all his actions, the worst Devadatta purportedly committed were causing a schism in the Sangha, killing a nun, and wounding the Buddha. This last act resulted in the earth swallowing up Devadatta and condemning him to Avichi, the darkest of hells. Often, religious persecutors call on the memory of Devadatta to denounce Buddhist practitioners and their practices as heretical.

The violent and persecuted caricature of Devadatta is almost the reversal of another person who tried to kill the Buddha. Angulimala was a robber who had committed himself to completing his vow of killing 1,000 people. Angulimala had a necklace of fingers, one finger for every death, and as it turned out, his last intended victim was the Buddha. On meeting the Buddha, Angulimala renounced his bloody path and joined the Sangha. During his time in the Sangha, he endures attacks from lay communities but attains enlightenment under the guidance of the Buddha. Images of Angulimala represent the far-reaching redemptive power of the Buddhist path for the most violent of initiates.

In the Sri Lankan *Mahavamsa's* legendary war between the Buddhist king Dutthagamani and the forces of King Elara, Dutthagamani wields a royal spear endowed with a Buddhist relic. During scriptural accounts of battles, rulers are purportedly given amulets or relics that sacralize their weapons. Most of the time, these weapons or artifacts bestow on a person protection. In Thailand, soldiers believe that by consuming the wild animal one may absorb their spiritual and physical prowess. They wear various amulets, often images of Buddhist saints that prepare them for battle; some shield them from bullets while others repel bombs. These amulets became transnational commodities during the US war in Vietnam, when Thai Buddhist soldiers shared their amulets with US soldiers (Richard 2011: 134 and 189).

Buddhist images are suffused with brilliant colors and complex lines. Like the doctrine, tantric imagery is remarkably complex and contains several interpretive layers. Sand mandalas represent the microcosm of the body and the macrocosm of the universe, all the while reminding us of their impermanence. The Buddhist pantheon contains violent depictions of deities, bodhisattvas, and spirits—many wield bloody weapons with ferocious countenances such as the skull-crowned Mahakala. The bovine-headed Yama, the lord of death, is killed by the bovine-headed Yamantaka (which means "terminator of Yama"). There is even Kojin, the fiery, fanged bow-and-arrow-wielding Japanese god of the hearth. These violent depictions most often are meant not for practitioners but for the evil spirits that would prey on the practitioner, or they serve the metaphoric purposes of attacking the negative qualities within ourselves.

There are also myths about demons that are ritually murdered but are reborn as protectors of Buddhism. This transformation from foe into protector illustrates the power of compassionate violence. This notion of violence as a means of burning away the vices of an entity transcends Buddhist traditions (it is quite common with the use of Agni, god of fire, in Vedic and Hindu traditions). However, it has become a central theme for some Buddhist traditions. One prominent example comes from a Tibetan Buddhist foundational myth found in the Nyingma *Compendium of Intentions Sutra* in which tantric buddhas battle with the demon Rudra. In his analysis, Jacob Dalton considers the murder of Rudra "essential for anyone seeking to understand the place of violence in Tibetan Buddhism" (2011: 3). After numerous rebirths and confrontations, the conflict ends when a *heruka* buddha plunges a trident into Rudra's chest and swallows him whole. Within the heruka's stomach, Rudra is purified (ibid., 19–21). From Rudra's subjugation, death, and then rebirth emerges a protector deity of Tibetan Buddhism. This motif of demon into protector is found in other myths and legends, such as cannibalistic evil spirits who protect the *Lotus Sutra*, the sword-wielding Dorje Shugden that protects Tibet and its people, and damned Cittipatti, skeletons who after living lives of sin and misdeeds must work off their negative karma and guard the entrances to Tibetan and Mongolian Buddhist sites.

In addition to the Tantric images that contain violent figures, there are other images of notoriously nonviolent deities and bodhisattvas that are placed in violent contexts. When the Manchus conquered the Mongols in the late seventeenth century, they considered their rule an emanation of the bodhisattva of wisdom, Manjushri, even in their use of the death penalty (Wallace 2010: 96–97). The benevolent image of Manjushri is seen in other contexts, such as in tenth-century Japan, when Tendai abbot called on monks to embody Manjushri by carrying bows and arrows into battle. A thousand years later, the Japanese gave the bodhisattava of compassion, Avalokiteshvara, the rank of a shogun or generalissimo in World War II (Victoria 2006: 142).

Although tantric rituals of defense invoke symbolic (and actual) violence on animal sacrifices, the bulwark of symbolic violence comes from narratives and images. Buddhist traditions have their share of violent symbols, relics, and images, but a cursory review of these also reveals the dominant presence of context. Even the most peaceful of images, such as Avalokiteshvara, the bodhisattva of compassion, may become associated with violence given the specific circumstances.

Manifestations of Violence

People commit various atrocities on themselves and others, but what is distinctive about their violence that makes the actions Buddhist? To return to the parameters drawn earlier, Buddhists are people who follow the Four Noble Truths and hold the Buddha as the penultimate figure/deity. However, being Buddhist does not necessarily mean that one's acts are "Buddhist"; rather, Buddhist worldviews and codes of conduct influence one's behavior. Various Buddhist elements are embedded in acts of violence. Tanks have patrolled with Buddhist amulets on them, monasteries have served as military compounds for soldiers, and monastic Buddhist reliquaries (stupas) and pagodas have been used for military defenses. However, to narrow our focus, the most notably "Buddhist" acts are human actions that reflect the core values of the religion: The Three Jewels of Buddha, Dhamma and Sangha (or in Tantric Buddhism, the Four Jewels). Self-proclaimed bodhisattvas, *arahants* and buddhas (Buddha) have engaged in violence, violent acts are done in the name of Buddhist teaching (Dhamma), and monks have committed violence (sangha). This section will review these elements in regard to war, punishment, and social control.

War

Buddhists have engaged in wars since the time of Ashoka in the third century BCE. These wars contain a myriad of causes and factors but become sanctified to the participants through enlightened leaders, Buddhist rhetoric (dhamma/dharma), and Buddhist monks. Most Buddhist-inspired wars are either the result of a closely aligned monasticism and state or a movement that contains millenarian elements.

It was in the first century CE that Buddhist monks brought their traditions to China. Three hundred years later, there were Chinese Buddhist millenarian revolts and insurrections, often led by monks. Buddhist-inspired revolts also occurred under the Tabgatch Empire against the villainous Mara (402–517 CE), and messianic monks rebelled during the Sui and Tang dynasties (613–626 CE). It was in the Tang Dynasty that Faqing led his soldier-monks on a revolt in which ten deaths would enable them to complete their bodhisattva path (815 CE). The White Lotus Society incorporated messianic elements into its Pure Land practices. By the thirteenth and fourteenth centuries, they had staged armed uprisings to establish their own states and to overthrow the Mongol Dynasty.

Mahayana Buddhist traditions were transported from China to Korea in the fourth century CE. Korea embraced Buddhist practices during the bloody Chinese interregnum (220–589 CE.). The nascent Silla kingdom credited Buddhist protectors for causing the Chinese to make peace with them in 671 CE. Then Koreans brought Buddhist practices and beliefs to Japan in the sixth century CE. In Japan, powerful Buddhist monasteries gradually emerged, and armies were solicited to protect their landholdings. The close political ties between monasteries and state in the Heian period (794–1185 CE) drew monks into conflicts. During the twelfth century, Chinese and Korean monks fought in wars against the Jurchens, the Mongols, and the Japanese. In the next century, Japanese Shin adherents fought apocalyptic battles over Amita paradise.

Within the Theravada traditions, Thai chronicles in the sixteenth century reveal monks as spies and conspirators. From 1699 until the mid 1950s, Lao and Thai holy men (phumibun) staged dozens of messianic revolts against Thailand. The leaders claimed to possess extraordinary powers and drew on the lore of Phra Si Ariya, the Thai version of Maitreya, the Buddha-to-be (Nartsupha 1984: 112). This claim of supernatural powers was not solely a phenomenon of revolts. The Thai king Taksin liberated his people from Burmese occupation in 1767 and declared himself a stream enterer—the first of four stages to sainthood in Theravada Buddhism.

Monks became warriors in Chinese, Japanese, Korean, Thai, and Sri Lankan traditions. Perhaps the most widely known of these are the Shaolin monks of the Chinese Chan tradition, who developed martial arts for meditation and fighting. Japanese peasants, inspired by Pure Land teachings, fought a battle of cosmic relevance to promote a Buddhist paradise during the Warring States period of the 1500s, and Japanese Zen monks fought as soldiers in the Russo-Japanese War of 1904 and 1905 (Victoria 2006). Within the Tibetan traditions there is a fraternity of fighter monks (*ldab ldob*). Although these monks are not soldiers, they equip themselves with at least one weapon. They are notable fighters and have served in special all-Tibetan frontier forces in the Indian Army of the Republic. In recent years, Thai soldiers serve in covert operations as military monks (*tahan phra*). Unbeknownst to their abbots, these men fully ordain and retain their military status, guns, and monthly stipends (Jerryson 2011: 116–127).

In the colonial and postcolonial periods, Buddhists rebelled against the predominantly Christian colonialists and reasserted their identities. Burmese monks such as U Ottama led anticolonial movements against the British in the 1930s. During the early 1940s, Korean monks equated the United States' growing military influence with "Christian power" and sought to cleanse the world from demons and the evil of Mara (Tikhonov 2009: 8). Their sentiments were mirrored by Chinese Buddhists during the Korean War (1951–1953). Influential Chinese monks like Ven. Juzan challenged Chinese Buddhists to fulfill their patriotic duty and assist North Korea by resisting the encroachment of US influence, which he saw as the same as subduing evils (Xue Yu 2010: 142). However, Korean Buddhist movements against external forces turned internal in the 1950s. Korean Buddhist Chogye monks engaged in bloody conflicts with married monks over the issue of celibacy, claiming that monastic marriage practices were a by-product of Japanese colonialism.

In the twentieth century, monks became part of the intelligentsia that supported socialist revolutions. In the early 1900s, Mongolian monks were principal members of the socialist revolutionary party (Mongolian People's Revolutionary Party). After the revolution, the government embraced a more militant socialism and targeted and killed tens of thousands of monks (Jerryson 2007: 93). In a similar fashion, Cambodian monks were also early supporters of Pol Pot's efforts, only to find themselves victims after the regime was installed (see Erik Davis 2015). Communist movements such as these concerned Thai Buddhists. One of the most notable political activists was Kittiwuttho, who in the 1970s called on Thais to eradicate the communist rebels.

During the US war in Vietnam (1963–1975), Buddhist monks demonstrated their opposition to the suppression of Buddhism and US involvement by self-immolation. The most prominent of these was Thich Quang Duc's immolation in Saigon on June 11, 1963. Although Buddhist self-immolations were largely a Chinese or Vietnamese phenomenon, Tibetan lamas have adopted this practice of self-immolated for political protest. The earliest reported self-immolation was Thubten Ngodup who lit himself on fire during an Indian police crackdown on the Tibetan Youth Congress in 1998. The Tibetan self-immolation gained international attention in 2009 when it was used to protest the Chinese human rights violations and suppression of Tibetan Buddhism. Since then, more than 144 have died by self immolation, the most recent a Tibetan Buddhist monk named Kalsang Wangdu near Retsokha monastrey in the western Sichuan province, China, on March 2, 2016 (see Tsering Woeser 2016).

In South Asia, Sri Lankan monks became politically active and advocated strong forms of Buddhist nationalism. The socialist-leading Janatha Vimukthi Peramuna enlisted monks in an armed uprising during the 1980s. Vimukthi Peramuna were followed by a more politically focused and hardened Jathika Hela Urumaya (National Heritage Party) in 2004. In 2012, a splinter group broke off from the Jathika Hela Urumaya to become the Bodu Bala Sena (Buddha Power Army; see Jerryson 2015). Lao monks have supported resistance movements against the Lao communist government since the 1980s.

After the fall of the Berlin Wall, the Buddhist world changed. Among the more costly sites of Buddhist conflict in contemporary times are the Sri Lankan civil war against the LTTE (1983–2008) and the Burmese Buddhist nationalist groups, the 969 Movement and Ma Ba Tha, which have led a persecution of Rohingya Muslims in Myanmar (see Jerryson 2016). Regional conflicts persist with the continual Tibetan self-immolations in Chinese-controlled Tibet, and Buddhist-Muslim conflicts in Ladakh, India, and southern Thailand.

Punishment

Throughout the many iterations of the state over the centuries, Buddhists have supported their government's right to adjudicate punishments in order to maintain the Buddhist ethos. In addition to the state's function of preserving the dhamma, some interpret corporal punishments as executions of the law of kamma. For others, the system of punishment is itself an application of negative actions. As indicated earlier under doctrinal justifications, the majority of Buddhists condone corporal punishments, which includes torture as well as capital punishment.

The Buddhist position on punishments has changed over the centuries. In the sixteenth century, the Mongolian Khutukhtu Setsen Khung Taiji edited the *White History of the Tenfold Virtuous Dharma*, which advised measures such as blinding someone for stealing or cutting out a tongue for a lie (Wallace 2010: 93). Various punishments were carried out in Mongolia until the social revolution in 1921. Thailand does not maintain laws like those found in the *White History*, but it has been cited by nongovernmental organizations such as Amnesty International and Human Rights Watch for their torture techniques of suspects. Some torture techniques retain Buddhist connotations, such as the Sri Lankan *dhammacakke ghahana* (hitting the wheel of the dhamma). For this torture, people were forced to contort their bodies into the shape of a wheel; their bodies were then spun and beaten until the person passed out or bled to death (Abeysekara 2002: 230–231). Tortures are not always inflicted by force. Buddhists have applied forms of self-mortification in order to gain merit, display filial piety, or express devotion. These practices are most frequently seen in Chinese traditions, wherein Buddhist monks wrote in blood, sliced off parts of their body, and engaged in extreme ritual exposures to the sun (Yu 2012).

Some nation-states are not supportive of the death penalty. Sri Lanka has had a long history of opposition to the death penalty. In 1815, the British implemented the death penalty, but in 1978 it was revoked. Subsequently there have been periodic attempts to reinstate this policy.

Social Control

Social control is maintained through hegemonic systems, as well as through the execution of particular laws. Because of the visible state advocacy of Buddhist principles, Buddhist traditions have been used in authoritarian regimes such as Myanmar and its *karaoke fascism*, a term Monique Skidmore uses to describe the form of oppression and the Burmese response to a life of domination (Skidmore 2004: 7).

Religious texts are suffused with gender and racial stereotypes. In the heterosexually dominated narrative, women are subservient to men—either in recollections of the Buddha and his past lives or in the pantheon of deities and bodhisattvas. Buddhist traditions were among the earliest to grant women ordination (along with Jains), but this was not without con-test. The Buddha's favorite disciple Ananda had to ask three times for their admittance, and after the Order of Nuns was created, the Buddha explained the life of the dhamma was cut short because women were included. There were early female Buddhist saints such as those found in the collection of female hagiographies (*Therigatha*), but South Asian Buddhist women have learned to identify themselves from the perspective of male heroes (Wilson 1996: 5). Through the centuries most countries did not sustain their Order of Nuns; some, such as Thailand, never initi-ated it. In the alternative practices of Tantra, the division of sexual bodies and sacrality are not much different. Charlene Makley points out that par-adigmatically male bodies of Tibetan incarnate lamas (*tulkus*) act as cru-cial indexes of the local divine cosmos (2007: 25). There is much to say about a religion that focuses on overcoming attachment and depicts women as seductresses in texts and images (such as Mara's daughters). Viewed from this perspective, it is not a coincidence that sex ranks higher than murder among the highest offenses (*parajika*).

Buddhist practices have been used to sustain racial impositions. The earliest of these dates back to the South Asian Brahmanical caste system, which was officially rebuked by the Buddha. However, the monastic guide-lines contain a wealth of physical restrictions for those who wish to ordain, and the vast majority of his followers were of the higher castes (particularly of the merchant and priest castes). Within the early South Asian social system, racial divisions were physically mapped by skin tones; those people with darker skin pigmentations were designated as the lower castes. The preference for lighter skin pigmentation is largely the result of labor condi-tions. Those of the lower castes worked outside in the sun, whereas the wealthy could afford to stay indoors. This early method of racializing bod-ies is present within cotemporary Buddhist societies of South and South-east Asia and has been reinforced by global media and entertainment.

Sri Lankan society still maintains a caste system, and Thai society retains a preference for lighter skin tones as well. Within these nation-states, it is generally the White tourists who visit the beaches to tan; whit-ening creams are commonly advertised. The preference for lighter skin pigmentation is mapped onto Buddhist images, with light skin tones for the Buddha and darker skin tones for his adversaries. In some accounts, Mara and his minions are depicted with darker skin tones, such as in Thai Buddhist murals. These features suggest a structural level of violence that integrates Buddhist lore and racialized subjects (Jerryson 2011: 143–177).

In regard to slavery, Buddhist traditions do not have canonical prohibitions. We find examples of Buddhist intolerance toward slavery, such as in "Assalayana" in the _Majjhima Nikaya_, in which the Buddha rejects the view that people are born into servitude and are lesser beings than others. He espouses that all people, no matter the color of their skin, are equal to one another. However, Buddhist states (and monasteries) employed slaves until the late nineteenth century. In China, slavery continued under Buddhist influenced states, (the earliest records of slavery predate the introduction of Buddhism in the fourth century BCE), and there is record of the Sri Lanka Sangha receiving slaves as gifts as early as the first century BCE.

Laws on euthanasia and abortion differ with each nation-state and doctrinal grouping. The majority of Buddhist nation-states do not support the use of euthanasia or abortion. Humans must endure the fruits of their negative actions; in this light, the dying persons expiate their past kamma through their suffering. And because Buddhist notions of the self pinpoint life at conception, the abortion of a fetus is the ending of a self. This stance has created problems in some countries such as Thailand, where abortion is prohibited but abortions are performed. Thai Buddhists believe that the fetuses' spirits must be appeased, and so aborted fetuses are brought to monasteries for cremation. Japanese Buddhists perform a fetus memorial service (_mizuko kuyo_) for stillborn, aborted, or miscarried fetuses. During these ceremonies, offerings are made to the bodhisattva Jizo (Ksitigarbha), the guardian of children.

Conclusion

There is great strength in the Buddhist calls for compassion and acceptance. Among the various examples in the scriptures lies one from its founder Siddhattha Gotama, who abandoned his own familial allegiance for the sake of reconciliation. In the _Sutta Nipata Atthakatha_, the Sakya and Koliya kingdoms were close to declaring war over the use of the river Rohini, which flowed along the borders of both kingdoms. Each kingdom needed water for irrigating their crops, and a recent drought had deepened the severity of that need. However, instead of choosing his own kingdom of Sakya, Siddhattha counseled both sides to share the water since blood was more important than water.

We find more recent examples of Buddhist-inspired reconciliation in the Nobel Peace laureate, the Fourteenth Dalai Lama, whose advocacy of diplomacy with the Chinese government limits the violence within the

Tibetan region to small disparate acts. In the last several decades, movements such as the Sarvodaya Movement in Sri Lanka and the recent Burmese monks' use of civil disobedience in their Saffron Revolution exemplify the power of Buddhist peace activism. Like all religious systems, Buddhist traditions contain a great capacity for reconciliation. In order to make use of these strengths, we should not turn a blind eye to its shortcomings.

Bibliography

Abeysekara, Ananda. *The Colors of the Robe: Religion, Identity, and Difference.* Columbia: University of South Carolina Press, 2002.

Bartholomeusz, Tessa J. *In Defense of Dharma: Just-War Ideology in Buddhist Sri Lanka.* New York: Routledge Curzon, 2002.

Benn, James A. *Burning for the Buddha: Self-Immolation in Chinese Buddhism.* Honolulu: University of Hawai'i Press, 2007.

Bhikkhu Bodhi, trans. *The Connected Discourses of the Buddha: A Translation of the Saṃyutta Nikāya.* Boston: Wisdom Publications, 2000.

Broido, Michael M. "Killing, Lying, Stealing and Adultery: A Problem of Interpretation in the Tantras." *Buddhist Hermeneutics.* Ed. Donald S. Lopez Jr., 71–118. Honolulu: University of Hawai'i Press, 1988.

Chang, Garma Chen-chi, ed. "How to Kill with the Sword of Wisdom." *A Treasury of Mahayana Sūtras: Selections from the Mahāratnakūṭa Sūtra,* 41–72. University Park and London: Pennsylvania State University Press, 1983.

Chatthip Nartsupha. "The Ideology of Holy Men Revolts in North East Thailand." *Senri Ethnological Studies* 13 (1984): 111–134.

Collins, Steven. *Nirvana and Other Buddhist Felicities: Utopias of the Pali Imaginaire.* Cambridge, UK: Cambridge University Press, 1998.

Cowell, E. B., ed. *The Jataka or Stories of the Buddha's Former Births.* 1895. Delhi: Motilal Banarsidass Publishers, 1990.

Daishonin, Nichiren. "139: Strategy of the Lotus Sutra." Trans. Soka Gakkai International. *Writings of Nichiren Daishonin.* 1000–1001. Soka Gakkai International, n.d. 17 January 2009. www.sgilibrary.org/view.php?page=1000.

Dalton, Jacob P. *Taming the Demons: Violence and Liberation in Tibetan Buddhism.* Princeton, NJ: Yale University Press, 2011.

Davids, Thomas Williams Rhys. *Questions of King Milinda, Part II.* Oxford, U.K.: Clarendon Press, 1894.

Davidson, Ronald M. *Tibetan Renaissance: Tantric Buddhism in the Rebirth of Tibetan Culture.* New York: Columbia University Press, 2005.

Davis, Erik W. *Deathpower: Buddhism's Ritual Imagination in Cambodia.* New York: Columbia University Press, 2015.

Demiéville, Paul. "Buddhist and War." Trans. Michelle Kendall. *Buddhist Warfare*. Eds. Michael Jerryson and Mark Juergensmeyer, 17–58. New York: Oxford University Press, 2010.

Geiger, Wilhelm, trans. *The Mahāvaṃsa or the Great Chronicle of Ceylon*. New Delhi and Madras: Asian Educational Services, 1993 [1912].

Gethin, Rupert. "Can Killing a Living Being Ever Be an Act of Compassion? The Analysis of the Act of Killing in the Abhidhamma and Pali Commentaries." *Journal of Buddhist Ethics* 11 (2004): 167–202.

Gokhale, Balkrishna. "Dhamma As a Political Concept" *Journal of Indian History* 44 (August 1968): 249–261.

Gray, David B. "Compassionate Violence?: On the Ethical Implications of Tantric Buddhist Ritual." *Journal of Buddhist Ethics* 14 (2007): 238–271.

Horner, Isaline Blew, trans. *The Book of the Discipline (Vinaya-Pitaka): Vol. I (Sutta-vibhanga)*. Oxford, UK: Pali Text Society, 1992 [1938].

Horner, Isaline Blew, trans. *The Book of the Discipline (Vinaya-Pitaka): Vol. III (Sutta-vibhanga)*. Oxford, UK: Pali Text Society, 1983 [1942].

Horner, Isaline Blew, trans. *Milinda's Questions*. London: Luzac & Company, 1963–1964.

Jenkins, Stephen. "Making Merit through Warfare and Torture according to the *Ār ya-Bodhisattva-gocara-upāyaviṣaya-vikurvaṇa-nirdeśa Sūtra*." *Buddhist Warfare*. Eds. Michael Jerryson and Mark Juergensmeyer, 59–76. New York: Oxford University Press, 2010.

Jerryson, Michael. *Mongolian Buddhism: The Rise and Fall of the Sangha*. Chiang Mai, Thailand: Silkworm Books, 2007.

Jerryson, Michael. "Introduction." *Buddhist Warfare*. Eds. Michael Jerryson and Mark Juergensmeyer, 1–16. New York: Oxford University Press, 2010.

Jerryson, Michael. "Buddhists and Violence: Historical Continuity/Academic Incongruities." *Religion Compass* 9/5 (2015): 141–150.

Jerryson, Michael. "Buddhism, Conflict, and Peacebuilding." *The Oxford Handbook of Contemporary Buddhism*. Ed. Michael Jerryson. New York: Oxford University Press, 2016.

Jerryson, Michael. *Buddhist Fury: Religion and Violence in Southern Thailand*. New York: Oxford University Press, 2011.

Kent, Daniel. "Onward Buddhist Soldiers." *Buddhist Warfare*. Eds. Michael Jerryson and Mark Juergensmeyer, 157–177. New York: Oxford University Press, 2010.

Keyes, Charles. "Political Crisis and Militant Buddhism." *Religion and Legitimation of Power in Thailand, Laos, and Burma*. Ed. Bardwell L. Smith, 147–164. Chambersburg, Penn.: ANIMA Books, 1978.

McGranahan, Carole and Ralph Litzinger, eds. "Self-Immolation as Protest in Tibet." (special edition, April 9, 2012). Last modified on April 9, 2012. www.culanth.org/?q=node/526.

Maher, Derek F. "Sacralized Warfare: The Fifth Dalai Lama and the Discourse of Religious Violence." *Buddhist Warfare*. Eds. Michael Jerryson and Mark Juergensmeyer, 77–90. New York: Oxford University Press, 2010.

Makley, Charlene E. *The Violence of Liberation: Gender and Tibetan Buddhist Revival in Post-Mao China*. Berkeley: University of California Press, 2007.

Mayer, Richard. *A Scripture of the Ancient Tantra Collection, The Phur-pa bcu-gnyis*. Oxford, UK: Kiscadale Publications, 1996.

Meinert, Carmen. "Between the Profane and the Sacred? On the Context of the Rite of 'Liberation' (*sgrol ba*)." *Buddhism and Violence*. Ed. Michael Zimmermann, 99–130. Lumbini, Nepal: Lumbini International Research Institute, 2006.

Ming-Wood, Liu. "The Problem of the Icchantika in the Mahayana *Mahaparinirvana Sutra*." *Journal of International Buddhist Studies* 7.1 (1984): 57–81.

Reuter, Christoph. *My Life Is a Weapon: A Modern History of Suicide Bombing*. Princeton, NJ: Princeton University Press, 2004.

Ruth, Richard A. *In Buddha's Company: Thai Soldiers in the Vietnam War*. Honolulu: University of Hawai'i Press, 2011.

Schmithausen, Lambert. "Buddhist Attitudes toward War." *Violence Denied: Violence, Non-Violence and the Rationalization of Violence in South Asian Cultural History*. Eds. Jan E. M. Houben and Karel R. Van Kooij, 39–67. Leiden, Netherlands, and Boston: Brill, 1999.

Schober, Juliane. *Modern Buddhist Conjunctures in Myanmar: Cultural Narratives, Colonial Legacies, and Civil Society*. Honolulu: University of Hawai'i Press, 2010.

Sharf, Robert H. "The Scripture in Forty-Two Sections." *Religions of China in Practice*. Ed. Donald S. Lopez, Jr., 360–371. Princeton, NJ: Princeton University Press, 1996.

Skidmore, Monique. *Karaoke Fascism: Burma and the Politics of Fear*. Philadelphia: University of Pennsylvania Press, 2004.

Skidmore, Monique, and Trevor Wilson. *Dictatorship, Disorder and Decline in Myanmar*. Canberra: The Australian National University Press, 2010.

Tatz, Mark, trans. "Murder with Skill in Means: The Story of the Ship's Captain." *The Skill in Means (Upāyakauśalya) Sutra*, 73–74. New Delhi: Motilal Banarsidass, 1994.

Thanissaro Bhikkhu trans. "Kesi Sutta: To Kesi the Horsetrainer." *Anguttara Nikaya*. Access to Insight, 25 July 2010. www.accesstoinsight.org/tipitaka/an/an04/an04.111.than.html.

Tikhonov, Vladimir. "Violent Buddhism—Korean Buddhists and the Pacific War, 1937–1945." *Sai* 7 (2009): 169–204.

Victoria, Brian Daizen. *Zen at War*. Lanham, MD: Rowman and Littlefield Publishers, 2006.

Wallace, Vesna. "Legalized Violence: Punitive Measures of Buddhist Khans in Mongolia." *Buddhist Warfare*. Eds. Michael Jerryson and Mark Juergensmeyer, 91–104. New York: Oxford University Press, 2010.

Wilson, Liz. *Charming Cadavers: Horrific Figurations of the Feminine in Indian Buddhist Hagiographic Literature.* Chicago: University of Chicago Press, 1996.

Woeser, Tsering. *Tibet on Fire: Self-Immolations Against China Rule.* New York: Verso, 2016.

Yu, Jimmy. *Sanctity and Self-Inflected Violence in Chinese Religions, 1500–1700.* New York: Oxford University Press, 2012.

Yu, Xue. "Buddhists in China during the Korean War (1951–1953)." *Buddhist Warfare.* Eds. Michael Jerryson and Mark Juergensmeyer, 131–156. New York: Oxford University Press, 2010.

Chapter 3

Sikh Traditions and Violence

Cynthia Keppley Mahmood

THERE HAS BEEN a martial aspect to the Sikh tradition since the early stages of Sikh history. This is due, in part, to the social context of the emergent community. Were historical maps of resistance on the geographical peripheries of the Indian subcontinent constructed, they might show conflicts piled on one another like colored transparencies glowing through time, though expressed in differing idioms, sometimes religious, sometimes political. The Sikh tradition arose in one of these contested cultural regions and geographical peripheries and expressed itself in its own religious and political terms.

The Sikhs

Sikhism is among the youngest of the global religions. The seminal figure who is regarded as the founder, Guru Nanak, was born in 1469 in what is now Pakistani Punjab. While orthodox Sikhs believe that Nanak's message was totally new and divinely inspired, some Western scholars point to Hindu and Islamic elements in his teachings (e.g., McLeod 1989). It is clear that Nanak rejected much of what he observed in both religious communities and critiqued particularly the empty ritualism of Brahmanical Hinduism that he saw as an impediment to true spiritual understanding. He founded a community that would eventually comprise 2 percent of the Indian population, and count some 20 million members worldwide.

Nanak traveled through the subcontinent and beyond and gathered disciples or *Sikhs* (the term *sikh* comes from the verb *to learn* and implies those who learn from a spiritual teacher, a "guru"). He emphasized the importance of meditation on a unitary divine spirit and on rightful living in this world. In direct contrast to the position of Orthodox Hindus, the

Sikh community strove to ignore caste distinctions by interdining in a communal kitchen (*langar*). Also open to all were the Sikh temples or *gurudwaras* (a term that literally means "the doorway to the guru"). After Nanak died, the status of guru was passed to a loyal disciple, and the authority of guruship was subsequently passed from one to another through a series of ten gurus.

Three gurus are of particular interest here. Guru Arjun, the fifth guru (1563–1606), was not only the compiler of the *Adi Granth* ("the Ancient Scripture"), writings that would become in their final form the Guru Granth Sahib ("the scriptural lord guru"), the holy book of the Sikhs, but he was also the first of the Sikh Gurus to be martyred. Through the hideous tortures by the Mughal emperor Jahangir, Guru Arjun is described as remaining "unruffled" and "calm as the sea." Portraits of this first martyr adorn the walls of the homes of many Sikhs, including those who have attained political asylum abroad after suffering torture in contemporary Punjab.

The sixth guru, Hargobind (1595–1644), is a key to understanding another important strand of the Sikh martial tradition. He was the first to take up arms in defense of the faith. The double swords of Guru Hargobind represent the complementarity of temporal and spiritual power (*miri* and *piri*). Important to the Sikh understanding of "the just war" (*dharm yudh*) is the recognition that, while Hargobind was a valiant fighter, his battles were entirely defensive in nature. Hargobind also supplemented the symbol of the sword to defend the weak, with that of the kettle to feed the hungry. "Kettle-Sword-Victory" (*Deg Teg Fateh*) is a Sikh motto that remains popular in the militant community. Its symbolism is integrated into the *khanda*, an icon sewn onto flags, pinned into turbans, and representing the miri-piri philosophy. Today it is second only to the image of the words *Ek Oankar*, one god, in its prominence in Sikh life.

The tenth and last guru, Gobind Singh (1666–1708), took the most important step toward full militarization of the Sikh tradition: He established the army of the Khalsa, a group of respected Sikhs who vowed commitment to the faith. This took place in 1699, when Guru Gobind Singh called for a gathering of the entire *panth* (Sikh community). According to an account of this occasion that is remembered in the Sikh community, he drew his sword and demanded volunteers who would be willing to give their heads for their faith. Five volunteered, willing to make the ultimate sacrifice for their guru. They were called *panj piaray* or "five beloved ones" and were initiated by Guru Gobind Singh into a new order called the

Khalsa, "the pure." They were to be "saint-soldiers" (*sant-sipahi*) and were regarded as having the wisdom of saints and the courage of soldiers.

Rather than pass the guruship to another individual as his predecessors had done, Guru Gobind Singh chose to pass his spiritual authority to the holy scripture; it was after this occasion that the *Adi Granth* became known as the *Guru Granth Sahib* ("the Scriptural Lord Guru"). Sikhs today venerate the sacred book as a living Guru and do not accept intermediaries such as priests (although there are clergy who are scripture readers and caretakers of the *gurudwaras*). Insults to the *Guru Granth Sahib* are taken as direct affronts to the guru, a factor that plays a role in the development of the sense of outrage militant Sikhs feel toward those considered to have committed blasphemy against the holy book and, by extension, against their faith. Guru Gobind Singh passed his worldly authority to the community, or panth. Thus the book, and the community, were the two manifestations of Divinity in the ongoing Sikh tradition.

By the time of India's independence in 1947, Sikh activists had mobilized their community, reformed the gurudwara system, and won recognition as an important political force. Many Sikhs believe that it was at this moment of the political partition of the Indian subcontinent in 1948 that the Sikh nation of Sikhistan or Khalistan might have been established. Instead, Sikh leaders at the time chose to stay with the secular pluralist India led by Pandit Jawaharlal Nehru. They lost much of their territorial base to Pakistan, but the Sikh population in India's east Punjab formed a significant minority. In 1966, after the redrawing of Punjab's boundary lines to match the boundaries of the Punjabi language, Sikhs became a slight majority in the newly defined Punjab state of India. However, economic inequalities and rising unemployment in the 1970s resulted in a disenfranchised, unemployed rural youth, who formed the backbone of the Sikh militancy in the 1980s (see Fox 1985; Kapur 1986).

In the early 1980s, Sikh separatists began fighting for an independent state of Khalistan to be located in place of the Indian state of Punjab. This struggle connected the past with the present, with a central theme of martyrdom within the separatist discourse drawn from the valorization of death in battle expressed in Sikh religious history. The struggle for Khalistan was a resistance movement against the perceived injustices of the Indian state and a political movement aimed at sovereign rule, but it also provided an existential means of being a Sikh, independently of instrumental political goals (Mahmood 1996, 1–16). This combination is a particular point of interest to those concerned with religion and violence.

Sikhs and Militancy

Following the rise of the militant Khalistan movement in the 1980s, there has been a popular misconception in India and around the world that Sikhism is a violent religion and that Sikhs involved in the movement for Khalistan were terrorists. Some Sikhs attempted to defend their tradition by arguing that Sikhism is a peaceful religion and that members of the Khalistan movement were nation builders like Washington and Jefferson; but this position also ignored the complexity that actually characterized the state of *Sikhi* ("the Sikh way of life") during the insurrectionary period of the 1980s and 1990s. It is only now, in a period of reflection, that Sikhs and those in dialogue with them are finding ways to talk about militancy in more nuanced terms.

The discussion about Sikhism and militant protest begins with the debates about the nature of the first guru, Nanak. Though often portrayed as a reclusive meditative figure like the Buddha, with his eyes half shut in spiritual rapture, he was also recorded as having challenged the prevailing socioreligious order. The pacifist image of Guru Nanak was promoted by scholars who regarded him as a reconciler, taking the best of Islam and Hinduism and merging them into a new religion. Some British colonial observers such as Ernest Trumpp (1828–1885) went so far as to define Sikhism as a synthesis of Hindu and Muslim traditions. Sikhs almost uniformly reject the idea that Sikhism is a blend of Hinduism and Islam. Most Sikhs see Guru Nanak as a critic of both religions, since he quite firmly criticized what he saw as flaws in the Muslim and Brahmanical Hindu traditions, saying clearly that a Sikh was neither a Muslim nor a Hindu. It is true, however, that the Guru Granth Sahib contains ideas from Hindu, Muslim, and other predominant idioms of the times. The fact remains that the teachings of Guru Nanak were spiritually rebellious as much as they were politically benign.

As the community of Sikhs grew and the mantle of the guru's spiritual authority was passed from one to another, questions about definitions arose. Islamic dynasties were in power during the evolution of the Sikh community, and it was clear by the increasing persecution they faced that Sikhs were not regarded as Muslims. Were these Sikhs some sect of Hindus, then, who also bore the burden of Muslim political oppression? Sikh and Hindu communities at the time had permeable boundaries in the region; they intermarried; they worshipped at each other's temples; they enjoyed each other's festivities. In particular, the Sikhs of Punjab, who ended up fighting the long line of invaders coming into the subcontinent from the west, became colloquially known as "the sword arm of Hinduism." Many of the eldest sons in Hindu families were reared as Sikhs, just as a family might send one son off to military duty.

In the flurry of academic cogitations around the question "Who is a Sikh" (McLeod 1989), one thing that scholars cannot fail to note is the increasing stridency of the tone of the stories about the nine gurus who succeeded Guru Nanak. It is common to place the kind, fatherly, gentle visage of Guru Nanak, the first guru, next to the proud, martial and regal Guru Gobind Singh, the tenth and last, in Sikh homes and in classrooms teaching the development of Sikhi. Clearly, something has been trans-formed during the course of the teachings of the lineage of ten gurus from approximately 1500 to 1700 CE. The Sikhs were persecuted by either Hindu or Muslim rulers during nearly the entirety of this period. The revolutionarily egalitarian message of the gurus can be seen as a threat to any ruler of India, especially one who is dependent on a hierarchical social structure. Thus it is understandable that the Sikh tradition would be char-acterized with conflict, even violence, throughout its history.

In the mid twentieth century, the Sikhs were among the communities that were affected by the independence of India and the partition of the subcontinent that created the countries of India and Pakistan. Some of the Sikhs at the time considered the possibility of a homeland defined by reli-gion. Just as there would be a Pakistan for the Muslims, some representa-tives argued that there should be a Sikhistan for the Sikhs. For various reasons that historical opportunity passed, and the Sikhs, for the most part, threw their lot in with India on promises of secularism by the Central Government and room for all religious communities in India "to breathe," as it was said. So the need to define just who was a Sikh was put off for a time, but the issue arose again during the Punjabi Suba movement of the 1960s, which led to redrawing the state boundaries of Punjab on the basis of speakers of the Punjabi language. The issue became even more salient during the Khalistan insurgency of the 1980s and 1990s.

Sikhs wielding AK-47s and using RDX explosives were responsible for large numbers of deaths in the Punjab of the 1980s and 1990s, but it was a tiny minority of all Sikhs who engaged in this action and probably a minority who supported them. Moreover, the government of India, in the form of Punjab Police and other military and paramilitary groups, was responsible for at least as many, and probably more, deaths. Sikhi (the Sikh way of life) was irrevocably linked to violence in the Indian mind, and Sikhs were then seen as unworthy victims when desperate cries for solidarity against human rights abuses went unheeded by a frightened population.

This picture is out of sync with the Sikh army officer that every Indian knew from childhood as a figure to be trusted and respected. That moment of slippage from military defense to bloody violence is critical to a historical narrative of India that recognizes the interaction of minorities with the Centre as the key to civilizational structure. For scholars of Sikhi, it is the key to understanding how militancy became defined as a posture that is now linked to violence. Citizens of India showed themselves willing to tolerate, even applaud, the abrogation of their civil rights in the name of national security as threats such as Sikh separatism reared their heads.

A conflation of militancy with violence in the Sikh tradition has led to a widespread misunderstanding of Sikhi in the modern world, has contributed to the unfortunate "Sikhs as terrorists" propaganda, and has distorted the theological message of the tradition. This conflation has indeed led to a *meconnaissance* of a people with its own historical identity, limiting to some extent the current discourse that appears possible and the range of futures that appear feasible even within the Sikh community. My twenty years of ethnographic research among *amritdhari* and other Sikhs leads me to propose that elucidating the razor-thin line between militancy and violence opens a way forward for studies of comparative religion and violence, for dialogue between Sikhs and non-Sikhs in the Indian postconflict context, and for a healing dialogue within the Sikh community that has been badly damaged by the Khalistan conflict as well.

Recall that the Sikh stance of militancy evolved through the leadership of the ten gurus who originated and led the community; violence emerged as a last resort when all other means of maintaining Sikhi had failed. It is a narrow line when viewed etically (from outside) and particularly from an accusational posture, but it is a key distinction when analyzing Sikh tradition from within (emically). We can find a useful and new angle into Sikh discourse through this little-noticed distinction. Sikhs may find a path to a more peaceful and more unified future if they come to terms with just who their gurus asked them to be, contemplating not only when the time arrives to remove the sword from its sheath but also when it may be time to put the sword once again to rest, seeking alternate means of fulfilling the duties of Sikhi.

The Sikh Identity Today

Although the first several gurus did not explicitly teach about violence or nonviolence, the martyrdom of the fifth guru, Arjun, was seminal. This led the sixth guru, Hargobind, to take up the classic icon of double swords, *miri* and *piri*, denoting worldly power and spiritual truth. By implication, one could only find spiritual truth when worldly sovereignty was assured. And the Sikhs did attempt to ensure the political space for their search for truth by becoming *sant-sipahis* or saint-soldiers, trained as well in the martial as in the spiritual arts.

It was Guru Gobind Singh, the tenth guru, "rider of the blue steed," who in 1699 established the Khalsa, which committed five sant-sipahis, known as the Beloved Ones, to live with their heads in their hands, or in complete service and egoless dedication. Long ago Guru Nanak had described such service as the best way to "play the game of love" that was human life. In 1699 the five were given five Articles of Faith to keep at all times: uncut hair bound into a turban, a wooden comb signifying purity, a steel or iron bangle on the right wrist, a martial loincloth used for horsemanship, and, perhaps most important, the *kirpan* or sword. All were called Singh, lion (the women were called Kaur or princess), and were to live as one family. This lifestyle since has become a goal for all Sikhs, whether or not they adopt the five articles or take on the vows of lifelong dedication.

Today, the initiation into the Khalsa through *amrit* is a visually stunning, deeply moving ceremony. The applicant, who is "of age" in terms of conscience and conscious choice, has usually prepared for months or years for the amrit. It is an irrevocable change in status that can therefore not be undertaken lightly. Men and women both often wear the five articles for some time in preparation, and study the holy book day and night. There being no intercessors in Sikhism, every individual knows the prayers, the readings, the ways to approach the Spirit. Walking the path of guru is seen as an ambition that will demand a life's work, so the amrit ceremony—overseen by the Five Beloved Ones—is held in a spirit of deep humility. The vow to give one's head, to live one's life, for one's community and one's faith is the moment of martyrdom for a believing Sikh; the battlefield death, the physical death, is but an incidental in a guru-permeated life. This is why *amritdhari* Sikhs (those who have undergone the ceremony of amrit) are said to be "fearless." It is not exactly courage in the Western sense that is praised here; it is more akin to the Buddhist notion of "living as if already dead," that is, in a state of detachment. That is the Sikh state of grace.

The actual use of the kirpan (and, derivatively, other weapons) is governed by specific rules. It is to remain on the body at all times but is to remain sheathed. One may remove it from its sheath only to protect the weak, to correct an injustice, and to defend the faith and only when all peaceful means have failed. It is not to be used offensively, not even for the sake of one's own family. The level of defense must be when the identity of Sikhi itself is in trouble; that is, when it is existentially under assault. That is why Jarnail Singh Bhindranwale, the charismatic preacher who roused the Sikhs to action in 1984, emphasized the danger that Sikhism could disappear in India unless Sikhs did something about it. He saw the decline of the faith all around him, but never issued a call for separatism. A separate state would be necessary, he said, only if the Golden Temple itself came under attack.

Bhindranwale's urging that Sikhs become sant-sipahis by way of the amrit ceremony was prompted by several grievances. A major one was article 25 of the Constitution, which for purposes of marriage law groups Sikhs and Buddhists within the Hindu category, thereby eliding Sikhs with Buddhists and, ultimately, Hindus. There were other serious grievances such as the diversion of river waters to other states, agricultural pricing detrimental to Punjab's Sikh farmers, and the lack of a separate capital city for Punjab. However, these other grievances received little air time at the Golden Temple, because Bhindranwale understood well that the "the faith in danger" was the trigger point at which amritdhari Sikhs would take action. He spent much of his time initiating thousands of young Sikhs into the Khalsa, an activity which some criticized as a waste of (political) time. But in theological terms, the strategy makes sense. When Indira Gandhi proclaimed a state of national emergency from 1975 to 1977, the base of newly initiated Sikhs was motivated to "save the faith." These were the core of the Khalistani activists. They set their revolt in terms of the precondition laid down by Guru Gobind Singh—"all peaceful means having failed." In their perception, the move from militancy (the protesters refusing to comply with Indira Gandhi's emergency and instead being jailed by the thousands) to violence (the guerilla warfare of the Khalistan movement) was fully justified.

The political implications of the *panth-granth* principle are often overlooked. When Guru Gobind Singh noted, as did the Buddha and the Prophet Mohammed before him, the tendency of human beings to idolize charismatic leaders and form a cult around them rather than continuing to devote themselves to Spirit, he took radical action in announcing that there would be no more human gurus after him. Guru had always been a vaguely defined concept, not exactly "both human and divine" but conceived more as a human being who holds within himself or herself the flame of divinity—which is passed on to the next guru, as a candle lights another candle. Guru Gobind Singh, reflecting the two-in-one approach of miri-piri, the world and the spirit together, said that the whole of the worldly power he held as guru would be passed into the Sikh *panth* or community. His spiritual power, on the other hand, would be passed into the sacred texts, the *granth*. Hereafter there would be no human leaders; there would be instead, Guru Granth Sahib, the holy book, and Guru Panth, the community of Sikhs. This doctrine became known as *granth-panth*, and is one of the clearest expressions of the "religion and politics combined" thesis in existence.

Few theologians, philosophers, or political theorists outside the tradition have commented on the radical quality of this development, the vesting of Godhead in a book open to anyone to interpret (from the beginning there had been no priesthood or intercessor class in Sikh tradition) and, correspondingly, the deeply democratic affirmation that the people, students on the path toward God, hold the ultimate authority over themselves. This reality is the Sikhi in which Sikhs understand themselves to be the primary actors. A Sikh saint-soldier is one who lives in the state of grace allowed to those who have "already died" through committing themselves heart and soul to God (becoming Khalsa by amrit initiation), and martyring himself with joy in defense of God (the book/the community). The Sikh does not look forward to a further life in heaven, far less at the right hand of God the Father. Nor does he imagine a heaven in which seventy-odd virgins await his arrival. The Sikh's martyrdom is existential: an afterthought to the well-lived life on the guru's path.

As founder of the Khalsa, Guru Gobind Singh also defined the use of force within the Sikh path. "When all peaceful means have failed," he said, "then it is justified to take to the hilt of the sword." It is on this point that the internal controversy over the twentieth-century Sikh separatist movement in Punjab centered. Were the members of the Babbar Khalsa, and the Sikhs gathered with Jarnail Singh Bhindranwale in the Golden Temple Complex in 1984, "terrorists" the Indian state had the right to rout out of there, or were they revolutionary Singhs who were standing up for Sikh rights after more than a decade of peaceful protest and sacrifice in the name of democracy? Certainly there was violence, but what kind of violence? For the years during Indira Gandhi's emergency rule, Sikhs led the civilian protests, courting arrest in the thousands. Did this fulfill Guru Gobind Singh's caveat that "all peaceful means" had to be tried first, before taking up "the hilt of the sword"? If so, the militant violence of the

Khalistanis in the 1980s may be seen as religiously valid. The Anandpur Sahib Resolution of 1973 (there were later iterations), had called for a centrifugal dispersion of power from the Center to the states. This had been supported by many of India's minorities and peripheral states but was initiated by Sikhs working for the good of the community. The later "terrorist" label for Sikhs supplanted a considerable respect for the courage of the Sikhs in these early peaceful protests. (Likewise, historians agree that Sikhs contributed heavily to the Gandhian project earlier, at the front lines of peaceful protest against the British Empire; another fact easily forgotten once the accusation of terrorism took hold after 1984.) There are those, however, Sikh as well as non-Sikh, who believe that the avenues for peaceful protest had not been fully explored when, in the early 1980s, Sikh militancy became Sikh violence—pulling it thus beyond the validation offered by Guru Gobind Singh's maxim.

Guru Gobind Singh is said to have attached nuggets of silver to his arrows, so that the families of the enemies he had slain would have the money to sustain themselves. Bhindranwale, leader of the band of militants at Amritsar in 1984, also carried arrows around with him as a reminder of Guru Gobind Singh. But in discourses over the morality of killing, one notes a distinct failure of imagination to consider the victim, both historically and in the present time. One saw Khalistani fighters evaluated according to their courage, their brilliance, their clever strategies, and so on, with no room for the question of victims. The key humanitarian question was whether the victims were innocent bystanders or combatants? The way of thinking that valorizes the soldier but ignores his victims is a characteristic of warrior cultures but not of a professional soldiers in a modern war, who must uphold the humanitarian laws of war. Likewise, the granth/panth formulation of authority in Sikhism meant that it was virtually every person for him- or herself in terms of understanding what the sacred texts say about the morality of violence, and the "five beloveds" form of leadership meant that every small community on the local level had the power to take matters into its own hands (i.e., decide its own missions). Khalistani Sikhs expressed pride in these features of their religion and culture, saying they expressed basic democracy in action. In the battlefield setting, however, they meant, practically speaking, chaos. They also meant many innocent deaths.

The guerilla organizations organized themselves according to military ranks, but it would be hard to argue that these had much meaning except as honors for jobs well done. No one knew who was responsible for what, no one had the authority to establish rules over things such as the treatment of civilians and cross-border smuggling and, though they upheld the Sikh tradition of fighting and dying with stunning valor, the desire for martyrdom played at odds with the instrumental military goal of living to fight another day. Although the Sikhs had real grievances with the government of India and a generation of men and women gave themselves over to one more chapter in the rich narrative of Sikhs in revolution, in the end the movement faded away for two reasons. First, the population on which all guerilla movements depend simply grew weary of violence, death, fear, and the crime that had overwhelmed the military aspects of the moment. Second, the government of India had the power to crack down on Punjab with complete impunity, which it did not only during the Khalistan movement but even after it had bled away its existence. The core of true sant-sipahis simply had no resources left.

Conclusion

Sikhs in the past had been known for turning defeats into victories. But the fight for Khalistan was different, in large part because their side took all the blame for the violence that overtook Punjab while the Indian government, despite all manner of human rights reports and other attempts to publicize the atrocities Sikhs suffered in repercussion against Khalistani insurgency, got off scot-free. The Sikh-as-terrorist icon has spread across the whole world.

Interestingly, the theological formulation of *Guru Granth/Guru Panth* continues to be at issue today. In the first decade of the twenty-first century, there has been an increasing tendency, often unmarked, to cite *Guru Granth* and simply not mention the complementary *Guru Panth* at all. As the Khalistan movement wound down in the 1990s, many Sikhs lamented that all their community needed was a strong leader—a comment entirely contrary to the traditional Sikh notion of leadership by community. So powerful is the traditional notion of the panth that it is depicted iconographically by the scene in which the first Five Beloved Ones, having received amrit from Guru Gobind Singh, turned around and initiated him. On bended knee, head humbly bowed, sword on the ground by his side, the guru sipped from the bowl of nectar proffered by one of the newly sworn Khalsa. This early panth had the power even to initiate a guru; today, however, for some at least, faith in the community has apparently been shattered.

In an intriguing attempt to analytically separate the elite leadership of the Khalistan movement from the broad base of Sikhs who, in the late twentieth century, became alienated from the state of India and developed a collective forward identity, Jasdev Rai distinguishes between the first as a modernist movement for a territorial Sikh state, which failed, and the *lehar*, the body of ordinary Sikhs that has resisted assimilation to any other collectivity before and after the moment in time marking the Khalistan movement with its attendant violence. The Sikh lehar could never fit into a secular state that demands separation of the sociopolitical from the spiritual, because for Sikhs they are intertwined. Yet the response to the secular territorial state of India need not be a contrarian Sikh territorial state (of Khalistan). Rai's concept of lehar allows for a wider, postmodern range of futures for a Sikh panth that need not defer to the territorial state model of sovereignty (see Rai 2011).

In the twenty-first century, when it has been made clear that the path of arms has not led Khalistani Sikhs to victory in their struggle for a sovereign Sikh state, many Sikhs have turned to their holy book to try to figure out when the kirpan is to be appropriately returned to its sheath, even if Guru Gobind Singh's standard of when a turn to violence is justified had been met. Significantly, the guidance of the book is that Sikhs are only to return to a peaceful path when victory has been achieved. "All Victory to the Khalsa!" is a daily greeting of the initiated (amritdhari) Sikh. Unfortunately there is no advice as to when it may be appropriate to resheathe the swords and again attempt a peaceful path to the assertion of rights (or protection of the weak or the correction of an injustice—the other two grounds for the use of arms). Sikhs had been always expected to win, so the "if...then..." is not present in the text to offer guidance in the current situation. Facing a modern nation-state with a vast military machinery, Sikh warriors of course could never have won their war through the use of arms. Today groups of young Sikhs all over the world are rethinking what to do next; other means of achieving justice and sustainable coexistence consistent with Sikhi. (Jasdev Rai's proposal is one of these.) Some are reevaluating whether the bar had been met for the use of violence in 1984; perhaps there had been an overemotional rush to fight rather than a considered plan for the protection of the religion, the resolution of the economic issues, and the establishment of a capital city. Working to retain the militant, principled, and uncompromising stance that has kept Sikhi alive through the centuries and made Sikhs the embodiment of courage, integrity, and respect in all of India (prior to 1984), young men and women defining a new, global panth have high ambitions as they attempt to think through more thoroughly how Sikhi can avoid the chaos of unwarranted violence, while upholding its gloried principles.

Bibliography

Asad, Talal. *Genealogies of Religion: Discipline and Reasons of Power in Christianity and Islam*. Baltimore: Johns Hopkins University Press, 1993.

Embree, Aislee T. *Utopias in Conflict: Religion and Nationalism in Modern India*. Berkeley and Los Angeles: University of California Press, 1990.

Fox, Richard G. *Lions of the Punjab: Culture in the Making*. Berkeley and Los Angeles: University of California Press, 1985.

Kapur, Rajiv. *Sikh Separatism: The Politics of Faith*. London: Allen and Unwin, 1986.

Mahmood, Cynthia Keppley. *Fighting for Faith and Nation: Dialogues with Sikh Militants*. Philadelphia: University of Pennsylvania Press, 1996.

Mahmood, Cynthia Keppley. "Why Sikhs Fight." In *Anthropological Contributions to Conflict Resolution*, edited by Alvin Wolfe and Honggang Yang, 11–30. Athens, GA: University of Georgia Press, 1994.

Mamdani, Mahmood. *When Victims Become Killers: Colonialism, Nativism, and the Genocide in Rwanda*. Princeton, NJ: Princeton University Press, 2002.

McLeod, W. H. *The Sikhs: History, Religion and Society*. New York: Oxford University Press, 1989.

Oberoi, Harjot. "Sikh Fundamentalism: Translating History into Theory." In *Fundamentalisms and the State*, edited by Martin E. Marty and R. Scott Appleby, 256–285. Chicago: University of Chicago Press, 1993.

Rai, Jasdev. "Khalistan is Dead! Long Live Khalistan! *Sikh Formations* 7.1 (May 4, 2011): 1–41.

Tully, Mark and Jacob Satish. *Amritsar: Mrs. Gandhi's Last Battle*. Calcutta: Rupa and Company, 1991.

Chapter 4

Religion and Violence in the Jewish Traditions

Ron E. Hassner and Gideon Aran

THIS ESSAY PRESENTS the traditional violent themes in religious Judaism as they appear in sacred texts, rites, customs, and chronicles. It offers a survey of the components of Jewish religion relating to violence while analyzing and illustrating their development and influence throughout history.

Religious tradition is a reservoir of ideas and symbols, norms and values, information and moods handed down from generation to generation and stored in written and oral texts or objects, available for contemporary cultural, social, or political use. Tradition is not just a fixed rigid body inherited from the past, a fossil imposing itself on passive consumers of tradition. It is a vital and open-ended organism that lends itself to a wide variety of understandings and manipulations.

Jewish tradition preserved a harmony among countless interpretations, homilies, metaphors, sayings, ethical teachings, legends, and testimonies, which together constituted the material contained within the Aggadic (homiletic) and normative components of the Talmud, Midrash, Halakha, and Kabbalah. This included a fair number of categorical, embellished, and provocative statements that, in their wider contexts, were considered acceptable despite their problematic nature. All these sacred texts provided a wealth of ideas that proved crucial in the tradition's survival. They can be said to contain everything: arguments, on all their variants, including their opposites. This reservoir, limited but large, was harnessed by a wide range of ideological leanings and historical requirements. It also legitimated a vast array of interests and moral stances by providing them with a "traditional" authority. This included an abundance of materials that supported religious violence and an abundance of materials that opposed it.

Religious violence is, firstly, violence sponsored or performed by individuals or groups who self-define and are identified by those around them as religious. Secondly, these actors account for their violence in a religious language, invoking religious symbols and referencing religious norms and values.

The case of Jewish violence is especially complicated since Judaism is characterized by a close relationship and a substantial overlap between religious association and ethnonationalist ties, akin to the ethnic nationalism that characterizes Tibetan Buddhism, Tamil Hinduism, Shintoism, and Sikhism. In Christianity and Islam, religious affiliation does not necessarily involve attachment to any particular nation or ethnic group. In contrast, affiliation with the Jewish religion implies affiliation with the Jewish people and vice versa. For more than three millennia, until the late eighteenth or nineteenth century, it was difficult to differentiate between the religious and the "tribal" components of Jewish identity. In the modern era, however, this tight linkage was disentangled. With the disintegration of the traditional, basically medieval, Jewish community, new Jewish phenomena emerged, including Jewish secularism, on the one hand, and varieties of Jewish religion, on the other hand. Though one cannot be a religious Jew without belonging to the Jewish people, the vast majority of contemporary Jews are not religious, let alone Orthodox. Consequently if, before, the term *Jewish violence* was sufficient to describe our phenomenon and by definition referred to a complex of both religious and ethnonationalist violence, the recent two centuries require us to distinguish between two types of Jewish violence: secular Jewish violence, which is mainly associated with Jewish nationalism (i.e., Zionism), and religious Jewish violence, on which this chapter focuses.

Our intention in the following pages is not to depict Judaism as a violent tradition nor is it our intention to portray Judaism as a nonviolent tradition. The reality is far more complex, as it is in all religious traditions. Jewish tradition includes an abundance of material that has clearly violent implications but also a profusion of materials that support a nonviolent ethic. Jewish religious motifs are as apparent in the past and present struggle against Jewish violence as they are in justifying such violence. Most contemporary observant Jews have no violent tendencies and in today's Jewish world there are religious figures and movements dedicated to opposing violence. Many of these actors justify their peaceseeking positions by means of religious ethics and base their resistance to animosity and aggression on sacred texts.

We begin our survey by tracing the violence in Jewish tradition to its roots in biblical prescriptions and descriptions (the second and third parts, respectively). In the chapter's fourth part, we explore how postbiblical interpretation and mediation blunted the Bible's violent elements by discussing the motif of zealotry, exemplified in the Bible by the acts of Phinehas. Our survey then traces the development of the violent tradition from the four great revolts that occurred from 200 BCE to 200 CE through the composing of the extracanonical books (the fifth part), to the compilation of the Talmud (the sixth part). In the seventh and eighth parts of this chapter, we discuss the violent implications of two religious elements that are distinct and central in the Jewish legacy: mysticism and messianism. We conclude with a critical assessment of the nonviolent tradition attributed to medieval and early modern Judaism (the ninth part).

Biblical Prescriptions for Violence

The most fundamental element in the Jewish cultural reservoir, its very axis, is the Hebrew Bible. The Bible provides a rich source of antiviolent themes, humanist ideals, and descriptions of idyllic peace and justice. At the same time, the Bible, like its counterparts in other ancient Near Eastern civilizations, is a remarkably militant text that includes an extraordinary range of aggressive themes and models, often confusing and contradictory. Violence is evident in the image of God, his treatment of humanity, the manner in which he demands to be worshiped, and the rules he sets forth for social control. Violence is also apparent in the chronicles of the Israelites, replete with war, genocide, and internecine conflict, as well as in prophecies that envision a turbulent end of times.

The violence inherent in the Hebrew image of God is particularly significant because the divine serves as a model for human emulation (*imitatio dei*). The Hebrew God is a "Lord of Hosts", vengeful and militant. He ruthlessly kills individuals, annihilates groups, and punishes humanity with plagues, brutal wars, and natural disasters. He also commands killing on a "chauvinist" basis: His chosen people are instructed to implement his fury against inferior peoples that are accursed from the moment of their inception, like the Ishmaelites, Moabites, Ammonites, and Edomites.

The implications of God's wrath are both direct and indirect: God is wrathful, and he commands others to do violence on his behalf. Since he is a model of emulation, his exemplar permits or even requires mimetic violence, as exemplified by Phinehas. At the same time, violence committed in the name of God and in emulation of God can absolve the perpetrator of agency and responsibility.

Violent divine discrimination is twofold: God is intolerant toward lesser peoples but reserves his most extreme expressions of fury for the people he holds to the highest standard. His entire relationship with Israel, even in its ideal form, is based on the ritualization of violence: It begins with Abraham's "Covenant between the Parts" (*brit bein habetarim*), which involves a dismembering of animals, continues with the covenant of circumcision (*brit milah*), and ends with the cultic butchering, eating, and burning of animals in the Jerusalem Temple (*korban*). God requires constant sacrifice. Sacrificial offerings, ranging from sheep, bulls, and doves to wine, grains, and incense, were offered at regular festivals, as thanksgiving, after birth or disease, as atonement for sin, in fulfillment of vows, or as a voluntary deed. The ritual slaughter industry in Jerusalem was vast, requiring colossal administrative, architectural, and economic machinery. But it also undergirded a prohibition on human sacrifice, the likes of which had occurred in the valleys around Jerusalem. Prebiblical memories of child sacrifice to Moloch survive in the ominous tales of the sacrifice of Isaac and the story of Jephthah's daughter.

In prohibiting human sacrifice, homicide, and even the consumption of blood, the Bible places limits on violence. At the same time, the divinely ordained procedures designed to prevent crime, including violent crime, involve violence as a form of social control. The Bible commands capital punishment as a reprisal for violent acts such as murder, negligent homicide, brutality against parents, rape, and kidnapping. But it also requires capital punishment for sexual crimes (ranging from incest and bestiality to adultery) and for a long list of religious offenses (worshiping false gods, desecration of the Temple, blasphemy, desecration of the Sabbath, and witchcraft). The response to minor violent crimes is violent as well, in accordance with the *lex talionis* principle of "an eye for an eye."

Biblical Descriptions of Violence

Beyond prescriptions for violence, the Bible abounds in descriptions of violence. Key historical moments in the chronicles of the Israel stand out in their carnage. The Exodus begins with Egyptian genocide against the Israelites, features the retaliatory killing of a violent Egyptian by Moses as its turning point, culminates in the ten plagues (including genocide against the Egyptians), and ends in the drowning of Pharaoh's army in the Red Sea to the rejoicing of the Children of Israel. There follows the conquest of Canaan by Joshua, including the destruction of Jericho and Ai, the enslavement of the Gibeonites, the defeat of the Amorites, and the destruction of Hazor, all aided by divine intervention. Once settled in the land, the Israelites follow judges and kings in a sustained campaign against neighboring ethnic groups, including the Aramites, Moabites, Midianites, Amalekites, Ammonites, and, their most threatening rivals, the Philistines. These conquests are accompanied by a sustained struggle against idolatry, exemplified in the Prophet Elijah's massacre of four hundred priests of Ba'al. The period of peace and flourishing under King Solomon is brief: Civil wars, conquest by regional empires, and exile follow. Even in exile, the Jews suffer but also sanction violence, as described in the book of Esther.

The brutal wars that assume a central role in the Bible are regulated by laws of war that prohibit particular tactics but also compel ruthless killing. Deuteronomy 20, for example, prohibits surprise attacks and requires sparing women and children in wars outside Canaan. But it suspends these constraints in wars against the six peoples of Canaan (the Hittites, Amorites, Canaanites, Perizzites, Hivites, and Jebusites), in which none may be spared. Wars against these groups were regulated by the laws of the ban (*herem*), in which all the spoils of war were dedicated to God. Refusal to abide by these strictures, as in the case of Achan, prompt swift retaliation. Famously, King Saul loses his crown and his sanity for his refusal to execute the Amalekite king, a task that the Prophet Samuel promptly completes on his behalf.

The war against the six peoples of Canaan bore distinctly religious characteristics. The confederacy of tribes made a sacred commitment to participate in it. Combatants, their weapons, and their camp were consecrated. This purity was prompted by virtue of God's presence in the midst of the camp and by a perception of the enemy as unclean and contaminating. In battle, the Israelites were accompanied by the arc of the covenant, priests equipped with trumpets, and temple vessels. The victims and loot were "consecrated to destruction," gifts to God akin to sacrifices in gratitude for victory. While composed in the context of an existential struggle and confined to a particular time and space, the virulent hostility towards neighboring groups depicted in the scriptures beckoned the reader to relive and reimplement ruthless enmity in every passing generation, as epitomized in the commandment to "remember what Amalek did to you."

Even the rare moments of peace in the Bible's historical account are interwoven with brutality. The origins of man, depicted in the early chapters of Genesis, involve betrayal, expulsion, pain, multiple homicides, and the annihilation of all living things by means of flood. The Hebrew patriarchs engage in theft, deceit, abduction, and physical combat; conduct war; commit incest; and attempt fratricide and infanticide. The latter is of particular significance, because Abraham's willingness to sacrifice his son by divine edict, the *akedah*, supplies a model for Jewish martyrdom in later ages.

In the Bible, civil conflict also pits Israelites against one another as rival kings, clans, tribes, cities, and the two kingdoms, Judea and Israel, struggle for supremacy. For example, in Judges 19–21, a Levite avenges the rape and murder of his concubine by his Benjaminite hosts by hacking the concubine's corpse into twelve pieces and sending the sections throughout the territory of Israel. This macabre call to arms prompts a civil war in which the other tribes nearly exterminate the tribe of Benjamin.

The Bible, thus, offers an infinite yet paradoxical repertoire from which true believers can draw precedents, inspiration, and virtual blueprints for violent activity. The *herem* offers a script for violence but tempers the laws of war. The active role played by God in war suggests the feebleness and even innocence of the combatant, but the Bible's historical account emphasizes his pervasiveness and brutality. At times, the Bible glorifies war as a chivalrous game in which warriors prove their cunning and courage. At other times, it prophecies an end to war. These prophetic scenarios for the end of times can be equally shocking. Isaiah, Micah, Zechariah, and Jeremiah may envision a distant future devoid of arms, poverty, and aggression. But, on closer reading, these prophecies of global peace result from the death, devastation, or enslavement of the enemy. Apocalyptic visions are suffused with bloodshed, torture, and the annihilation of entire populations. Only the winners enjoy relief from fighting.

Even innocuous passages from the prophecies have received interpretations that are charged with intolerant implications. For example, Ezekiel 34:31 states: "And ye my flock, the flock of my pasture, are men [*adam*]." The Talmud interprets this quote to signify that "You [Israel] are called Man and gentiles are not called Man" (Talmud, Baba Me'zia 114b). A statement in the Mishnah that expresses unconditional love toward all humans received similar treatment. "Beloved is man, for he was created in God's image" (Avot 3:17) was interpreted by several leading rabbis as referring to Jews only. In his commentary on this passage of the Mishnah, the sixteenth-century rabbi Judah Loew of Prague argued: "Though it says 'Beloved is man' this does not include all of mankind, because the sages said 'You are called man and gentiles are not called man.'"

Coping with the Violent Implications of the Bible

Judaism has distanced itself from the Bible by placing interpretation (the Oral Torah) as an intermediate between itself and the Bible (the Written Torah). With the passage of time, this interpretation assumed primacy. The Talmud, intended as an exegesis of the Bible, became its substitute. The essence of Judaism became the interpretation and application of the Bible to historical realities. This involved a neutralization of the Bible and a defusing of any embarrassing and complicating segments that encumbered this adaptation to changing circumstances. Thus, Judaism is at one and the same time a religion in which the Bible is crucial and a different religion that developed after the Bible was sealed, canonized, yet rendered less relevant with the destruction of the Temple in Jerusalem and the Jewish exile from the holy land. In the absence of a kingdom, a territory, or priesthood, the wars of the Bible, its sacrifices, and other violent elements lost their validity as a model for emulation.

Interpretation and mediation have blunted the Bible's violent elements. Biblical violence experienced the same process of castration as biblical eroticism did: Both underwent symbolization, spiritualization, and ritualization. The foundation of postbiblical religion, which forms the core of Jewish tradition, is a product of the systematic effort to "deviolence" the ancient Israelite inheritance. The rabbinical treatment of zealotry in the Bible is instructive of this process.

Numbers 25 narrates the paradigmatic case of zealotry. While the Israelites were camping in the desert of Moab before crossing the Jordan River on the way to Canaan, they whored with Midianite women, and worshiped a pagan deity. This double sin angered God who ordered Moses to hang the wayward Israelites, but Moses did not dare to confront the people. At that point, a prominent Israeli aristocrat challenged the divine power, transgressing both the sacred law and the authoritative leadership by committing an outrageously wicked act of blasphemy: He had sex with a local princess while worshiping the local gods. The act took place in public, near the Tabernacle. In reaction, God punished his people with a plague that caused the death of thousands. However, Moses and the judges did nothing to stop the scandalous situation. In contrast to the impotence of established authority, a man named Phinehas took the initiative and slew the mixed couple. His impulsive brutal action, committed out of true belief, appeased God, thus stopping the plague.

Phinehas's zealotry was rewarded highly. He was granted God's covenant of peace and the high priesthood was guaranteed for him and for his descendants. According to this biblical precedent, zealotry is defined as religious violence aimed against those who are perceived as opposing the divine will, particularly by violating the boundaries of the collectivity and thus threatening its identity. From this formative religious moment on, zealotry in general, and Phinehas's zealotry, in particular, were sanctified. For more than two thousand years, Phinehas and his zealous act have been a quintessential ideal of monotheistic religious virtuosity. His epic deed became a morally, if not legally, binding precedent among Jewish and Christian devotees.

Yet the text can be read in many different ways, as the Judeo-Christian record has shown. It can be read literally as an incontrovertible precedent calling for brutal action. It can also be interpreted critically, a move that necessitates a great deal of creative sophisticated religious rationalization. Between these exegetical alternatives lies a vast array of resourceful maneuvering.

Phinehas had embarked on his deadly mission without any official license, ignoring all legal procedures. Yet he was not sentenced even after the fact. Zealotry amounted to undermining authority, law and order, thus threatening anarchy. It threatened to harm the very religiopolitical culture whose banner it bore. The traditional Jewish handling of the Phinehasic issue, developed through hundreds of years of exilic rabbinic life, is a qualified and reluctant attempt to diffuse the sting of zealotry.

Over the course of generations, the Jewish zealotry tradition has become mostly subterranean or marginal, while the antizealot tradition became the dominant traditional culture. The religiopolitical leadership sought to avoid presenting zealotry as a guiding ideal lest it endanger the status of traditional authority, threaten the internal integration of the collectivity, and endanger its ability to cope with its external environment.

These mixed feelings are reflected in the Palestinian Talmud, which argues that Phinehas and his zealot act are contrary to the rabbinic spirit (Jerusalem Talmud, Sanhedrin 27:2). The Mishnah rules that a person who "copulates with a Syrian (Gentile) woman . . . zealots are permitted to hit [i.e., kill] him" (Babylonian Talmud, Sanhedrin, 81b). At the same time, the traditional convention is to effectively annul this rabbinical decision by introducing this passage into the peculiar category of "this is religious law but the rabbis do not so instruct" (*halakha ve'ein morin ken*). The ruling regarding zealotry is one of those rare cases referred to in the Oral Torah in which there is a general consensus about the legitimacy of a certain behavior in principle, but it is modified by the fear that license for such behavior would be expanded beyond acceptable bounds.

The sages demanded that zealotry should be enacted in a public place, witnessed by many. A zealous act witnessed by less than ten people was regarded a punishable crime. The sages also placed time constraints on the act. Zealotry is a matter of a clear-cut specific moment. The sages declared religious violence that is initiated a few seconds too early or terminated a few seconds too late to be illegitimate. Thus the distance between the most elevated zealous act and sheer murderous criminality is miniscule but, nevertheless, critical. The Talmud contends that a zealot who approaches religious authorities to ask for their advice and sanction should not be granted such a license: "The one who comes to consult, they do not approve" (*ha'ba lehimalech, eyn morin lo*). Zealotry has to be an individualist and spontaneous act. A person who commits religious violence can be defined as a zealot only in retrospect, never beforehand. The Talmud also sets a terminal time limit on the act: Had Phinehas killed the couple after their bodies had parted, the act of killing would have been considered illegal and liable for punishment. Furthermore, had the would-be victim reacted quickly enough to kill Phinehas, he would have been found innocent. Seconds suffice to turn an exemplary deed into a despicable act.

Between the Torah and the Halakha, on the one hand, and the implementation of the precepts derived from them, on the other hand, thick strata of rabbinical interpretation qualify and refine the law based on changing historical circumstances. The interpretation, rationalization, adaptation, and application of Phinehas's zealotry are representative of the rabbis' sustained effort to disarm violent motifs in the Bible. This marks the transformation of the ancient Israelite cult to what became known as rabbinical Judaism, represented in modern times mainly by Jewish orthodoxy. This old-new religion, basically an exegetical enterprise, became the crux of Judaism's distinct religious tradition.

It is contained in a corpus that can be divided into four parts. The first, and least important, is the extracanonical books. The second consists of the writings of the sages, starting with the Mishna and continuing with the Halachik and Aggadic elements in the Talmud, composed between the second and the sixth centuries CE. The third consists of the medieval heritage that includes explanatory reading of the Torah (e.g., Rashi), Halachik rulings (such as responsa and treaties, including those by Saadia Gaon, Maimonides, and Joseph Karo), theology and philosophy (e.g., Nachmanides, Yehuda Halevi, and Judah Loew of Prague), and mystical writings (particularly the Zoharic and Lurianic Kabbalah). The fourth component consists of rabbinical writings in recent centuries and in modern times, mostly Halakha (notably Chafetz Haim, Chazon Ish, and Ovadia Yosef) and *Machshava*. The latter combines simplified versions of theology and politics, moral-didactic teaching (*musar*), and mysticism (prominently, work by Abraham Isaac Kook and his son Zvi Yehuda Kook).

A Legacy of Rebellion and Destruction

In the period between second century BCE to the second century CE, the Jewish community in the Land of Israel experienced four great revolts: the Hasmonean Revolt against the Seleucid Empire (167–160 BCE), the Great Revolt (66 CE–73 CE), the Revolt of the Diasporas (also known as the Kitos War, 115–117 CE), and the Bar Kokhva Revolt (132–136 CE) against the Roman Empire.

These four revolts shared three characteristics. First, all exhibited a clear nationalist component in addition to their religious facet. All occurred against the background of a Jewish striving for overthrowing foreign occupation and establishing political sovereignty and religious autonomy. Second, each revolt was suffused with a messianic spirit. Third, in all revolts, violence was directed not only against a foreign occupier, as part of a liberation struggle, but was also inwardly directed, aimed at political and religious deviants or collaborators who were not sufficiently radical. During the Hasmonean Revolt, much of the bloodshed was directed at Hellenisers, seen as undermining both the ritual and the ethnic purity of Judaism. During the Great Revolt, the Sicarii assassinated many who rejected their suicidal stance of combat without restraint against all odds.

Due to the excessive violence of these rebellions, particularly the inwardly directed violence, and because they ended in military, political, and religious catastrophes (primarily the destruction of the Temple and exile), they are remembered as traumatic events in Jewish historiography. After all, the violence resulting from repression of these revolts exceeded by far the violence initiated by Jews. Of the Bar Kokhva rebellion, for example, the Jerusalem Talmud notes that the Romans "went on killing until their horses were submerged in blood to their nostrils" (Ta'anit 4:5).

As a result, traditional Judaism has a deeply ambivalent attitude toward each of these episodes, which tend to be condemned or repressed and forgotten. The Masada episode, at the culmination of the Great Revolt, was absent from Jewish chronicles until it was rediscovered by Zionists. Bar Kokhva was initially perceived not only as a national savior but as a veritable messiah (hence his name, son of the star). But after the failure of his revolt, the sages described him as "Bar Koziba" (meaning both "son of a lie" and "son of disappointment," i.e., a false messiah), until his image was rehabilitated by Zionists.

The period of the revolts was a period in which Jewish violence was conspicuous and consequential. At the same time, this period was distinguished not merely by its disastrous violence but by virtue of being the only such episode in Jewish history. No less significant than its occurrence was the systematic effort by the guardians of Jewish traditions to relegate this interlude to oblivion or to regard it with loathing, from the period of the sages until the modern era.

This period, in which the last books of the Bible were written, the centuries before the Common Era, was a tumultuous period of changing governments, wars, civil wars, rebellions, the destruction of the Temple, and exile. All were momentous events in ancient Israel, upheavals of geopolitical, national, and religious dimensions. It seems that different varieties of Judaism existed side by side in this period in the Land of Israel and its surroundings. One of these Judaisms was the Pharisee movement that ultimately prevailed to imprint itself on Jewish tradition, which in retrospect was considered the most authentic and legitimate and which found its expression in the writings of the sages. Another movement was to eventually become Christianity. In the range between the two, a variety of movements provided textual innovations in response to the decline of the Jerusalem-centered priestly cult.

Several of these more-or-less Jewish books were excluded from the scriptures due to theological resistance or because they were completed after the sacred writings were sealed. Some of these texts have been lost, some survived only in Greek translation, and some were only recently discovered. For these reasons, this literature has had a negligible influence on later Jewish worldviews and on Jewish behavior, but the apocrypha and other documents from this period can testify to the moods prevailing in this revolutionary period. The status of these documents, in particular their representativeness and influence, continues to be hotly debated. The Dead Sea Scrolls, discovered in the 1940s and 1950s, offer a dramatic example. The texts are replete with violence, concentrated particularly in the scroll about the "War of the Sons of Light against the Sons of Darkness." This scroll offers a detailed Manichean account of a brutal confrontation in the future between Israel and a coalition of nations that will result in redemption.

The expressions of violence in texts from the Second Commonwealth period take one of two literary forms: apocalyptic visions and mythohistorical accounts. The prophecies, such as the books of Enoch, Ezra, and Baruch, are reminiscent of the catastrophic visions of the biblical prophets, such as the book of Daniel and the New Testament prophets, such as the book of Revelation. Among the mythohistorical accounts, Jewish tradition respects but has not canonized the books of Maccabees, which describe the Jewish rebellion against Seleucid rule in Judea. These two books are our most important source about this period. First Maccabees, a Hebrew text addressed to local Judeans, is sympathetic to the rebellion's leaders, the Hasmonean priestly family, who strain for ritual purity and national militancy, emphasizing heroic zealotry. Second Maccabees, written in Greek and addressed to Jews in the Diaspora, tends to be more critical of the revolt. It argues that it was not an inevitable clash between two cultures but unnecessary bloodshed caused by corrupt and alien parties.

These texts have also offered behavioral models for later Jews, in particular Zionists. This includes the most gruesome incident of Jewish martyrdom: the legendary tale of the woman and her seven children who are willing to undergo horrific torment and, ultimately, painful death rather than agree to consume pork. The narrator comments: "Most admirable and worthy of everlasting remembrance was the mother, who saw her seven sons perish in a single day, yet bore it courageously because of her hope in the Lord" (2 Maccabees 7:24). Sure enough, generations of schoolchildren in Israel have been taught to revere this woman as a symbol of Jewish courage and dignity.

The Oral Torah and Rabbinic Ruling

Present day orthodoxy is a Judaism that is centered on the Halakha. It inherited, fostered, and developed the normative ritual code from traditional Judaism, which now regulates its way of life. The Halakha dictates how a Jew is to behave in any situation. Orthodox doctrine considers the source of these laws to be divine and regards the laws as having been transmitted to the Jewish people in a revelatory act at Mount Sinai. The laws were initially recorded in the Written Torah (i.e., the Hebrew Bible, particularly the Pentateuch). The Oral Torah is a sequel and interpretation of the Written Torah. Officially, the Oral Torah is slightly inferior to the Written Torah in holiness and authoritativeness but in practice it replaces and supersedes the Written Torah.

The writings of the sages and the Halakha combine elements from different sources with different agendas, expressing various schools, periods, and places. Nonetheless, future generations, including contemporary Orthodox Jews, conceived of these as made of one cloth. Moreover, they are organically bound with the great pillars of the medieval and early modern Halakhic literature.

The number of rabbinical rulings has grown exponentially over time. Generations of rulings, rendered generally as answers (*responsa*) to questions from community members analyzed the commandments and adapted them to the changing situations with which Jews had to contend. In this manner, the rabbis compiled a rich corpus covering almost every conceivable topic. Thousands of compendiums have since collected, reworked, and updated these rulings.

The oral law, in general, and the Halakha, in particular, are not merely an exegesis of past writings but also a foundation for future writings, an infrastructure for a new Judaism that would have to survive unknown circumstances. The Bible, composed in ancient times, had to be adapted for a people without a temple, a homeland, territorial concentration, a shared language, independence, or politics. The oral law can be seen as Judaism's adjustment project to thousands of years of life in exile. To so adjust, the Oral Law and the Halakha had to suppress nationalism and repress messianism. This also involved a sublimation of the Bible in an effort to supervise and qualify the violence of Judaism, until it could no longer be expressed. This denationalizing and demessianism required the severing of the Gordian knot between religion and territory and religion and politics. Thus, the sages emphasized the sanctity of the Land of Israel and its ritual significance over its historical significance and its function as a sovereign base. In the first four or five centuries of the Common Era, the counterviolent trend may well have been one current among others, perhaps not even the primary current. Only later on, given the exilic reality, did this current prove to be the most adaptive. It alone prevailed and became identified with Jewish tradition.

The sages used several strategies in order to curb the violent elements of Judaism, particularly those hidden in the religion's national and

messianic aspect. First, Jewish tradition underwent a fundamental theological transformation: It transferred the focus of responsibility to the
heavens and placed sovereignty exclusively in the hands of God. The
Jewish collective and the individual were absolved of the need to take an
active role in history. Second, Jewish fate was reinterpreted: The failure of
rebellions and exile were presented as a divine punishment for transgressing religious law, "because of our sins" (*mipney chata'enu*) as evident in
the *musaf* prayer that Jews continue to recite on holy days. This allowed
the believer to come to terms with his circumstances and to turn his
efforts to contemplation and ritual and away from politics. Since persecution was divinely ordained, failure to submit to God's instruments (the
Assyrians, Babylonians, Greeks, or Romans) merely invited further suffering and delayed redemption. The focus of conflict shifted away from military clashes between Jews and their enemies and to the tension between
Israel and God. Here, Israel's power lay in the opposite of self-determina-
tion: in negating power, subjecting itself to God, and repenting.

Changes in religious conceptions were accompanied by changes in
Jewish identity that had implications for violence. A clear example was the
revolution in the masculine image in Judaism. The biblical hero, who
worked the land, administered the state, and participated in combat was
gradually replaced with the man of books and the man of faith. The great
virile conquerors underwent near effeminization: Joshua became a Torah
scholar, and David became the head of a yeshiva. From now on, their distinction was wisdom and piety. An exemplary expression of this revolution can be found in the tale of an emperor who asked a rabbi: "Who is a
hero?" According to the Mishnah, the rabbi replied: "He who conquers his
lust" (Avot 4:1).

A parallel twist occurred in stories about the Bible and the Second
Common-wealth. The emphasis shifted from physical to spiritual force
and from the political to the miraculous. The Passover Haggadah retold the
Exodus as deliverance by divine hand in which Jews were passive participants and Moses, the Bible's charismatic leader, was completely absent.
Similarly, the Chanukah epic ceased to be about a war in which the weak
cunningly and courageously overcame Seleucid troops equipped with ele-
phants, as reported in First and Second Maccabees. The Talmud transformed this military account into a story about the miracle of the small pot
of oil. Here, as in the rabbinical treatment of Bar Kokhva, the rabbis strove
to ensure that violent legacies would not lead to risky imitation.

This new Jewish stance also led to significant Halakhic innovations, including a moderation and restraining of the laws of war. The Halakha suggested that the launching of war involved prudence and caution. It distinguished between mandatory war (*milkhemet mitzvah*), which was essentially defensive, and discretionary war (*milkhemet reshut*) that could be launched only with permission from the Sanhedrin (the parliament of seventy-one sages) and with the support of the high priest. Since both the Sanhedrin and the priesthood had been dissolved, some argued, these conditions precluded war altogether.

Other Halakhic changes related to the regulation and humanization of war. It was said that even Amalek must be offered peace conditions before attacking. Maimonides, for example, ruled that one cannot surround a city from all sides but only from three sides so that the enemy can escape. Nachmanides prohibited pillaging the enemy's livestock and property. Judah Loew of Prague ruled that one could not harm civilian bystanders.

At the same time, the sages placed limits on violent criminal penalties. Though the list of capital offenses in the Bible was long, in practice the death penalty was enacted only under the most extreme circumstances and only after particularly complex legal procedures, so much so that Rebbi Elazar ben Azariah regarded a court that executed one criminal in seventy years as a "murderous court." Maimonides stated that that it is better to set a thousand criminals free than to punish a single innocent man.

Kabbalah and Mythology

Analyses of the traditional sources of Jewish violence tend to focus on the Bible and the Halakha while ascribing a significantly lesser role to the mystical or moralistic literature. Yet even these disregarded texts have shaped the ethos of Jewish believers, particularly in the modern era. Like any religious mysticism, the Kabbalah deals with the secret of the divine and the wonders of creation and of man. Mysticism seeks to create an unmediated link between the believer and his God and to arrive at a knowledge of a reality that is both sublime and internally hidden. This reality is authentic, while apparent reality is only its symbolic reflection.

The roots of Jewish mysticism lie in the Second Commonwealth era. It flourished in the Middle Ages, both in the Land of Israel and in the Diaspora, in parallel to Jewish philosophy, its rival and complement. Because of its esoteric and individualist tendency and its preoccupation with higher realms, mysticism is usually associated with the tendency to withdraw from worldly matters, with an indifference and alienation toward the surrounding environment or a striving toward harmony with the environment. Consequently, the Kabbalah has a naturally quietist and conciliatory dimension. At the same time, the Kabbalah has a facet that can lead to worldly activism and even to Jewish violence.

Jewish mysticism can be divided into two currents. The ecstatic Kabbalah focuses on meditative procedures to create a direct contact with God. This type of Kabbalah has a prophetic and an occult aspect, which can gravitate to practical Kabbalah. The second type of Kabbalah is theosophical. It develops an elaborate theological system to intimately and profoundly know God, his environment, deeds, and plans. For hundreds of years, the ecstatic Kabbalah has been linked to violent rituals that have a clear magical element. This violence is neither central nor prominent in the Kabbalah, but it is a noteworthy offshoot of this tradition. These rituals include complex cultic procedures aimed at affecting the well-being of individuals and groups, such as rituals that can cause material and physical harm, even death. The best known of these is the secret spell Lashes of Fire (*pulsa dinura*), rumored to be in use even today by Israeli political activists who wish to neutralize opponents.

More surprisingly yet are the subtle and effective implications of theosophical Kabbalah for Jewish violence. First, the Kabbalah gives rabbinical Judaism vitality by introducing a mythical component to what is otherwise an intellectual and legalistic tradition. The Kabbalah overflows with mythology, in the strict sense of the word: the epic exploits of the divine. Second, the Kabbalah offers tools for theurgy, the ability to influence God and manipulate the heavens. The Kabbalah does so by supplementing the halakhic practice with *kavana,* a concentrated awareness of the mystical implications of one's normative actions. With *kavana,* the believer can redeem the divine and thus redeem the world. The Kabbalah makes possible an activism pregnant with religious energies. It presents historical reality as a mirror and integral component of a larger cosmic drama in which the Jew and the people of Israel can play a vital role.

The two most influential Kabbalistic texts are the Zohar, composed in thirteenth-century Spain, and the Lurianic Kabbalah, composed in Galilee in the sixteenth- century. The Zohar allows the reader to become thoroughly acquainted with the nature of God and to fathom the secrets of the universe by means of the ten *sefirot,* emanations of the divine that create and sustain the world. Of the many interesting ideas in the Zohar, the most relevant to Jewish violence is the distinction between the exalted Jew and inferior non-Jew. The Zoharic tradition treats the Jew as unconditionally and undeniably holy whereas the gentile is of low moral standing, regardless of his behavior. The Jew draws from the divine light whereas the gentile is impure, beastly, corrupt, and sinister. This dehumanization of non-Jews makes them potential targets of Jewish violence.

The Lurianic Kabbalah can be read as confirming this discriminatory attitude toward gentiles and can be exploited to back calls for violence against non-Jews. For example, according to the Lurianic myth of *berur* ("selection"), evil achieves its reign over human existence and can struggle against the divinity and harm humans by capturing sparks (*nitzotzot*) in shells (*klipot*). Whereas divinity is the sole supplier of life energy, evil, the essence of matter, has no independent source of power. It draws its vitality from its hold on holiness, which is the substance of the sparks. The devil can only exist by joining the divine source, taking it hostage by stealth or force and drawing it out. Rescuing the sparks from the grasp of matter is the key to destroying the powers of evil. There is no repair (*tikkun*) for heaven and earth without a clear selection between the emissaries of good and evil. This esoteric account has been read as identifying the sparks with Jews and the shells with gentiles, whose force derives entirely from their hold on Jews. Destroying the gentile will release the Jew from captivity, will eliminate chaos (*tohu vabohu*), and will restore order to the world.

The Lurianic Kabbalah has an even greater impact on violence by virtue of linking mysticism with messianism. This mystical messianism is suffused with national ideas and symbols that encourage the believer to become an agent for change. For these and other reasons, this Kabbalah is particularly popular and has impacted multiple facets of Judaism, including normative Halakha, the seventeenth-century Sabbatian messianic surge (discussed ahead), and eighteenth-century Hassidism. It has many followers among religious Jews in Israel, particularly those of Middle Eastern origins.

According to Luria, at the root of all evil and chaos was a primal event, the breaking of the vessels (*shvirat kelim*), a cataclysmic cosmic rupture. Overcoming this catastrophe requires repair (*tikkun*), which means redeeming the divine and the world, in particular Israel. This process is not merely cosmic in which good and evil struggle over the future of the universe but delegates a seminal role for the individual Jew. Redemption does not occur of its own accord but requires human awakening from below (*itaruta diletata*) through the improvement of religious behavior.

This unites the mystical and the messianic goals: perfecting the world (*tikkun olam*). It creates an overlap between the redemption of God and the cosmos from a state of fragmentation, the redemption of the nation from its exile, and the redemption of the individual Jew's soul. This is an activist and protonationalist approach that places responsibility on each and every Jew and on the Jewish people as a whole. The Jews' task is to usher in the Messiah by separating from the gentiles and discarding them. They do so by fulfilling the commandments of the Torah in a focused matter that leads to awareness of their deeper significance, a penetration of the heavens and their manipulation. A particular mystical-messianic power is ascribed to the commandment to conquer the land and settle in it. Thus the forceful treatment of Palestinians has cosmic significance.

The atmosphere of mystery and awe that surrounded the Kabbalah, in addition to the explicit rabbinical ban on the study of the Kabbalah, limited its circulation. Only in certain periods did the preoccupation with the Kabbalah become relatively widespread. In these periods, it underwent concretization and simplification. This occurred in the seventeenth century, when the trauma of the expulsion from Spain created fertile ground for redemptive ideas.

Messianic Ideas and Messianic Movements

Messianism is one of Judaism's most important contributions to the Western heritage. This motif is not to be found in a distinct corpus of sacred books or in a particular genre of Jewish thought. Rather, it is manifested in a broad variety of sources that have infused Jewish tradition throughout the ages. Judaism conceived of messianism, developed it, and spread it. Judaism has also done its best to restrain messianism and neutralize it of its revolutionary and aggressive elements. Even the sages of the first centuries of the Common Era espoused messianism while proclaiming it to be detrimental "to awe" (of God) "and love" (of man).

As in other religions, Judaism displays an affinity between messianism and violence. The books of Isaiah and Daniel, the apocrypha, the legends of the Talmud, the Kabbalah, and even current prophecies envision the end of days in apocalyptic terms. It is difficult to think of historical incidents of acute messianism that did not degenerate into violence. In Jewish history, the variable intervening between messianism and violence is nationalism. The rebellions of the Second Commonwealth are prime examples of outbursts of Jewish national messianism that involved violence.

As a rule, with the exception of several brief episodes, Jewish tradition has treated messianism with ambivalence. It praised the messianisms of the past and future but deplored present-tense messianism. Excessive messianism would endanger the existing order, make tradition superfluous, undermine the authority of the Halakha and the rabbis, and undercut political power. An example for this attitude is the famous Talmudic assertion that "There will be no difference between the current age and the Messianic era except for [our emancipation from] subjugation to the [gentile] kingdoms" (Berachos, 34b). Maimonides interpreted this as a bold claim to defuse the explosive revolutionary and miraculous element of messianism and turn redemption into a normal political process. At the same time, Judaism took care to maintain messianism on the back burner because it recognized that a measured and contained drive was necessary for sustaining religious vitality.

Exilic quietism was interrupted by messianic incidents that are mere historical curiosities, as in the case of Shlomo Molcho (a sixteenth-century Portuguese Marano and mystic who is recorded in Jewish historiography as a "pseudo-Messiah"). The famous exception that problematizes the linkage between messianism and violence is the seventeenth-century Sabbatean movement. This was a particularly intensive messianic outburst that lasted two years and swept much of Judaism, from the Middle East to Europe. Yet the movement provoked no violence at all. The Turkish sultan was threatened by Sabbatai Sevi's "kingdom" and arrested the messiah, but the enthusiasm that seized hundreds of thousands of Jews from all sectors of society was contained within the bounds of religion and did not cross the line into social and political unrest. It most certainly did not manifest as rebelliousness and violence. Sabbatai alone was assigned the burden of realizing redemption while his followers were expected only to focus on his personality and deeds by means of faith and rite. It is tempting to hypothesize that the presence of a figure that personifies the messianic urge releases the followers from the burden of activism.

The Sabbatean movement was echoed in several movements in the century after its decline, such as the Frankists. Their messianism became more esoteric and antinomian over time, until it lost all political and activist potential. A final element of Sabbateanism appeared in yet another great historical Jewish movement, the eastern European Hassidism of the eighteenth century. This movement was also messianic, but its messianism was curbed by displacing mundane religious energies into the soul.

The paradox of messianic quietism in the Middle Ages is even more surprising in light of several characteristics of Jewish messianism. First, both the redeeming agent and the redeemed unit are not the individual but the collective, namely the Jewish people. Second, redemption occurs not merely on the spiritual level but first and foremost on the historical level. Both characteristics distinguish Jewish messianism from its Christian counterpart and grant it a national-political quality. Even at its most fanciful, when it conjectured the redemption of God and the cosmos, Jewish messianism maintained a nucleus of Jewish territorialism and sovereignty. The fulfillment of the messianic vision, in all its variants, posited the ingathering of the exiled in the Land of Israel and the establishment of an independent state that will guarantee security, affluence, and dignity for Jews. It can be said that the Jewish conception of redemption always contained a proto-Zionist element.

In regard to the human role in God's redemptive plan, Jewish scholars tended to adopt an intermediate stance. Although redemption is up to heavenly forces, man has a role to play, be it minor. Human behavior is not a sufficient but a necessary condition. Human involvement is limited to ethical and ritual behavior at some times and necessitates historical action at other times. Religious behavior that contributes to redemption can be limited to the fulfilling of commandments and the strengthening of faith, or it can necessitate an involvement in the social and political order. The latter involvement risks being interpreted as a signal of distrust in divine providence. Consequently, activism is trivialized and minimized as an effort to "merely" hasten the pace of redemption, as a trial of determination to signal to the divine that one is deserving of redemption, or as a mechanism of selection that sets apart those willing to take action into their own hands. Yet, even though it fulfills a minor role, human participation in the dynamics of redemption is often violent.

Human intervention in the messianic process can take on a paradoxical character. When belief in messianic determinism is particularly strong and the redemption is particularly imminent, when redemption is practically behind the door, logic dictates passive waiting with full trust in the divine. Ironically, it is precisely then that the believer loses his patience and violently bursts through the door in a manner that tends to be cruel and deadly. When the messianist is active in history, his action tends to be assertive precisely because he is playing a role in a divine process, feels omnipotent, is released from ethical restraint, and can overcome all political hurdles. After all, the responsibility for his actions is not truly his. These conditions create the perfect storm for messianic violence.

In Jewish history this has occurred two times, separated by two millennia: once in the period immediately before and after the destruction of the Temple and once in the last four decades. The most resourceful and dominant Jewish revival movements in recent times are the overtly messianic movements Gush Emunim, the Lubavitch Hassidism (Chabad), and, to a lesser extent, the Breslav Hassidism. All three contributed substantially to the remessianization of religious Judaism and all involve right-wing militant ethnonationalism. Members of the first have been implicated in violent acts whereas members of the latter two movements seem to sympathize with and even admire perpetrators of Jewish violence.

Several idioms related to the messianic tradition involve catastrophic eschatology that is unavoidably violent. The pangs of the Messiah (*chevley mashiach*, often also *ikvata demeshicha*) refer to the period that precedes the realization of the full redemption, typically characterized by a radical deterioration in religious and political conditions. This concept suggests that the messianic process is not necessarily linear but involves digressions, regressions, and most importantly, a dramatic crisis just prior to the consummation of the process. This catastrophe has a moral-spiritual and a physical-historical aspect. The pangs of the Messiah can take the form of heavy wars involving Israel. There are those who seek such a war to ensure redemption in their time.

The messiah from the Davidic branch is the idyllic messiah whose appearance signals the End of Days. He is the embodiment of harmony and peace. Some Jewish traditions claim that his reign is preconditioned by a different messiah, "Messiah, son of Joseph" (*mashiach ben yoseph*), a man of war, who fiercely fights for the fulfillment of redemption. According to the Talmud (Sukkah 52a–b), as interpreted in the rabbinical apocalyptic literature, only his death in battle opens the opportunity for the arrival of the Davidic messiah.

Redemption is a matter of timing. Its date is clouded in mystery and dread. This tormenting uncertainty can be overcome by anxiously searching for hints (*simanim*) in regard to the definite time and by calculating the end of days (*chishuvey kitzin*). On occasion, this search can escalate into taking impatient action to provoke the appearance of these indices. For example, those who read Jeremiah's prophecy that "evil begins from the North" (1:14) as a precondition of messianic timing find a degree of comfort in Israel's armed confrontations with Syria and Lebanon.

The War of Gog and Magog (the equivalent of the Christian Armageddon) is the ultimate military clash between Jews and the nations that hate Israel and seek to conquer Jerusalem. After great suffering and sacrifice,

the Jews will be victorious and will usher in the full redemption. Any identification of a contemporary military confrontation with the War of Gog
and Magog might encourage certain Jews to support the war enthusiasti-
cally and take great risk in the certain knowledge that the end will involve
victory and redemption. The Jewish messianic tradition describes this war
as a day of judgment (*yom ha'din*) on which all accounts will be settled.
This will be a day of darkness, suffering, blood, and death but also a day in
which justice will prevail.

When messianic Jews lose their patience, they seek at all costs to
change reality in order to force it to match their vision. A different strategy
to fulfill the vision is to turn it from a future aspiration to a present reality
by declaring that the current order, as it stands, is a redeemed world. Both
approaches are potentially dangerous from the religious establishment's
point of view. It is no coincidence that orthodox authorities are deeply
concerned about the realization of the dream held high by their followers.
Rabbinical authorities, from ancient times to this day, have fought every
messianic phenomenon by declaring it to be a false messianism as soon
as it manifests itself. In addition to endangering traditional religion and
conventional morals, which are rendered obsolete by the messiah, there is
also a danger of violence. Believers experience a dissonance between their
internal reality, which acknowledges redemption, and external reality,
which they experience empirically, that is abundant with the characteristics of an unredeemed world. The frustrating gap between these levels of
consciousness has to be bridged without reservations, even violently if
necessary.

1,800 Years of Nonviolence?

Between the suppression of the Bar Kokhva Revolt and the modern era,
most Jews settled in the European and Middle Eastern diasporas as a
minority that survived by virtue of Christian and Muslim tolerance. This
relative peace was interrupted occasionally by violence against Jews. The
survival of Jewish communities, let alone their well-being and prosperity,
depended on curtailing violent initiatives. Gradually, this nonviolence
transformed from an existential expediency into a religious principle.

In the Middle Ages, the effort to curb violence was accompanied by a
parallel effort to neutralize messianism, gradually distance Judaism from
the written Bible (the Torah) in favor of the Oral Torah (the Talmud), condemn violent episodes, and reduce the nationalist elements associated

with Jewish violence, such as territory and sovereignty, to a symbolic level. For example, rituals and memories of the holy land, such as prayer eastward, came to replace immigration and settlement. Techniques for neutralizing the threat of activist messianism include spiritualization, ritualization, and co-optation.

A well-known example is that of the "three oaths." At the origin of this principle is a verse in the Song of Songs: "I adjure you, O maidens of Jerusalem, by gazelles or by hinds of the field: Do not wake or rouse love until it please!" (2:7). The Babylonian Talmud invokes this verse and relates that God made the Israelites swear to "not ascend the wall," traditionally understood as a prohibition against mass immigration to the Land of Israel. The second oath is "not rebel against the nations of the world," interpreted as a command to refrain from politics and violent activism. Many quote a version of these oaths that imposes an additional prohibition: "Do not press the end," abstain from coercing God to bring the redemption before its preordained time.

In this protracted exilic period, which provided the roots of religious Judaism as we know it today, violence was rare and a tradition of victimhood developed. But in this same period, new cannons, customs, and rituals developed that undoubtedly had a grain of violence in them. The two most prominent examples are the Passover *Haggadah* that was compiled over the course of the Middle Ages and Purim celebrations that drew on the book of Esther. The reader will be familiar with the ceremonial Seder meal in which religious Jews repeat the line from the *Haggadah* "Pour out your wrath on the nations that refuse to acknowledge you—on the peoples that do not call upon your name. For they have devoured your people Israel." Participants sing hymns of victory accomplished through cruel acts of violence against Egyptians (which are often identified with contemporary villains). They also recount with triumphalism each of the ten plagues with which the Egyptians were afflicted, including the killing of their firstborns.

The violence in Purim celebrations takes two forms. The first, not unlike Passover, revolves around a ritual reading of a biblical text, the book of Esther, which expresses superiority over gentiles, hatred, and a great deal of verbal violence. Readers rejoice at the hanging of Haman, the villain of the tale, with his ten sons at gallows intended for the hanging of Jews. The second element is a carnival atmosphere that may have led on occasion to modest physical violence against gentiles.

The prototypical medieval carnival involved not only the overturning of fortunes, which is a central principle of this holiday, but the upending of all social hierarchies and categories. This reversal found expression in the donning of costumes and in the commandment to consume alcohol until one cannot distinguish friend from foe. But this carnival atmosphere also confined aggression in time and space (such as the synagogue, on one particular day of the year). The same emancipating subversiveness that enabled measured expressions of Jewish violence during Purim also contributed to restraint during the rest of the year and thus bolstered the existing social order in which Jews were passive and subordinate.

There is a clear gap between the Halakhic, theological, and ceremonial preoccupation with violence and the ability to actualize that violence. It is precisely the certain knowledge that violence cannot be exercised that gave free reign to violent fantasies. One can speculate that the textual and ritual acting out of violence betrays impotence as an overcompensation for the inability to take violent action.

Three final comments conclude this discussion of Jewish quietism and bring to a close our survey of violence in Jewish tradition. First, there is some evidence of violence directed by Jews against other Jews in the context of social control. This violence relates primarily to rabbinical rulings designed to penalize deviants in the community by means of humiliation or excommunication. A conspicuous example is the struggle against informers, particularly in periods of Jewish persecution in Europe. The community's fear that its autonomous social and economic arrangements would be exposed to the authorities and the Christian environment led it to view informers as one of its greatest menaces. Ashkenazi communities often circumvented Jewish legal institutions when dealing with informers (categorized as *moser* in Halakhic law). On rare occasions, Sepharadic communities condemned informers to death, with the assent of Christian rulers. The most common and effective control mechanism was the *herem* that, in distinction from its biblical namesake, was akin to an excommunication. This banishment was proclaimed in a terrifying ceremony and was experienced as a particularly violent measure, given the precarious nature of Jewish life outside the community.

Second, the ancient Jewish tradition of "sanctifying the name of God" (*kiddush ha'shem*) reached its apex during the Middle Ages. This martyrdom tradition developed in response to extreme acts of violence directed against Jewish communities, such as the slaughters of the Crusades. As part of this tradition, Jews murdered their families or committed suicide to avoid conversion. These defiant acts contained a measure of aggressiveness toward the Christian perpetrator, perhaps even an internalizing of the perpetrators' aggressiveness. Medieval Jewish and Christian martyr-dom traditions influenced each other in mutual and cunning ways. Several elements of the medieval Jewish martyrdom tradition diffused from Christian models of martyrdom and assimilated them until they appeared to be authentically Jewish. Such martyrdom was violent not merely by virtue of the aggression directed toward oneself and one's family. The martyr also snatched the prerogative of killing from his opponent, thus appropriating mastery over his own death. Finally, by undergoing a noble death that sanctified the name of God, the martyr provoked the divine to avenge his death, unleashing God's violence against his opponent.

Third, the medieval period saw the emergence of a Jewish tradition of victimhood. For long and formative periods in history, Jews were targets of violence by non-Jews, as exemplified by forced conversions and expul-sions in fifteenth-century Spain, nineteenth-century pogroms in Russia, and so forth. This violence tended to be lethal and was driven by ideological-religious (mostly Christian) justifications in addition to an economic and political logic. Moreover, it was directed against Jews as a collective, affili-ated with a particular ethnic and religious group. In the two millennia in which Jews were victims of anti-Semitism and its violent derivatives, an elaborate tradition of Jewish victimhood emerged.

The issue of victimhood is particularly conspicuous in the post-Holocaust era. Contemporary Jewish life takes place under the shadow of the most extreme case of anti-Jewish violence, the Shoa. Jewish collective memory and collective identity as victims of violence has two implica-tions. On the one hand, it has led Jews to be acutely aware of issues con-cerning violence, leading to toleration and moderation. On the other hand, a distinct minority of Jews use their own victimhood as a license to inflict violence on others by way of compensation or revenge.

Thus, to the two parallel and complementary Jewish traditions, vio-lence and antiviolence, one should add another Jewish tradition, that of victimhood. These three traditions can be viewed as an integral triangle, each corner of which has a dialectical relationship with the other two.

Bibliography

Ben-Sasson, Haim Hillel, A. Malamat, et al., eds. *History of the Jewish People.* Cambridge, MA: Harvard University Press, 1976.

Berger, Michael S. "Taming the Beast: Rabbinic Pacification of Second-Century Jewish Nationalism." In James K. Wellman, ed. *Belief and Bloodshed: Religion and*

Violence across Time and Tradition, 47–62. Lanham, MD.: Rowman and Littlefield Publishers, 2007.

Eisen, Robert. *The Peace and Violence of Judaism: From the Bible to Modern Zionism.* Oxford, UK: Oxford University Press, 2011.

Horowitz, Elliott. *Reckless Rites: Purim and the Legacy of Jewish Violence.* Princeton, NJ: Princeton University Press, 2006.

Idel, Moshe. *Kabbalah: New Perspectives.* New Haven, CT: Yale University Press, 1988.

Inbar, Efraim. "War in Jewish Tradition." *The Jerusalem Journal of International Relations* 9 (1987): 83–99.

Niditch, Susan. *War in the Hebrew Bible: A Study in the Ethics of Violence.* Oxford, UK: Oxford University Press, 1995.

von Rad, Gerhard. *Holy War in Ancient Israel.* Grand Rapids, MI: Wm. B. Eerdmans Publishing, 1991.

Scholem, Gershom. *Major Trends in Jewish Mysticism.* New York: Schocken, 1995.

Scholem, Gershom. *The Messianic Idea in Judaism: And Other Essays on Jewish Spirituality.* New York: Schocken, 1995.

Schwartz, Regina M. *The Curse of Cain: The Violent Legacy of Monotheism.* Chicago: University of Chicago Press, 1997.

Steinsaltz, Adin. *The Essential Talmud.* New York: Basic Books, 1984.

Urbach, Efraim Elimelech. *The Sages: Their Concepts and Beliefs.* Cambridge, MA: Harvard University Press, 1979.

Yuval, Israel. *Two Nations in Your Womb: Perceptions of Jews and Christians in Late Antiquity and the Middle Ages.* Berkeley: University of California Press, 2008.

Chapter 5

Religion and Violence in Christian Traditions

Lloyd Steffen

OVER THE CENTURIES Christian people have engaged in acts of violence believing that they were, on religious grounds, justified in doing so. This is a matter of historical record, as is the fact that Christian people have also opposed violence on the same grounds. Any discussion of violence in this faith tradition must acknowledge at the outset that Christianity, with more than 2 billion adherents the world's largest religion, does not advance a single consistent perspective on the issue of violence despite the assertion of many Christians that it does—the religion is simply too large and too complex for any such claim to uniformity in belief or practice on this or any number of other issues.

Christianity continues to be today what it has been historically: not one religion but three distinct overarching faith traditions—Catholicism, Orthodoxy, and Protestantism. Each of these Christianities houses a multiplicity of discrete, sometimes ethnically distinct, smaller groupings of Christian communions, to the point that it is estimated today that what we perhaps too confidently refer to as "Christianity" breaks down into more than 34,000 denominations, rites, or distinct "sects" worldwide, many of them independent churches or church collectives not wanting to affiliate with larger ecclesiastical bodies or denominations (ReligiousTolerance.Org).

Each of the major Christianities has a history of involvement with violence. Theological differences have naturally arisen among the wild diversity of Christians who have believed their particular interpretation of the faith possesses an exclusive—and excluding—access to the truth of God's way with humanity. These differences have occasioned conflicts that Christian people have sometimes sought to resolve by resorting to force.

The conflicts have been many, but they have occurred in basically three arenas.

1. Christians have come into conflict with other Christians, not only one Christianity against another but sometimes within the same tradition, denomination, or even within the same local church body.
2. Christians have resorted to violence against people of other faiths. Christian anti-Jewishness is perhaps the most notable example of a nefarious and sometimes murderous bigotry directed against another religion, but a more broadly conceived anti-Semitism has historically been directed as well against Muslims and the religion of Islam.
3. The close relationship of Christian authority to political power, especially in Europe, has led to numerous situations over the centuries in which the state has called on Christian spiritual authority to sanction and legitimate uses of force against perceived enemies. This development affected Christian theological reflection on the state as well as on the state's use of coercive force as it pertains to war, punishment, and social control.

Added to these general reasons for involvement with violence is the status of Christianity as a conversion religion. People engaged in the work of spreading the Christian faith have often resorted to coercion in the effort to "Christianize" the world or, in a more inward turn, to purge the faith of perceived theological impurities. So Christianity has had a major role to play in colonialist missionary efforts that have been coercive and oppressive to indigenous peoples, and the three Christian traditions, in their own claim to exercise coercive power, have had occasion to direct violence against those who self-identified as Christian but who were deemed subversive to church authority. Historically, Christians have claimed the power to use force as an instrument of institutional self-governance.

The story of the Christian religion traces back to an execution, an act of political violence directed at a first-century itinerant teacher, a Palestinian Jew, and leads, according to the final book in the Christian scriptures, Revelation, to an apocalyptic vision of the end of history. Violence and destructiveness are inseparably linked to the Christian self-understanding, from beginning to end, and are clearly integral to the unfolding story of Christianity in the Western historical record. The involvement with violence is not a surprising development given that the religion early in its history became the official religion of the Roman Empire and thus became a player embedded in the world of power politics. That Christian people have resorted to violence to settle conflicts believing that using force is consistent with Christian values contrasts, however, with other, more irenic teachings in the tradition that offer a compelling, even beautiful vision of forgiveness, reconciliation, and peacemaking. The twentieth-century ecumenical movement and interfaith dialogue efforts designed to turn from religious conflicts based on differences among Christians and between Christianity and other faiths serve as an implicit acknowledgement that Christian people have in the name of their religion too often acted in ways at odds with the noblest values of the faith. Such efforts have constituted an attempt to repudiate the violence and destructiveness that have been so much a part of Christian history.

The story of the Christian involvement with violence is long and complex, but some summarizing, highlighting of major developments, and an inescapable simplifying can be useful in the effort to clarify how Christianity relates to questions about violence, coercion, and uses of force in particular issues such as war, punishment, and social control. In the overview that follows, three issues will be discussed. The major focus will be to examine the theological justifications for violence within the sources of the traditions. A brief look at the symbolic representations of violence in the history of the tradition will be followed by a consideration of some specific issues that have provoked Christian people to condone or even resort to violence while believing themselves faithful to Christian teachings and values. We turn first to theological justifications.

Theological Justifications
Paul

Christianity began as a Jewish reform movement intended to reorient Jews to a belief that the long-expected promise of a "messiah," an "anointed one" or in Greek, *Christos*, had in fact been realized in the life and work of Jesus of Nazareth. Oppression of the Jewish people by Rome in first century Palestine lent regional fervor to the hope for a messiah, who, for many Jews, was to be a new King David sent by God to unite the people of Israel and usher in an age of justice and peace. Aggressive missionary work by early church leaders took Christian ideas beyond the originally targeted Jewish audience, and Christianity owes its status as a world religion to the vision and work of Saint Paul, who can rightly be said to be the true founder of the religion of Christianity, for it was he who took the message of Christianity to the gentile world, connecting Jewish and Greek thought in a way that offered a universal message that attracted a diverse following of people. Jewish and gentile converts formed the communities of faith that became institutionalized as "church" (Gk: *ecclesia*), and Saint Paul articulated ideas that would become the theological basis for Christian doctrine. Saint Paul endorsed a notion of basic human equality before God, freedom from Jewish legal constraints, an eschatological hope for Christ's return and a preaching pronouncement that, because of the person and work of Jesus Christ, sinful humanity had been restored to a right relationship with God.

The successful organizing activity of the early church in the Mediterranean basin did not escape the watchful eye of the Roman authorities. Tacitus and Suetonius, two first-century Roman historians, both reported that Rome viewed Christianity suspiciously, considering it an atheistic superstition out of line with the older religious traditions that helped order the state. The early Christian church did experience persecutions, especially under the emperors Nero and Domitian. According to Tacitus, Nero held Christians responsible for the great fire of Rome in 64 CE and in retaliation had Christians rounded up and summarily executed, which included hoisting them on pikes and setting them afire in his garden to illumine the walkways (Tacitus 15.4).

Although the violence directed against Christians by Rome was probably not as widespread as is sometimes portrayed, the dangers some Christians faced were real. Saint Paul was arrested and executed, and there is no doubt that despite efforts to evade persecution—Paul, a Roman citizen, appealed to Rome to defend his preaching activity—the early Christian community became a victim of state-sponsored violence due to repression by the Roman authorities, and suffering persecution at the hands of governmental authority is a major theme in the Christian scriptures. Saint Paul had been an active opponent of Christians prior to his conversion, even participating in the killing of the first church martyr, Stephen (Acts 7:58–8:1a), after which "a severe persecution began against the church in Jerusalem" (Acts 8:1b). Jesus noted the potential for violence and persecution against his followers when he offered the beatitude in the Sermon on the Mount: "Blessed are those who are persecuted for righteousness sake" (Matthew 5:10). Christians came to honor as "saints" those victims of lethal violence "martyred" at the hands of the enemies of the faith; and Christians came to understand "persecution" as important to their history and integral to their identity.

Paul's writings, the earliest we have in the Christian Scriptures, advance an ethical view in which the faithful are charged to love one another, to extend hospitality to the stranger, to bless one's persecutors, to live in harmony, and to refuse to repay evil for evil but overcome evil with good. He does not advocate any uses of coercive force in response to harms and persecution but takes the psychological view that by returning kindness to one's enemies "you will heap burning coals on their head"(Romans 12:20). Romans 13:1–7a, however, offers these comments from Saint Paul about the state and what it is owed:

> Let every person be subject to the governing authorities; for there is no authority except from God, and those authorities that exit have been instituted by God. Therefore whoever resists authority resists what God has appointed, and those who resist will incur judgment. For rulers are not a terror to good conduct but to bad...if you do wrong you should be afraid, for the authority does not bear the sword in vain! It is the servant of God to execute wrath on the wrongdoer. Therefore one must be subject, not only because of wrath but because of conscience. For the same reason you are also to pay taxes, for the authorities are God's servants.

In this passage, it appears that Paul is recognizing the right of government to use coercive force to maintain the social and political order, for he acknowledges the power of the sword, an image of lethal power, although he also is saying that Christians should recognize and accede to this power not out of fear of wrath or terror, but out of conscience—because all authority comes from God. Christians will, then, pay their taxes and meet other obligations to the state because the state wields power on authority from God who sanctions the state's activities, including the coercive power to tax and even the power of the sword itself, which would appear to fall justifiably on one who offends the state through bad conduct.

Mennonite theologian John Howard Yoder has argued against a theological view that justifies state violence on the grounds that there exists "a very strong strand of Gospel teaching which sees secular government as the province of the sovereignty of Satan" (Yoder 1972:195). Government may have a legitimate ordering function to perform, but the power of the state is restricted and akin to that of the librarian who puts the books on the shelves in an orderly way so that they might be readily found and used effectively. Government has such an ordering function, but Yoder will argue that it does not receive any blessing from God for the use of violence or coercive force. Violence and coercion are anti-Christ—activities appropriate to the province of Satan.

Romans 13, because it invokes and acknowledges the "power of the sword," undoubtedly provides Scriptural support for the perspective that the coercive powers of the state are divinely sanctioned, but what those powers are specifically is not spelled out. The reference to the power of the sword apparently endorses the view that such power is an extension of God's own. Important as this passage is in providing a justification for state-sponsored uses of coercive power, Paul's invocation of "the power of the sword" challenges and even befuddles Christian interpreters, who cannot agree on its exact meaning. Nevertheless, this passage does provide a Christian scriptural warrant to justify the use of force—thus violence—by governing institutions, which includes not only the state but also the church when it has acted as a governing authority.

Jesus

Saint Paul had almost nothing to say about the actual life of the person who became the focus of the Christian faith, Jesus of Nazareth. For one thing, he believed, as his own earliest writings make clear, that Jesus as the victorious Christ would return in Paul's own lifetime—Christianity was an eschatological faith awaiting an imminent "end time" (Gk: eschaton). Paul's interest, therefore, was not in past history but in the person and work of Jesus as the Christ, and his letters to the various Christian churches in the Mediterranean area established the backbone of theological interpretation concerning Christ that are still affirmed in the main by Christians the world over. In his theology of the cross, Paul presented Jesus's execution and subsequent resurrection as the salvific events and atoning means whereby God and humanity were ultimately reconciled and even the power of death was overcome. Stories about Jesus's life and his teachings, however, are not to be found in Paul but in later writings—the Gospels. These writings were produced in and for Christian communities acting to preserve memories of Jesus as they awaited his eagerly anticipated return—that eschatological "second coming."

Jesus is well known to Christians but obscure to history. The Gospels must necessarily contain historical truth about Jesus, but the extent of it cannot be determined with confidence. Jesus was no doubt a healer, a teacher, and a person who attracted a significant and deeply loyal following.

The Gospels present the church's understanding of Jesus's teaching on a variety of subjects, including the appropriate response to enemies and even to the government. With reconciliation, forgiveness, and equitable sharing among his followers hallmarks of his ethic, Jesus offered, as Paul had earlier averred, a message that emphasized love of one's enemies, returning good for evil and doing good even to one's persecutors. The Gospels portray Jesus preaching about a kingdom of God that would exclude those not willing or ready to accept it but that demanded of the faithful a life lived in and toward love of God and neighbor and opposed to violence, vengeance, retaliation, and hatred—all that is opposed to love of God and neighbor. According to the Gospels, Jesus, upon being asked his views on the question of taxes, acknowledged a role for government and the obligation to "render to Caesar what was Caesar's" (Matthew 12:17), but he offered no specific justification for uses of force or a defense of the "power of the sword" except to say that "all who take the sword will perish by the sword" (Matthew 26:52). Furthermore, he did not condemn people who served the state but was known—and criticized—for associating with tax collectors, one of whom, according to Matthew 10:3, became a disciple (Matthew), and with members of the military, once doing the kindness of healing the paralyzed servant of a Roman centurion whose faith Jesus praised (Matthew 8:13).

The Gospel's picture of a nonviolent even pacifist Jesus, however, does have some cracks in it, and it cannot be said with certainty that what breaks through is historical truth. One crack is to be found in the cryptic comment, "I did not come to bring peace but a sword" (Matthew 10:34). He offers this comment in an "instruction" that finds Jesus saying in acknowledgment of the many conflicts his followers will experience: "I have come to set a man against his father, and a daughter against her mother" (Matthew 10: 35a). Although many Christians interpret this entire passage as a metaphor for ideological conflict, Jesus is not making an impartial observation about the inevitable consequences of following him; he is claiming as his intention that setting such conflict in motion is his mission. A more significant crack appears in the story of the cleansing of the temple, where, according to the Gospels, Jesus in a fit of rage overturned the tables of merchants selling goods and animals for sacrifice and chased them out of the Jerusalem temple. The Gospel of John adds the detail that he did this having fashioned a "whip of cords" to drive out the animals and apparently the money changers as well (John 2:15). So Jesus not only showed anger but engaged in what from a moral point of view must be considered acts of violence even if Christians would interpret this event as completely justifiable righteous indignation. Jesus did not peacefully negotiate or reason with the temple merchants but resorted to a use of coercive force in this instance—the Gospels are all agreed on this point.

A central issue related to the Christian understanding of violence involves the Crucifixion. For all that Christians would do to pin the death of Jesus on the Jews, there is no doubt at all that his death was a rather ordinary dispensing of Roman justice. Although the Gospels tell a story of Jewish leaders scheming for that death because of Jesus's apparent blasphemy, Jesus does not suffer the punishment for blasphemy set down in Mosaic law—stoning. Moreover, scholars are skeptical of such details in the Gospel passion narratives as the midnight trial before the Jewish elders at the Sanhedrin, which never met at night. The historical fact evident in the passion narratives is that Jesus was accused and tried under Roman law and sentenced to a specifically Roman means of death—crucifixion—for a specific crime—sedition.

Despite the overwhelmingly pacifistic portrayal of Jesus in the Gospels, it is possible that Jesus actually posed some kind of threat to the established order of his day and that he was guilty of sedition. One challenge to the Jesus-as-pacifist portrayal surmises—it is all surmising—that because the first-century church was suffering persecution from Nero, one way to blunt any possible justification for Roman action against the Christian community was to reassure Rome that Christianity posed no threat to its authority. As part of that effort at reassurance, the church presented Jesus as an otherworldly preacher of love and forgiveness, a peacemaker. To support the point, the passion narratives in a sense exonerate the Romans from their obvious part in Jesus death, for as Jesus will say to the Roman procurator, "My Kingdom is not from this world," for if it were "my followers would be fighting to keep me from being handed over to the Jews" (John 18:36). No one fights for Jesus, evidence that his is an otherworldy kingdom and, thus, of no threat to Rome, but he here imagines a justifiable use of force. Even in the moment he faces Roman legal judgment Jesus displays no hostility to Rome—he is portrayed as one who understands that it is the Jews who are making the trouble, with Rome caught unwittingly in a political drama and forced to accede to Jewish demands for Jesus's death.

The Gospels misrepresent and excoriate Jews, especially the Pharisees, who were liberal interpreters of the Torah, and present Jewish leaders as not only plotting Jesus's death but taking responsibility for it and even welcoming any consequences. When Pontius Pilate, the Roman governor hearing Jesus's case, addresses the Jewish crowd assembled by "the chief priests and elders," they shout back at him, according to the Gospel of Matthew: "His blood be upon us and our children!" (27:25). The Gospel of Matthew was written sometime between the years 70 and 100 CE, more than thirty years after Jesus's death, so that this story, despite its inclusion in a Gospel addressed primarily to a Jewish audience, reflects the deep anti-Jewish sentiment rampant in the early Church. The Gospels are infected with anti-Jewish attitudes, and the story of a Jewish crowd calling for Jesus' blood would undoubtedly provide comfort to later Christians seeking justification for acts of violence against Jews.

The Gospels shift blame for Jesus's death from a cruel Roman justice to Jewish conspiracy, and in the first century CE the refusal of many Jews to convert to a belief in Jesus as messiah would have further fueled Christian animosity toward Jews. Attributing Jesus's death to Jewish intrigue added an additional support and justification for anti-Jewish attitudes and actions that might not have led to profound consequences except for an unforeseeable accident of history, which Christians of the time did not see as fortuitous but as God willed. Emperor Constantine converted to the faith in 312 CE and following his victory over the Eastern emperor, Licinius, he consolidated power and became sole Emperor in 324 CE, a date that traditionally marks the beginning of the "Christian Empire." What this meant for Christians was this:

> The Kingdom of God had come down to earth. Christians now accepted the sacred nature of the emperor, whom they naturally enough looked to as the head of the Christian people: a new Moses, a new David.... The clergy obtained legal privileges; the Episcopal tribunals had a civil jurisdiction, and the bishops were considered to be on an equal footing with governors.
>
> (Comby 1992: 68, 75)

In 380 CE, Emperor Theodosius proclaimed Christianity the official religion of the state.

As Christianity and the developing religion of rabbinic Judaism broke into separate religions over the first four centuries of the Common Era, conflicts between the two intensified, with each tradition undergoing transformation and taking on a new historical role. James Carroll writes:

Christianity went from being a private, apolitical movement to being a shaper of world politics. The status of Judaism was similarly reversed, from a licit self-rule, a respected exception within a sea of paganism, to a state of highly vulnerable disenfranchisement. What might be called history's first pogrom, an organized assault on a community of Jews, because they were Jews, took place in Alexandria in 414, wiping out that city's Jewish community for a time. Even in Palestine, Jews became a besieged minority.

(Carroll 2001: 176)

Theologically, the Christian community came to understand itself as having replaced the Jews as God's chosen people—the conflict is referred to in Christian theology as supersessionism. What made this self-understanding dangerous was that Christian people involved with the wielding of imperial power could take political, legal, and even military action consonant with supersessionist beliefs. Jews were a target of deep animosity and viewed, as reflected in anti-Jewish Gospel stories, as dangerous enemies of Christian faith. Accordingly, Emperor Constantine, a powerful Christian scornful of Jews, issued an edict in 315 that made it a crime for Jews to proselytize. This offense would be upgraded a century later to a capital crime. This latter action symbolizes what can happen to a religion, even one that remembers its founder as nonviolent and as the victim of unjust state violence, when it becomes enmeshed in governmental power. Jews came to be viewed as fair game for political exclusion and legal retaliation. Justification for acts of violence against these perceived enemies of the faith was found in the fact that Christians had actually come to hold the levers of imperial power, that is, Christians came to believe that they were justified in their hostility toward Jews by history itself, for unfolding in history was God's own divine plan for Christian supremacy.

Justification for Christian involvement in violence is not found so much in explicit Scriptural sources, with Saint Paul's "power of the sword" notion a possible exception, but in an interpretation of history. Christianity, like Judaism and Islam, is a historical religion, meaning that the faithful believe history is the arena of divine activity where God acts to reveal the divine will. On this belief, Christians came to understand that their rise to power was an expression of God's will, the successful advance of Christianity evidence that God was authorizing Christians to seize the power of the sword in order to use it to God's greater glory. On this understanding Christians were authorized to use coercive power to maintain the supremacy of Christian faith against all adversaries, be they from within the faith or external to it.

Christian theological justifications for violence continued to develop over the course of European history. The development of a tradition of just war thinking, the Crusades, the internal purging of dissidents, and missionary activity represent arenas in which such justifications were advanced.

Just War

The Christian approach to the problem of violence includes an important tradition of pacifism, but Christian thinkers have also addressed in a "realist" mode the possibility that force or violence might be used justifiably even to go to war. Since the fourth century, Christian moral theology has advanced a tradition of thinking about justified uses of force associated with the idea of just war.

Just war thinking harkens back to Cicero and to older natural law philosophy, so this is not explicitly a Christian doctrine. Just war thinking, however, was developed within the Roman Catholic Church by significant natural law theologians so that that it can be said that it emerged as a teaching of the church. Just war realism is today advocated by many Christians, including Roman Catholics but other Christians as well. It enjoys wide acceptance in various secular arenas and is used by governments and militaries, and it frames international law on the question of war. Just war theory, as it is understood today, advances several criteria that structure the morally relevant issues that must be examined in light of empirical particulars. These broad, nonspecific guidelines or *jus ad bellum* criteria include legitimate authority, just cause, right intention, last resort, an outcome in which the good achieved outweighs the pain and destruction of war, preservation of values that could not otherwise be preserved, reasonable hope of success, with two other criteria governing the conduct once hostilities have commenced (*jus in bello*): noncombatant immunity and a proportionality of means, also called the prohibition on inherently evil means of waging war. These criteria taken together, if satisfied, outline a justification for violence and uses of force in a "just war."

Just war thinking as a Christian-friendly philosophical tool in specifically Roman Catholic moral theology has its origins in Saint Augustine (354–430). Augustine's view was that war was a great evil because it expressed human selfishness and the disorder that arose from "love of violence, revengeful cruelty, fierce and implacable enmity, wild resistance and the lust of power and such like" (Augustine 21). For Augustine, a justified war was not a war of self-defense but a punitive action: "It is generally to punish these things [these disorders just mentioned], when force is required to inflict the punishment, that, in obedience to God or some lawful authority, good men undertake wars" (Augustine 22). Augustine famously said that wars are waged for peace and order, that they are the result of necessity and not choice, and he advanced three ideas that are still vital to the contemporary formulation of just war criteria: legitimate authority, just cause, and right intention.

Saint Thomas Aquinas (1225–1274) moved away from the punitive notion of just war and developed what is considered the classic form of just war thinking. Aquinas adds to Augustine's "criteria" a different content to the "just cause" criterion, arguing that wars could be justly waged if they were for the purpose of righting wrongs, which would include restoring what has been unjustly taken away or punishing a nation that has failed to punish crimes committed by its own people. As Thomas wrote ("Of War"):

> In order for a war to be just, three things are necessary. First, the authority of the sovereign by whose command the war is to be waged. For it is not the business of a private individual to declare war.... Secondly, a just cause is required, namely, that those who are attacked should be attacked because they deserve it on account of some fault. [Quoting Augustine] "A just war is wont to be described as one that avenges wrongs, when a nation or state has to be punished, or to restore what it has seized unjustly." [and] Thirdly, it is necessary that the belligerents have a rightful intention, so that they intend the advancement of good, or the avoidance of evil.
>
> (Aquinas 578)

Aquinas made another significant contribution to just war thinking. In discussing the permissibility of natural self-defense in the *Summa Theologica* (II-II, qu. 64, art.7)—"Whether it is permissible to kill a man in self-defense?" was his actual question—he introduced the principle of double effect. "Nothing hinders one act from having two effects, only one of which is intended, while the other is beside the intention.... Accordingly, the act of self-defense may have two effects: one, the saving of one's life; the other, the slaying of the aggressor." (190–191) The "double effect" came into play to emphasize that individual Christians subjected to unjust aggression could justifiably repel attackers with a use of force that could prove lethal but only as long as any killing occurred as an unintended and secondary consequence (double effect) of the legitimate just war aim of repelling the unjust attack.

The intention and just cause criteria of just war have long centered on self-defense and resistance to unjust aggression, and these notions are current today in article 51 of the United Nations Charter, which acknowledges an "inherent right" of both individual and collective self-defense. Thomas held that it was natural for individuals to act to preserve their "being," but the repelling of an unjust attack must be proportional and not excessive and "it is not lawful for a man to intend killing a man in self-defense" (191). Thomas emphasized that using force with the specific objective in mind of killing an enemy is not a legitimate aspect of just war, and a criterion of proportionality developed over the centuries to indicate that a use of force must always be proportional to the end of restoring peace.

After Aquinas, the Spanish Scholastics Vitoria (d. 1546) and Suarez (d. 1617) and the Protestant Dutch theologian Hugo Grotius (d. 1645) offered further developments in the idea of just war. Often regarded as the founder of international law, Grotius, for instance, held to the view that "war is not in conflict with the law of nature," so that the rules of war were naturally binding. His treatment of war in the context of "the laws of nations" included the premise that "[b]y nature all men have a right of resistance against injury" and that this natural right could not be changed, not even by God (Grotius, 385–437). As the idea of a Christian commonwealth disintegrated during the Reformation, with the nation-state emerging along with increasingly secularized political and cultural shifts, just war thinking began to attend to the problem of limiting the destructiveness of war, a development caused by the devastation of the religious wars of the sixteenth century.

In both the Reformation and post-Reformation era, just war thinking shifted to address conduct of war or *jus in bello* concerns for means. New attention was paid to the issue of proportionality, and double effect was invoked beyond killing of combatants to include justification for the killing of noncombatants. Under just war thinking, such deaths, regrettable as they would be, could be deemed morally permissible as long as they were not intended and every effort was made to avoid them. Just war theory came to have more and more of an influence in international law and in secular thinking in general, and appeals to just war ideas play an important role in international law today, appearing often in United Nations deliberations and resolutions (Vaux 1992: 120–145).

Just war has evolved and modified over the centuries, but one constant in the background of just war thinking is the view that war is a terrible state of affairs, much to be avoided, and even if uses of force are considered legitimate, they must be restrained. Roman Catholic theologian Richard McBrien has written, "The purpose of just-war theory...was not to rationalize violence but to limit its scope and methods" (McBrien 1981: 1036).

Today, both the secular and the religious worlds invoke just war ideas, but the action-guides do not of themselves settle any particular issue in any particular conflict. The criteria provide, rather, the structure within which uses of force can be deliberated. The criteria serve to guide the moral reflections of policymakers, the military strategists and critically minded citizens who worry about violence and its use by the state.

A widely noted and inescapable criticism of just war thinking concerns the ease with which just war ideas can be used self-servingly, even cynically, to "rationalize violence" and to justify political and military incursions that require the patina of moral justification to garner public support. Despite those dangers, however, the great value of the just war structure lies in its ability to call reasonable people of good will together to employ a common language within a rational structure designed to assist in the public deliberation over the appropriateness of considering the use of force.

Just war thinking is Christianity's clearest institutionalized, church-related justification for using coercive force. Just war ideas have been criticized for rationalizing violence and serving national self-interest while failing to serve justice and peace. Many Christians join other reasonable people in holding that just war is an oxymoron given that wars, however justified they may seem at the start, spin out of control into injustice, with the just war idea of imposing rational constraint on violence lacking the realism about war that its proponents criticize pacifists for ignoring.

Although now thoroughly secularized, just war thinking still represents the major Christian perspective on justifying uses of force to resist evil and restore peace, and in as much as it provides a structure for determining when and under what circumstances violence might be applied to resist injustice, it continues to expresses the central justification for violence in Christian moral theology.

The Crusades

The Crusades offer another justification for violence that has arisen within the Christian experience—holy war. Holy war means, in its simplest generic sense, a war undertaken because it is divinely authorized, and all the monotheistic religions of the West have had their experiences with generic holy war. *Crusade* was the name for holy war given by the church, and eight Crusades to Palestine were undertaken from the eleventh to the thirteenth centuries (1095–1291)—this age of Christendom when Christianity was both the temporal and spiritual backbone of European society.

The origins of the Crusades can be traced to two causes: Christian pilgrimage and Turkish threats to the Eastern Byzantine Empire. European Christians had often made pilgrimage to Palestine, Jerusalem especially, to experience the early life and sufferings of Jesus and as an act of penitence for sins. Muslims and the eastern empire centered in Constantinople, Byzantium, had been in constant conflict for centuries, but in 1071 Muslim Turks defeated the Byzantine forces at Manzikert, took over Asia Minor and threatened the Byzantine Empire. This created serious problems for continued pilgrimage to Muslim-controlled Jerusalem, and the threat to the eastern empire affected all of Christendom. The Byzantine emperor Alexis asked Pope Urban II for assistance, and in 1095 the Pope convened the Council of Claremont from which he issued the first call to crusade. Pope Urban saw the Crusade as a way to heal the rift between eastern and western Christendom, which had divided in the Great Schism of 1054, and it is estimated that by spring and autumn 1096, ten armies of more than 160,000 soldiers accompanied by numerous pilgrims and church officials joined in the first Crusade (Armstrong 2001: 3). Pilgrims to the holy land had previously been forbidden to take weapons, but now they were authorized to do so. The Crusades became armed pilgrimages.

The official justification for the Crusade was religious. The Pope, Christ's vicar on Earth, was sending forth an army with a holy commission to return Jerusalem and Christ's tomb to Christian hands. One twelfth-century report of the Council of Clermont—no contemporary account of Urban's speech exists—observed that "the pope, a prudent man, summoned to war against the enemy of God all those who were capable of bearing arms and, by virtue of the authority which he holds from God, absolved from all their sins all the penitents from the moment they took up the cross of Christ," that is, resolved to go on the Crusade (Vitalis

1992: 156). In his call to crusade, Urban II described the Muslim Turks as "an accursed race, a race utterly alienated from God, a generation, forsooth, which has neither directed its heart nor entrusted its spirit to God," so that Christians were duty bound "to exterminate this vile race from out lands" (Armstrong 2001: 3). Urban endorsed taking up arms to liberate Jerusalem from the Muslims, to which his crowd of listeners responded, "*Deus hoc vult* [God wills this]" (Armstrong 2001: 67).

Pope Urban had hoped by his call to crusade to expand the territorial reach of the papal church into Byzantium and improve relations between the eastern and western empires. The Pope cast the Crusade as a spiritual journey, reminding his listeners at Clermont that Jesus had said that those who followed him should be prepared for death. Urban even quoted the words of Jesus traditionally offered to monks entering the cloister: "Everyone who has left houses, brothers, sisters, father, mother or land for the sake of my name will be repaid a hundred times over" (Matthew 19:29; Armstrong 2001: 67). There is no doubt that, for all the political purposes served by the Crusades, the justification for the call to crusade was religious. The Crusades were a call to arms authorized by God, a holy war against the enemies of Christianity—Muslims. Karen Armstrong observes that with this move "Urban had made violence central to the religious experience of the Christian layman and Western Christianity had acquired an aggression that it never entirely lost" (Armstrong 2001: 67).

Anti-Islamic sentiment would prove to be a central factor in uniting Christendom for war on Muslims. Justification for holy war goes directly to divine authority, and the Pope acted explicitly as God's representative and directly on God's behalf. The Crusades may have created for knightly European societies "a perfect way to unite their love of God with their love of war," in Karen Armstrong's words (Armstrong 2001: 150), speaking about the Franks; and there is no doubt that Christians faced a military threat. But any appeal to a defensive "just war" was overshadowed by the holy war justification, which is always difficult to counter, for if God, the ultimate arbiter of truth and justice, commands an action, it is the duty of the faithful to respond with the question of right and wrong being beyond question and settled because God has willed the action. In response to the Pope's call, significant numbers of people would for the next two centuries be involved in bloodletting, demonstrating how sacred places can give rise to destructive behaviors, a phenomenon still seen today.

Although they fostered interaction between East and West and helped to consolidate papal power and even a sense of Christian unity and solidarity, the Crusades failed to accomplish the original end of expelling Muslims from the Holy Land. They also created what would turn out to be even greater divisions between eastern and western Christians. The attempt to create unity among Christians was accomplished by identifying a common enemy—Muslims—who were vilified and demonized as a "vile race" outside God's protection. The Crusades may have failed to defeat Islam, but they did succeed in exposing a Christian supremacist attitude toward yet another Semitic group of non-Christian monotheists, who, along with the Jews, were to be viewed as enemies of God whom God wanted resisted and defeated through violence. The Crusades left a legacy of bloodshed and massacre and reinforced the view of many Christians that God willed the use of violence to settle conflicts against enemies of the faith.

Heresy and Inquisition

If the Crusades were an example of Christians using violence to respond to external threats to the faith, the church also resorted to violence to deal with internal threats. Saint Augustine had expressly forbidden execution for heretics, a view maintained until the eleventh century. Heresy was a religious offense, a denial of the articles of faith, but because society in the Middle Ages was theocratic, heresy was also a form of treason—it challenged the claim of rulers that their authority came from God and tore at bonds of societal unity. The Second Lateran Council (1139) had stipulated imprisonment and confiscation for heretics; and in 1231 Emperor Frederick II, following legal precedents, issued this legislation:

> Anyone who has been manifestly convicted of heresy by the bishop of his diocese shall at the bishops's request be seized immediately by the secular authorities of the place and delivered to the stake. If the judges think his life should be preserved, particularly to convict other heretics, they shall cut out the tongue of the one who has not hesitated to blaspheme against the Catholic faith and the name of God.
>
> (Comby 1992: 167)

In February 1231, Pope Gregory IX issued *Excommunicamus*, which set up courts to try heresy cases, pronounce judgment and dole out punishment, although the convicted were handed over to civil authority to carry out sentences (O'Brien 9). Thus Pope Gregory set in motion what would become by 1233 the Inquisition tribunals, which relied on Dominican inquisitors who received under papal power the authority to bring suit against any person even rumored to be a heretic. The purpose of the Inquisition was to suppress heresy, to return heretics to the Catholic Church and to punish those who would not recant their errors (McBrien 1998: 9). The most common punishment was burning at the stake.

Following the medieval Inquisition, other inquisitions would follow, including the Spanish Inquisition (1478–1834), which was independent of the Pope and royally administered; it addressed political issues as well as heresy and was directed at Muslims, Jews, and, later, Protestants. Various groups, including the Bogomils, Waldensians, Cathars, and Lollards (Edwards 1997: 43, 266–268) suffered persecution and execution for heresy; and these groups, along with many others, were the target of Frederick II's legislation, for heretics were believed to threaten the stability of the government. Although inquisitions are associated with Roman Catholicism, Protestants rooted out heresy by means of ecclesiastical tribunals as well. In John Calvin's theocratic Geneva, for instance, the governing council condemned Michael Servetus to the stake as a heretic in 1553. Calvin defended the action on the grounds that it is the duty of the state to establish true religion. The state, he wrote, "exists so that idolatry, sacrilege of the name of God, blasphemies against his truth and other public offenses against religion may not emerge and may not be disseminated" (Calvin 123). The severe reaction to a humanist and non-Trinitarian such as Servetus arose from fear of the consequences of letting heresy proceed unchecked. For false doctrine destroyed souls; heretics tore the church apart; and the great fear was that heretics would bring down on the faithful a divine wrath, which could take the form of war, famine, or plague.

Inquisition and heresy trials employed violence on the grounds that if a heretic was not reclaimed, others would be endangered. Thomas Aquinas had said as much when he defended execution "if the church gives up hope of his conversion and takes thought for the safety of others, by separating him from the church by sentence of excommunication, and further, leaves him to the secular court, to be exterminated from the world by death" (*Summa Theologica*, IIa, IIae, 11, art. 3). The Inquisition used torture to extract confessions, sometimes resorted to mass executions, and in the Inquisition period, between the fourteenth and seventeenth centuries, a war on witchcraft was undertaken with Protestants and Catholics in apparent competition to put witches to the stake. Luther said, "I would burn them all" (McBrien 1997: 122), and a chronicler of the day noted that the Holy Office had burned 30,000 witches who, "if left unpunished, would easily have brought the whole world to destruction" (O'Brien 123). It is estimated that the number of witches killed as enemies of Christian faith numbered anywhere from hundreds of thousands to millions (McBrien 1997: 127). Although women were not the exclusive target of the witch mania, most were women—the move by the male-dominated churches to exterminate witches expressed a murderous repression of women, an assault on women that one historian has described as "a vast holocaust" (McBrien 1997: 126).

Missionary Movements

Being a religion that actively seeks converts, Christianity has had a missionary history since the time of Saint Paul. Christianity spread through the Mediterranean basin and had become the official religion of the Roman Empire by the time of the empire's fall in 476. Missionaries took Roman Catholicism to the kingdom of the Franks and into Germany as early as the fourth century; Saint Patrick helped establish monasteries in Ireland; and by the seventh century monasteries were to be found in England and Scotland with missionaries spreading out over the European continent.

As Europe extended itself into the world, Christian mission work was deemed an extension of colonial power. Christian missionaries undertook evangelizing activity in the Americas, in Asia (India, China, and Japan), Africa—all over the world. Missionaries from Spain, France, and Portugal were sometimes persecuted in various settings due to resistance from indigenous people. Japan, for instance, outlawed Christianity in 1614 with a subsequent massacre of 35,000 Christians in 1636, after which missionaries were prohibited in the country. But in their service to Empire and imperial ambitions, missionaries contributed to the colonial efforts that brought warfare deaths and such European-based diseases as measles and smallpox to indigenous people, at times decimating the populations subjected against their will to colonial rule. When the Spanish and Portuguese invaded Latin America in the sixteenthth century, estimates are that native populations decreased from 70 million to about 3.5 million due to massacre, European-based diseases, overwork in mines, and enslavement (Edwards 1997: 512–513). Spaniards enslaved Indians, and replacing Indians killed by war and disease opened up a slave trade in the Christian West. The demand for labor after the discovery of the Americas gave rise to trade in Africans, with an estimated 20 million blacks being transported from Africa to the Americas, one of the justifications for it being that it allowed the African blacks to come into contact with the Christian faith. Some missionaries actually had slaves and participated in the slave trade (Comby and McCullough 1992: 69).

Serious students of missionary activity may argue, as Lamin Sanneh has, that assessing this evangelizing and conversion work is difficult, because "missions in the modern era has been far more, and far less, than the argument about motives customarily portrays" (Sanneh 1989: 331), but there can be no doubt that Christian missionary activity colluded with colonialism and participated in some heinous activities, including enslavement, warfare, murder, rape, and economic exploitation. Christian missionaries have performed positive, life-affirming, and self-sacrificing chores on behalf of the Christian faith and the church, including founding schools and building hospitals, providing health care, and working to support the development of indigenous peoples in many ways. But in assessing the relationship of Christianity to violence, missionary work must be included as having played a role in subjecting non-Christian people to violence and at times atrocity, and even today accusations are made that Christian missionary activity continues to pursue its goals through violence ("Conversion Tactics").

Concluding Statement

In discussing the problem of Christianity's relationship to violence, it is worth noting that Christian people have, in the name of their faith, also acted in ways opposed to violence. The Reformation spawned what are known today as the historic peace churches. The Protestant churches that hold pacifistic positions include the Quakers, the Mennonites, and the Church of the Brethren. Christian involvement in the ecumenical movements and inter-religious dialogue efforts begun in the twentieth century and that continue today constitute implicit recognition of the violence Christians have engaged in over the centuries with those both inside and outside the faith. These efforts at dialogue and understanding across the barriers of tradition and belief represent a repudiation of the legacy of violence that has characterized Christian history. The easy association of Christianity with a willingness to resort to violence has of course been offensive to many Christians over the centuries who have stood opposed to violence, war, and social injustice. Martin Luther King, Jr. repudiated violence as a means for achieving social and racial justice, locating his source of justification for active but nonviolent resistance to evil in the teachings of Jesus (and Gandhi). The Christian Peace movement of the 1970s and 1980s, a time when Protestants and Catholics were engaged in mutual terrorist actions against each other in Northern Ireland, put forward a Christian opposition to war and the means of war, nuclear weapons especially. The important work undertaken by Christians as citizens informed by their faith or working through their faith communities in support of environmental integrity, economic justice, women's rights, and inclusion of gays and lesbians and transgendered people in the life of the church express contemporary efforts to oppose violence—the violence of environmental degradation, structural injustice, and attitudes of discrimination. Christians have justified violence over the centuries by appealing to scripture and by developing theological interpretations that sanction violence in the belief that it is in accord with God's will, but many are today working with a new consciousness of this history and a new resolve to create dialogue in religious affairs and to connect faith to action in ways that repudiate reliance on uses of force.

Symbolic Representations of Violence in the Christian Tradition

Symbols, rites, and rituals permeate all aspects of Christian belief and practice, and violence is disclosed in various symbolic representations. Christian symbols, being multifaceted, can suggest meanings in the context of religious faith at odds with obvious historical or empirical connections to violence, suppressing moral meaning while effecting a transformation to transcendent meaning. Consider Christianity's most important symbol, the cross.

Every Christian knows that the cross was a brutal mode of Roman execution and that Jesus of Nazareth suffered a tortuous death on the cross, having been scourged and then crowned with thorns by Roman soldiers. For Rome, the cross symbolized imperial power and effective criminal justice. Crucifixion was a mode of execution designed to maximize pain and suffering so that its terror and brutality would serve the utilitarian purpose of deterring any who might want to foment resistance or rebellion against the state.

For Christians, the cross could certainly symbolize state power in service to injustice, for Christians believe in the main that Jesus was an innocent man who had done nothing to deserve such a death. It might be expected that Christians would hold the cross in contempt as a symbol of the worst injustice human beings can deliver to one another—using the enormous power of the state to crush and cruelly kill an innocent. Some Christians undoubtedly hold firm to this meaning of the symbol, but this represents a moral interpretation of the cross.

The cross came to represent something other than injustice. It came to represent sacrifice and redemption. Theological interpretation, offered by Saint Paul and transmitted through the tradition, has long held that the cross provided the means of human salvation. The logic of this line of theological interpretation is that God's justice demanded human accountability for sin but that the atoning and sacrificial death of Jesus as the Christ was sufficient to appease the divine wrath and thus that death provided the means of salvation for all of humanity. The cross, then, rather than being simply a symbol of violence, became a symbol for preventing a more important metaphysical violence than the Romans could imagine—the damnation and loss of souls due to God's just but wrathful judgment. The cross was transformed in the Christian community into a symbol of human salvation—and it is Christ's sacrifice that is honored by Christians and actually reenacted at every Mass in the Roman Catholic Church.

The cross, then, as horrible as it was for Jesus to experience, was more importantly a metaphysical or theological necessity, for without it, there would have been no resurrection and thus no salvation. The cross, a symbol of earthly injustice, was transformed to symbolize a most fortunate boon for fallen humanity, now redeemed and saved. The cross endures as a violence-bearing symbol that identifies Christians as Christians—and it has been worn on the breastplates of crusaders going off to war and by contemporary Christians going off to the office. The cross came to symbolize membership in the Christian community and to demonstrate confidence that the wearer is among those whom the cross has saved. Christians have transformed the cross from a symbol of violence into one of salvation and eternal life, and on such a reading the cross is actually a good thing indeed.

This transvaluation of symbolic meaning can be found in other symbols important to Christians. Blood, for instance, transforms bloodshed in the violence of crucifixion into a sign of Christ's enduring presence. Blood is of course a symbol of life, but rather than the horror of the blood loss Jesus experienced through crucifixion leading to death, which it did, that loss of blood is transformed in and by the faith community to symbolize the "new life" to be enjoyed "in Christ." Christ shares his blood, and imbibing this blood in the memorial ritual of Eucharist or communion, for all the many different meanings this sacrament can have, takes the life that Christ has to offer into oneself, so that the violence that results in bloodshed is suppressed and transformed through a sacramental ritual to express thanksgiving and symbolic union with Christ, the transcendent source of the blood that symbolizes life eternal. Blood comes to represent the presence of the Christ and the new life the Christian can have with Christ and "in Christ."

Another important symbol for Christianity is fire, which can be a destructive as well as a creative power. In the story of the founding of the Christian church in the book of Acts, fire comes to serve as a symbol of God's presence and spirit—the Holy Spirit; yet in the book of Revelation, the apocalyptic punishment of the enemies of God is accomplished by consigning them to eternal torment in a lake of fire that does not consume them, fire now a symbol of violent purification and judgment.

Christianity has other symbols associated with violence, some of which have been obscured by history. For instance, in one nonlethal punishment imposed by the medieval Inquisition, some repentant individuals found guilty of offense were compelled to wear a yellow cloth star on the outside of their clothing, a punishment particularly detested by those who received it, because it was humiliating and elicited jeering (McBrien 1981: 18). Christian images or religious statements, including those that were musical and incorporated into hymnody, such as "Onward, Christian Soldiers," found their way into Christian practices, even worship, as well as into the broader life of Christendom. So, since the time of Constantine, Christian images or religious statements consistent with a Christian majority's status have appeared on imperial or national currencies, thus demonstrating the close relationship of the state with Christian values and wishes. The use of clergy, mainly chaplains, to provide religious connection to government continues to exist to this day in various governmental settings, including the US Congress, which holds power to declare war and authorize violence in support of national defense and policies; and military chaplains have been employed to provide not only counsel and comfort to soldiers but to pray for God's protection and support of military causes. One of the important rites of the Christian church that was practically involved in violence during the Middle Ages was excommunication, because this ecclesiastical rite of cutting individuals off from the church was usually preliminary to delivering offenders to the state for execution. Christian clergy and prison chaplains have traditionally been fixtures at state-sponsored executions.

Christianity preserves connection to its history of involvement of violence—both as recipient as well as dispenser—in a variety of symbols, rites, and rituals. Christians have of course been on the receiving end of violence as is made clear in Christian art, with Jesus's crucifixion a major theme, but also with portrayals of martyred saints and their icons of violent death hallmarks of the tradition. Such symbols preserve a Christian memory of persecution and honor martyrs who died for the faith. But Christians have also been dispensers of violence in such matters as war, execution, serving governments, and providing religious sanction for acts of state violence. What is most remarkable about the valence of meaning attached to these the various symbols, rites, and rituals associated with violence in Christianity is the way in which they come to be used by the faithful as disclosures of transcendent meaning. By attending to a transcendent meaning, Christian symbols come to emphasize transcendence while relativizing and even suppressing the "earthly" violence that naturally associates with them, the result being that religious sensibilities are not directed to the rational moral meaning of those justice issues to which the symbol point but beyond morality and justice to theological matters such as salvation and redemption.

Manifestations of Violence: Warfare, Punishment, Social Control

Although it would be a philosophical mistake to attach agency to religion and argue that religion is a direct cause of violence, there is no doubt that religions sponsor viewpoints and attitudes that affect the decisions people make about what to do and how to act, and this is certainly true on the issue of violence. Christian people have turned to their faith tradition to seek justification for what they do even when their actions are morally suspect. Religion and morality are not equivalent notions, and what may be questionable, unjustifiable, or even wrong from a moral point of view may yet find religious justification because religion involves ultimate matters and transcendent resources that can effectively trump the ordinary moral thinking of reasonable people of good will. Christian people have appealed to such transcendent resources—a "higher" authority—over the centuries to justify actions involving violence that are not only morally questionable but which are at odds with values and ideals also endorsed in the tradition. A brief examination of several issues where the issue of violence is at stake will expose how Christian thinking about violence is manifest in the world of practical affairs.

War

Christians have a long history of involvement in warfare, not only against other religions, as in the Crusades, but among other Christians. In the post-medieval period of Protestant Reformation and Roman Catholic Counter-Reformation, wars between these two Christianities were pervasive in Europe. The sixteenth-century French wars of religion pitted the royal Catholic League against the Protestant Huguenots (1652–1698); and the Great Peasant War in Germany (1524–1525) protested, with religious overtones, the injustices of medieval serfdom. When Luther's attempt at reconciling the parties failed, he encouraged landlords to "stab, strike, strangle these mad dogs" thus ensuring that Catholics would continue to dominate southern Germany (Edwards 303). The seventeenth century saw civil wars in Sweden and Poland, and the Thirty Years War in Germany (1618–1648) began to separate the longstanding partnership of pope and emperor. These national and civil wars led to political upheavals, including the Protestant challenge to Catholic monarchy, which culminated in the overthrow and execution of England's Charles I in 1649. The bloodshed and political instability in Europe from religious wars led to a begrudging realization that religious tolerance was necessary if there was to be peace and stability in political life. As far away as such conflicts seem, it is also the case that Protestant and Catholics fought against each other in Northern Ireland for most of the twentieth century.

Christians have in their history advocated, defended, and justified war, viewing it essentially as a way of combating evil and defending values, such as one's nation or the faith itself, by means that may be undesirable and contrary to Christian ideals but that practical realities necessitate as a lesser evil. Christians who stand willing to support the use of force to resolve conflicts, presumably on the basis of just war thinking, have been designated Christian "realists" in contrast to Christian pacifists. Realists have included such influential theological minds as the twentieth century's Reinhold Niebuhr (1892–1971), realism's major advocate and arguably not a defender of classic just war thinking. Niebuhr recognized the love and nonviolence ethic of Jesus as the Christian ideal but advocated a pragmatic ethic of responsibility that would allow decisions for the use of force to be made as lesser or necessary evils. For Niebuhr, a theologian influenced by Augustine's view of human fallenness and sin, resisting with force of arms the evil and destructive power of the Nazi regime was a necessary and lesser evil that constituted responsible action. Niebuhr was a champion of anticommunism during the cold war and supported the development of nuclear weapons as a way of balancing power. This attitude of realism and a willingness to use violent force in the realm of practical politics expresses an attitude toward the use of force widely held by many Christians who would justify force similarly today in the face of threats like terrorism.

Just war thinking is still a useful tool for many Christians, and its employment has taken some interesting turns. In the 1980s, the American Catholic Bishops declared themselves nuclear pacifists on the grounds that nuclear weapons were a disproportionate means for conducting warfare since the effect of such weapons would prove damaging to innocent human life long after use in a tactical situation. This position did not receive Vatican approval but indicated, nonetheless, that just war's demand for restraint on violence could provoke a critical response to modern warfare, which was also extended to biological and chemical weapons on the same grounds. Many Christians opposed the United States' preemptive invasion of Iraq in 2003 as unjustified under various just war criteria last resort, just cause, just intention, and reasonable hope of success. Appeals to just war, as said earlier, go well beyond the Christian community, but this approach to the question of war and violence, which has maintained life due to the active transmission of just war in and through the church continues to have effect. Many Catholics and Protestants invoke just war, and Orthodox Christianity has supported just war thinking and armed defense against oppression and violence in certain circumstances but considers any killing that takes place in war a sin for which repentance is required. Holy war is not in favor in Christian circles, although it may appear in the unwavering support many evangelical Protestant Christians extend today to Israel and its often violent actions toward Palestinians on the grounds that doing so is prophetic of the end time and presages Christ's Second Coming.

Christianity's long history of involvement with power politics, contributing theological and ethical resources in support of using force of arms to resist evil and oppression, will prevent it from ever unifying around the pacifism so much associated with Jesus's ethic of forgiveness and love of enemies. A challenge facing Christians who continue to support the use of force concerns consistent application of this ethic of resistance to evil, for if Christians apply the ethic selectively and do not call for the active defense of those suffering persecution and genocide, as happened in Cambodia under Pol Pot or in Rwanda or Darfur, it might appear as if this ethic of justified uses of force is in reality a tool of nationalistic self-interest rather than a true moral perspective grounded in faith. The argument could be made that a Christian moral perspective that endorses just war ought not to consider geographical location when innocent people—all being equal in the eyes of God—are in need of active protection from evils such as genocide. The options of realism and just war, on the one hand, and pacifism and nonviolent resistance, on the other, identify a constant tension in Christian ethics, and the challenge of consistent application is a difficult moral issue for realists who want to maintain a Christian identity when addressing the question of war.

Punishment

Christian people have supported both the state and the church in dispensing retributive justice that has as its purpose the inflicting of pain and suffering on offenders and miscreants. They have supported everything from public humiliation, shunning, corporeal punishments, and imprisonment to executions. Christians have also opposed the death penalty and worked for prison reform, with Quakers in Philadelphia creating the first penitentiary 1829 designed to provide work and solitary confinement as penance in place of corporeal punishment—little did the reformers realize the cruelty of solitary confinement. Christian clergy have provided spiritual support for prisoners as visitors and prison chaplains.

Christians have supported harsh retributive justice on the model of "an eye for an eye," a notion that harkens back to the Code of Hammurabi and was picked up and transmitted through Hebrew scriptures and culture (Leviticus 24:20). Jesus explicitly repudiated the retribution teaching and did so in a story in which a woman accused of blasphemy was about to be stoned. Jesus stopped it (John 8:3–11). That story would seem to lend serious scriptural support to a Christian antideath penalty stance, but as on other issues, Christians are divided. Many Protestants oppose the death penalty but many also support retention of the death penalty on the grounds that the practice is biblical, and the Hebrew Bible, to which appeal is made, reports thirty-six different capital crimes (Steffen 1998: 147). Official Catholic teaching supports the right of the state to execute but

Pope John Paul II moved closer to an abolitionist stance on the grounds that society can be protected by means other than killing an offender. Various Orthodox Christian statements have condemned the death penalty because it eliminates the possibility of an offender's repentance.

That so many Christians support capital punishment may seem odd given that at the heart of the Christian story is an execution considered by Christians to be unjust and the victim innocent. The symbol the cross is multivalent and is so framed metaphysically that its meaning as an instrument of moral terror is dissipated; so for many Christians, the cross is not charged with negativity. In addition, many Christians appeal to the "power of the sword," believing Saint Paul gave executions legitimacy by that image, overlooking the fact that Paul made this reference in a prison letter when he was facing execution—why would he provide the temporal powers a justification to kill him when he had appealed his case to avoid such a fate?

The death penalty is a direct and intentional killing of a human being, a practice of extraordinary violence by whatever method, and many Christians continue to support the retributive practice even as many Christian bodies, including many Protestant denominations, Orthodox councils, and patriarch and papal statements, oppose it.

Social Control

Christians have been concerned to both preserve and extend their faith by various means of social control. Missionary efforts, the founding of Christian schools and institutions of higher learning, and support for hospitals, nursing homes, and orphanages point to the kinds of institutional developments that have been concerned to structure societies in conformity with Christians values and beliefs. Christians have sometimes entered the political arena with the express purpose of advancing Christian values or specific church teachings.

Christian people have expressed discriminatory and even demeaning attitudes toward people outside the community structures of faith. The exclusion of certain people from full societal participation as well as from various church communions expresses the primary means by which this is accomplished. In society, attitudes of discrimination and exclusion have been directed for centuries toward Jews and Muslims and peoples of non-Christian faith traditions; in the church it has expressed support of racial supremacy as well as in patriarchal structures to the exclusion of women—

women still cannot become priests in Roman Catholicism, Orthodox Christianity, and in many Protestant denominations. Hatred of gay, lesbian, and transgendered people has led to their censure and exclusion in many Christian communities, highlighted in the contemporary United States by the nondenominational, independent Westboro Baptist Church of Topeka, Kansas, whose members actually advocate making sodomy a capital crime in accordance with Leviticus 20:13. Of course there are Christians who are working for full inclusion of women and gay persons into church life and leadership, but attitudes of hatred and discrimination express violence in that they inflict injury on people by disrespecting them and denying them their full humanity.

Many Christians in the twenty-first-century United States consider same-sex marriage a moral abomination or at least a violation of the Christian understanding of marriage; thus many same-sex couples are denied certain civil liberties in virtue of being denied the legal protection of marriage. The abortion issue is very much related to social control and violence. The Roman Catholic Church hierarchy, the undisputed leader of the opposition to abortion rights in the United States, has associated abortion with murder and denied that a fetus could ever be a material aggressor. This stance however puts women at risk of losing their own lives since some abortions are therapeutic for life-threatening situations, but no abortion as an intentional killing, even to save mother's life, is permitted under Catholic teaching. Several American abortion providers have been murdered by individuals claiming religious sanction for their action. Religious advocates of abortion rights, such groups as Catholics for Choice and the Religious Coalition for Reproductive Choice, provide a counterpoint faith perspective and oppose the violence to women they hold is at issue in denying women reproductive freedom.

Christian people will reflect—as well as instigate—many of the conflicts that arise in contemporary society. At one time churches in the United States in regions where slavery was legal defended slavery on biblical grounds, the Pauline book of Philemon in the New Testament carrying an instruction that slaves should return voluntarily to their masters. Christian people have endorsed and supported the institution of slavery, and even when slavery has been abolished, attitudes of racial superiority have led to social structures of extreme discrimination and oppression, as was certainly the case in South Africa and the United States. Racial discrimination and attitudes of racial superiority have been a part of Christian culture in many settings and persist to this day. Christian churches are racially segregated today in the United States, as are American public schools, although the churches are so voluntarily.

In all manner of social justice issues, Christians have played important roles on both sides of the violence question as advocates and opponents. Christianity contributed to the identity of the Ku Klux Klan, a murderous vigilante lynching group that terrorized blacks beginning in the post Civil War era. On the other hand, the black Southern Baptist Church was the institutional foundation for the American civil rights movement and Jesus's Gospel teachings an inspiration for Martin Luther King's nonviolent resistance.

On social issues, on questions of war and punishment, Christianity fails as a religion to present a fixed consistent message. Some Christian people have expressed through their faith enormous respect for God's creation and for human life, while others have appealed to their faith to justify acts of horrendous violence. The violence in Christian history is unmistakable and not to be denied or diminished. But the story is complex, and the brightest hope for the faith being an instrument of peace comes from Christian people making moral decisions about how they will express their faith. Violence is a moral issue even when religion plays a role in motivating it, for people can appeal to religion to justify even horrendous or despicable acts: religion is infinitely interpretable and can serve many masters. In the end, Christian people are moral agents who have to make decisions not only about how to act but how to act religiously; they have to make decisions about what kind of Christian they shall choose to be. This is a moral rather than a religious question, but it is relevant to every religious person and will determine, finally, if the religion they practice expresses values that are life affirming or destructive (Steffen 2007).

Bibliography

Aquinas, Saint Thomas. "On War." *Summa Theologica, II, II Q. 40.* Trans. Fathers of the English Dominican Province. Chicago: Encyclopedia Britannica, 1952.

Aquinas, Saint Thomas. "Whether It Is Permissible to Kill a Man in Self-Defense?" *Summa Theologica,* II-II, Q. 64, article 7. Reprinted in *The Ethics of War: Classic and Contemporary Readings.* Eds. Gregory Reichberg, Henrik Syse, and Endre Begby, 169–198. Malden, MA: Blackwell 2006.

Armstrong, Karen. *Holy War: The Crusades and Their Impact on Today's World.* New York: Anchor Books, 1988, 2001.

Augustine. St. *Contra Faustum Manichaeum*. In John Langan, "The Elements of St. Augustine's Just War Theory," *Journal of Religious Ethics*, 12.1 (Spring 1984): 19–38.

Bible. New Revised Standard Version. Oxford, UK: Oxford University Press, 1989.

Calvin, John. *Defensio orthodoxae fidei*. In T.H.L. Parker, *John Calvin: A Biography*. Philadelphia: Westminster Press, 1975.

Carroll, James. *The Sword of Constantine: The Church and the Jews*. Boston: Houghton Mifflin, 2001.

Comby, Jean. *How to Read Church History, Volume 1: From the Beginning to the Fifteenth Century*. New York Crossroads, 1992.

Comby, Jean and Diarmaid MacCulloch. *How to Read Church History, Volume 2: From the Reformation to the Present Day*. New York: Crossroads, 1992.

"Conversion Tactics." 20 December 2010. www.christianaggression.org/tactics_violence.php.

Edwards, David L. *Christianity: The First Two Thousand Years*. Maryknoll, NY: Orbis Books, 1997.

Grotius, "The Theory of Just War Systematized (On the Law of War and Peace)." Reprinted in *The Ethics of War: Classic and Contemporary Readings*. Eds. Gregory Reichberg, Henrik Syse, and Endre Begby, 385–436. Malden, MA: Blackwell, 2006.

McBrien, Richard P. *Catholicism: Study Edition*. Minneapolis: Winston Press, 1981.

ReligiousTolerance.Org. "Number of Adherents." 4 December 2010. www.religioustolerance.org/worldrel.htm.

Sanneh, Lamin. "Christian Missions and the Western Guilt Complex." *The Christian Century* (8 April 1987). 2 December 2010. www.religion-online.org/showarticle.asp?title=143.

Steffen, Lloyd. *Executing Justice: The Moral Meaning of the Death Penalty*. Cleveland: Pilgrim Press, 1998.

Steffen, Lloyd. *Holy War, Just War: Exploring the Moral Meaning of Religious Violence*. Lanham, MD: Rowman & Littlefield, 2007.

Tactius. *The Annals*, 15.44. 28 December 2010. http://mcadams.posc.mu.edu/txt/ah/tacitus/TacitusAnnals15.html.

Vaux, Kenneth L. *Ethics and the Gulf War: Religion, Rhetoric, and Righteousness*. Boulder, CO: Westview Press, 1992.

Vitalis, Ordericus. *History of the Church* (1135). Cited in Jean Comby. *How to Read Church History, Volume 1: From the Beginning s to the Fifteenth Century*. New York: Crossroads, 1992.

Yoder, John Howard. *The Politics of Jesus*, Grand Rapids, MI: Eerdmans, 1972.

Chapter 6

Muslim Engagement with Injustice and Violence

Bruce B. Lawrence

IN THINKING ABOUT Islam and violence, when do we begin to track the connection of the two? Do we begin with 9/11 or 611? 9/11 is all too familiar: It conjures the stealth attack of Arab/Muslim suicide bombers, co-opting two planes, on the twin towers of the World Trade Center, a third plane attack on the US Pentagon, and a fourth crashed plane in Pennsylvania. After 9/11 and as a result of the traumatic death of more than 3,000 people, the US government declared war on two majority Muslim nations, global airport security forever changed, and American Muslims, as well as Muslims coming to the United States, became potential terrorist suspects.

But if 9/11 redefines Islam and violence, does it not also distort the long historical view of Muslims and their multiple responses to violence? If one begins not with 9/11 but almost 1,400 years earlier with 611, the story of Islam and violence changes dramatically. There was no Islam in 611, just an Arab merchant who felt called to be a prophet. The previous year, 610, when Muhammad ibn Abdullah experienced revelation for the first time, only his wife and a few others accepted his claim. His claim to prophecy depended on intermittent revelations, delivered in the face of hostility from local tribesmen, merchants, and idolaters in his hometown of Mecca. When Muhammad began preaching publicly, as he did in 612, the public reaction was not only negative but violent. From 612 till 622, there was continual, punitive violence directed against Muhammad and his tiny band. It was expressed at many levels: disregard of his lineage, since he had been orphaned, then raised by an uncle; disdain for his relative poverty, since he was not among the wealthy elite of Mecca; and outright rejection of his claim to represent a superior divine channel, a single all-encompassing God called Allah, rather than a pantheon of competing deities with several names.

Violence in the Earliest Phase of Islamic History
The Time of the Prophet: Societal versus Military Violence

If we begin in 611 rather than 9/11, the first expression of violence and Islam is not violence directed by or sanctified through Islam but rather violence against Muslims. Often that violence was a response to efforts by early Muslims to curtail pre-Islamic forms of violence. Throughout human history, societal violence has been as prevalent as military violence, and in early seventh-century Arabia one finds numerous forms of societal violence. These included, for instance, female infanticide, along with the abuse of orphans, the poor, and marginal. Against such forms of societal violence, the revelations mediated through Muhammad were clear, incontrovertible challenges to the social order of tribal Mecca. For instance, they prohibit the pre-Islamic Arabian practice of female infanticide as well as other bodily and social abuses through directives set down, transmitted, and encoded in the Qur'an. Consider the following:

> *And when the infant girl who was buried is asked*
> *For what offense she was killed*
> *[the person who killed her will have to answer*
> *for his sin on Judgment Day].*
> *(Surah al-Takvir, Qur'an [Q] 81: 8–9)*[1]
> *Do not kill your children out of fear of poverty;*
> *We will provide for them, and for you.*
> *Indeed, killing them is a great sin.*
>   (Surat al-Isra, Q 17:31)

What these two passages reflect is that in pre-Islamic Arabia killing of female infants was very common; often the moment a female was born she was buried alive. Islam not only prohibits female infanticide, but it forbids all types of infanticide, irrespective of whether the infant is a male or female. Consider the following:

> *You should not kill not your children on account of poverty—*
> *We provide for you and for them.*

And do not approach the property of the orphan,
except with what is better till he comes of age.
Take not life which God has made sacred.

(Surat al-Anam, Q 6:151–152)

In 2011 it is difficult to imagine how precarious life was in 611 and not just for children and women but also, and especially, for orphans. Consider the following directive, set forth in the chapter dedicated to women:Give orphans their property,

Without exchanging bad for good;
—And if you fear you cannot
Do justice by the orphans,
Then marry women who please you,
Two, three, or four;
But if you fear you won't be equitable,
Then one, or a legitimate bondmaid of yours,
That way it is easier for you not to go wrong.

(Surat an-Nisa, Q 4:2–3)

The irony of the preceding passage is its misapplication during subsequent Muslim history. In the course of centuries, Islamic law overlooked both the context for this revelation—to care equitably for the orphan—and its qualification—if you cannot be equitable to two, three, or four women (who have been previously married and have children now orphaned without a father), then marry but one woman or cohabit with a legitimate bondmaid, as Abraham did with Hagar producing Ishmael. Caring for orphans is the crucial rationale for plural marriage during the earliest period of Islamic history. It could even be argued that it is the sole rationale for plural marriage, and so the first signpost of violence in Islam is not the violence inherent in Qur'anic dicta but rather the greater violence of the preceding, non-Islamic period known as *jahliyya*, or period of ignorance. And the revelation of the Qur'an, along with the formation of a Muslim community (*ummah*), was intended to curtail rather than to expand or export violence.

The Qur'an as Guidepost for Early Muslims

It was difficult, however, to sustain the purity of thought and the dedication of purpose indicated in those early surahs. They were revealed to the

Prophet intermittently over twelve years, from 610 to 622, and during that time Muslims were the nonviolent members of Arabian society, in general, urban Mecca, in particular. At one moment, it seemed that Muhammad's nonviolent responses to the provocations of his hostile countrymen would jeopardize the entire Muslim experiment. In 617 the Prophet sent some of his closest followers and relatives next door, across the Red Sea, to Abyssinia (Ethiopia). Their enemies followed them and demanded that the traitorous Muslims be handed over to them and returned to face justice, that is, certain death, in Mecca. When the Christian king asked the fearful Muslims to explain their faith, one of their band recited to him a revelation that had just come to the Prophet. It included the first forty verses of Surat Maryam, and so closely did it parallel Christian scripture, belief, and hope that the king granted them asylum. That first *hijrah*, or exodus, was yet another instance when violence was prevented, rather than abetted, by the earliest Muslims, and the medium of their pursuit for justice, peace, and equality were those revelations that later became the Noble Book, the Holy Qur'an.

Later the bar of restraint moved higher and higher for Muhammad and his followers. By 622, life had become intolerable for the hardy cohort of Muslims. Consider the power of their enemies. All of them were connected to Mecca, either to Muhammad's close relatives or to tribesmen who had resolved to defeat him and, if possible, to kill him. The early followers faced curses and death threats from prominent Meccans, some of whom were relatives of the prophet. Public spectacles were made of converted slaves, for instance, who were targeted for verbal shame and physical harassment. In instance after instance, violence was directed at Muslims, not perpetrated by Muslims.

The First Instances of Muslim-Initiated War

Once Muhammad established a community of followers in Medina, he had no choice but to fight his Meccan enemies who continued to pursue him. As the Qur'an represents it, God had declared:

> *Permission to fight is given*
> *to those on whom war is made.*
> (Surat al-Hajj, Q 22:39)

But war was always and everywhere to be defensive. The war Muhammad waged against Mecca was not a struggle for prestige or wealth; it was, in his view, a war for survival, of both the community and the faith. His helpers from Medina joined the migrants from Mecca. They provided the migrants with food and with shelter from their own resources, but they were all stretched to the limit. They had to raid caravans. They raided only small caravans at first and never attacked during those times when fighting, especially blood feuds, was prohibited by Meccan custom. As someone who had guided many a successful caravan to its destiny, Muhammad knew the routes. He knew the seasons. He also knew the wells where Meccan traders would pass with their camels and their goods.

In December 623, more than a year after the beleaguered Muslims had fled to Medina, Muhammad ordered a small detachment to spy on a caravan to the south. It was proceeding along the route to Yemen, at the oasis of Nakhlah that links Mecca to Taif. Since it was a holy month, he had ordered his followers not to attack but they disobeyed. Killing some, they took others captive and brought the caravan back to Medina. Muhammad was appalled. Not only had his followers disobeyed him; they had disobeyed the divine command to fight only in defense of one's own life and property. Their actions mirrored his leadership. He was responsible. The prophet who had pledged to be a divine mediator had betrayed his own prophecy. Riven with distress, he prayed to God. He needed guidance from above. And when it came, it was at once clear and compelling:

> *They ask you about war in the holy month.*
> *Tell them:*
> *"To fight in that month is a great sin.*
> *But a greater sin in the eyes of God is*
> *to hinder people from the way of God,*
> *and not to believe in Him,*
> *and to bar access to the Holy Mosque*
> *and to turn people out of its precincts.*
> *And oppression is worse than killing."*
> *They will always seek war against you till*
> *They turn you away from your faith, if they can.*
> *But those of you who turn back on their faith*
> *and die disbelieving will have wasted their deeds*
> *in this world and the next.*
> *They are inmates of Hell,*
> *and abide there forever.*

(Surat al-Baqarah, Q 2:217)

This revelation had replaced a rule of principle with one of practical moral value. Yes, killing is forbidden in the sacred month (Q 2:191), but worse than killing is oppression, hindering people from the way of God. Empowered by this divine dictum, Muhammad accepted and divided the spoils of war from his followers at Nakhlah.

More war would follow. Muhammad and his followers entered into an unending conflict with their Meccan kinsmen and opponents. From 623 to 632, Muhammad planned thirty-eight battles that were fought by his fellow believers. He led twenty-seven military campaigns. The nonviolent protestor had become a general, waging war again and again. The first full-scale military campaign came at the wells of Badr, in 624, less than four months after the skirmish at Nakhlah. Muslims chose to attack a caravan coming south from Palestine to Mecca. The Meccans learned of their attack, opposing them with a force that far outnumbered the Muslim band. Muhammad and his followers should have lost; they would have lost, except for the intervention of angels (Q 3:122–127).

While the Battle of Badr projected the small Muslim community onto a stage marked as cosmic, with divine intervention as the basis for military victory, its outcome provoked fear in the Meccans. It also made them resolve even more firmly to defeat the upstart Muslims. By 625 the mighty Meccan general Abu Sufyan had assembled a huge army of both foot soldiers and cavalry. He marched toward Medina. The Muslims countered by moving out of the city proper. They engaged their rivals on the slopes of a nearby mountain, Uhud. Despite the superior numbers of the Meccans, it went well for the Muslims till some of Muhammad's followers broke ranks too early, in anticipation of another victory such as Badr. The Meccans then counterattacked, and Khalid ibn al-Walid, one of the brilliant Meccan nobles, led his squadron to the unprotected rear of the Muslim formation and, catching them unawares, began a great slaughter. The Muslims were soundly defeated, Muhammad wounded in the mayhem that day.

Yet the Prophet resolved to learn the deeper lesson behind this bitter defeat. He regarded the defeat of Uhud to be as important for Islam as the victory of Badr, for in defeat as in victory the Muslims had to acknowledge that their fate was not theirs but God's to decide.

> He knows what lies before them and what lies after them (i.e., what is in their future and in their past), and they understand nothing of His Knowledge expect what He wills (to disclose to them).
>
> (Surat al-Baqara, 2:255)

The aftermath of the Battle of Uhud also reinforced Muhammad's resolve to secure the loyalty of all his followers—both those who were Muslims and those who were non-Muslims yet bound to him by treaty. There followed some difficult, often bloody purges of tribes near Medina, and then the major Battle of the Trench in 627. A mighty Meccan army was led again by Abu Sufyan, the architect of Uhud. Abu Sufyan had tried to invade Medina, to defeat and destroy Muslims once and for all. Yet as understood by Muslims, God—and God alone—granted Muslims victory there. In the aftermath of this victory, fierce foes such as Abu Sufyan and the fiery Khalid ibn al-Walid ceased to oppose the Muslims and instead joined their ranks.

Beyond the battlefield, Muhammad never ceased trying to convert his Meccan opponents to the religion of Islam. Though he had forsaken non-violence, he had not embraced violence as a way of life, only as an expedient to a higher end. He contacted the Meccans to propose a peaceful pilgrimage. He assured their leaders of his intention, but they doubted him. It took until 629, seven years after he had left Mecca, before he and his followers were allowed to reenter their native city. At last all Muslims—those Meccans who initially had emigrated to Medina, those Medinans who had joined them, and other tribes who had become their allies—then also submitted to God, and all were able to return to Mecca in a peaceful pilgrimage.

When they returned in January 630, Muhammad made a singular decision. Instead of vengeance, Muhammad forgave all but his bitterest enemies. Yet another military encounter quickly followed on the heels of the peaceful pilgrimage. It happened one month later, in February 630. It was a bigger battle than any Muslims had seen since Uhud, and it came not from Mecca but from beyond. Many Bedouin tribes who were opposed to Islam saw the reentry to Mecca as provocation for their own ferocious, full-scale assault on the Muslims. Hunain was a fierce battle. Many of Muhammad's followers panicked. Once again, from the Muslim point of view, it was the Almighty and the angelic host—not Muslim numbers or their military prowess—that brought them victory. The Qur'an once again marked the event:

> Indeed God has helped you on many occasions,
> Even during the battle of Hunain,
> When you were elated with joy at your numbers
> Which did not prove of the least avail,

So that the earth and its expanse became too narrow for
you,
And you turned back and retreated.
Then God sent down a sense of tranquility
On His Apostle and the faithful;
And sent down troops invisible
To punish the infidels.
This is the recompense of those who do not believe.

                    (Surat al-Tawbah, Q 9:24b)

Muslims had scarcely moved beyond the victory of Hunain when other challenges beyond their borders arose. They had to engage the Byzantines, they had to levy taxes among recalcitrant Bedouin tribes, and above all, they had to purify their central rite, the pilgrimage or hajj, removing every vestige of pagan practice.

Muslim Wars after Muhammad: The Special Case of Ridda and the Problem of Retaliation

After the death of Muhammad in 632, his experiment, based so squarely on his personal authority, almost came unhinged. It was a delicate moment when a new leader, one of his trusted followers, Abu Bakr, was elected his successor, or *khalifa*. When several tribes tried to withdraw from the treaty that bound them to Muhammad, Abu Bakr fought them in what became known as the Ridda wars, the wars of apostasy or repudiation of Islam. For many scholars, this period initiates the practice of open warfare in the name of Islam. It is said to be the time when jihad, or war in defense of the faith, came to be associated with Islamic expansion. Yet according to Fred Donner, the Ridda wars, while testing the new Muslim state's capacity to integrate and organize Arabia's tribesmen, did not meet the standard of jihad, and neither the Ridda wars nor the expansionary wars that continued through the next period of nascent Islamic history should be defined as jihad.

According to Donner, three interlocking concepts defined the nascent Muslim experiment. They were: a single, indivisible community united by faith, that is, "the universal community of believers, reflecting its character as the body of worshipers of the one and universal God"; an absolute authority mediated through a binding, divine law; and the notion of a central human authority transferable from Muhammad to his successors (Donner:

54–61). The second concept—absolute authority mediated through divine law—was crucial since it curtailed without quite eliminating the protocol of retaliation, requital, or *lex talionis*. Qur'anic passages support this shift:

> *Believers, requital is prescribed*
> *For you in cases of murder;*
> *The free for the free, the slave for the slave,*
> *And the female for the female.*
> *But if anyone is forgiven*
> *Anything by his brother,*
> *Let fairness be observed,*
> *And goodly compensation.*
>
> (Surat al-Baqarah, Q 2:178)

> *And do not take a life*
> *That God has made sacred,*
> *Except for just cause*
> *And if anyone is killed unjustly,*
> *We have given his next of kin*
> *A certain authority;*
> *But he should not be excessive in killing;*
> *For he has been given divine support*
> *(to be restrained).*
>
> (Surat al-Isra, Q 17:33)

Especially crucial is the protocol for requital among believers, announced in Surat an-Nisa. It is long but pivotal and consequential for Muslim attitudes toward interpersonal violence:

> *It is never right*
> *For a believer to kill a believer,*
> *Except by mistake;*
> *And one who kills a believer by mistake*
> *Is to free a believing slave,*
> *And compensation is to be handed over*
> *To the family of the deceased,*
> *Unless they forego it to charity.*
> *If the deceased was from a people*
> *Warring against yours,*
> *Yet was a believer,*

> *Then free a believing slave.*
> *But if the deceased was from a people*
> *With whom you have a treaty,*
> *Then compensation is to be paid*
> *To the family of the deceased,*
> *And a believing slave is to be freed.*
> *And if one has not the means,*
> *Then one is to fast*
> *For two consecutive months,*
> *As an act of contrition granted*
> *As a concession from God.*
> *And God is all-knowing, most judicious.*
>   (Surat an-Nisa, Q 4:92)

All of these conditions—God as authority, the community as resource, the successor as leader—are crucial for defining both the Islamic state and its impetus for expansion through war. Jihad, when it does occur, appears only as an ancillary, incidental concept. Of course, early Muslim warriors were motivated by the prospect of either booty (if they survived) or paradise (if they were slain), but jihad entered as "a product of the rise of Islam, not a cause of it—a product, to be exact, of the impact of the new concept of the *umma* on the old (tribal) idea that one fought, even to the death, for one's own community (Donner: 295–296)." While there is a lot of fighting depicted in Islamic histories, such military encounters are known mostly as *maghazi* ("raids") or *futuh* ("conquests"). Whenever jihad is invoked, it is a sidebar, not a central feature of the narrative of early Muslim warfare.

Jihad Invoked, Redefined, and Reawakened

Over time what had been an incidental, qualified part of the Qur'anic message, and the earliest Islamic worldview became an independent force on its own, so much so that some have declared jihad to be a sixth pillar (beyond the standard five) that defines Islamic belief and practice. The seminal text cited by all proponents of jihad as a collective duty incumbent on all Muslims is Surat at-Tawbah (Q 9). Here, Muslims are told that idolaters must be fought, polytheists leveled, and that the reward for those who struggle will be paradise:

> *(But) the messenger*
> *And those who believe with him*

> *Struggle with their possessions and their persons.*
> *So the good things are for them,*
> *And they are the successful ones.*
> *God has prepared gardens*
> *Under which rivers flow,*
> *Where they will abide.*
> *That is the great attainment.*
>
> (Surat at-Tawbah, Q 9:88–89)

Yet neither this verse nor other Qur'anic verses motivated Muslims to engage in perpetual warfare against Byzantines, Sassanians, and other "people of the Book" after the death of Muhammad. In an analysis marked by consummate concern with detail and context, Carole Hillenbrand has shown how by the early eighth century, Muslim navies had given up their century-long quest to conquer Constantinople. "It became the practice for both empires to engage in annual campaigns, described in the Islamic sources as jihad but these gradually became a ritual, important for the image of the caliph and the emperor, rather than being motivated by a vigorous desire to conquer new territories for their respective faiths" (Hillenbrand: 93).

It was not until the eleventh century, with Saladin and the crusader conquest of Jerusalem, that jihad was revitalized. The crucial events were the fall of Jerusalem to the Crusaders in 1099; the recapture of Edessa from the Crusaders by Saladin's father, Zengi, in 1144; and then, in 1187, Saladin's recapture of Jerusalem. It was during the fateful twelfth century that the doctrine of jihad was revived and heralded as a paramount duty to preserve Muslim territorial, political, and symbolic integrity. "The process of the reawakening of jihad," notes Hillen-brand, "must have been slow and gradual, and in some part at least it must have come as a direct response to Crusader fanaticism, witnessed first-hand (Hillen-brand: 108)."

One scholar has even gone so far as to argue that "the Crusades triggered the jihad mentality as we know it now." It was in response to the Crusades that Zengi and Saladin produced, for the first time in Islamic history, "a broad scale propaganda effort to praise jihad and jihad-warriors. Jerusalem became the center of jihad propaganda, and Saladin extended its sanctity to Syria, reminding everyone that Syria (too) is the Holy Land and that Muslims are responsible for defending and protecting it (against foreign assaults) (Mourad)."[2]

Later, the doctrine of jihad was amplified and applied anew in the thirteenth and fourteenth centuries after the Mongols plundered Baghdad,
ravaged the Muslim world, and then themselves became Muslims. It was
Ibn Taymiyya (d. 1328), one of the most influential jurists in Islamic history, who inveighed against the Mongols, and his favorite tool for anathe-
matizing them was jihad. "With Ibn Taymiyya," observes Hillenbrand,
"jihad to (save) Jerusalem is replaced by an internal movement within the
Dar al-Islam itself, both spiritual and physical.... Ibn Taymiyya sees the
Muslim world assailed by external enemies of all kinds, and in his strong
desire to purify Islam and Islamic territory from all intrusion and corruption, he advocates as "the only solution to fight [is] jihad so that 'the whole
of religion may belong to God' " (Hillenbrand: 243).

Violence in the Gunpowder Empires
The Ottoman Case

Is violence waged by an Islamic empire or nation always an expression of
jihad, or religious violence? One could argue that it is less jihad than other
features of structural violence that came to characterize the major Muslim
empires of the premodern era. Beginning in the fifteenth century and, in
part, due to the violence unleashed by the Mongols, a simpler political
map of the Nile-to-Indus region, or the core Islamic world, emerged. It
was characterized by three regionally based empires: the Ottoman, Safavid,
and Mughal. They represented the core population of the Muslim world
by 1800, perhaps 70 percent of all Muslims, and much of what today is
regarded as Muslim expressions of violence can be traced to the structural
elements that characterized each of these empires.[3] For clarity of insight
into violence—its causes, expressions, and outcomes—the focus will be
on the Ottoman Empire. The Sunni Ottomans, based in Anatolia and
southeastern Europe, absorbed nearly all of the Arabic-speaking lands
with the exception of Morocco and parts of the Arabian Peninsula. Theirs
became the dominant regional power, although Shia Iran emerged as a
formidable foe and bloody conflicts between the two countries erupted
periodically. Mughal India, officially a foe of neither the Ottomans nor the
Safavids, benefited from their mutual antagonism. Especially the persecution and expulsion of non-Shia Muslims from Safavid Iran provided some
of the human resources—artistic, intellectual, and religious—that made
possible the splendor of the Great Mughals. Islam remained a central

focus of identity as well as the ideological underpinning for a variety of social and political movements. The period saw the establishment of Shiism as the state religion of Iran, with the forced conversion of its largely Sunni population under Safavid pressure. New Sufi orders emerged throughout the region, one of them actually serving as the precursor to the state sponsored Shiism of Safavid Iran. Often Sufi orders became vehicles of protest against the establishment, nowhere more evidently than the Naqshbandi-Mujaddidi movement of north India. Toward the end of this period in Arabia, the Muslim puritanical movement of the Wahhabis rose to challenge Sufi practices and Ottoman authority.

Violence must also be traced through its implication in the political order, not least in the way that it was managed for the preservation of the empire so that the rulers of various Muslim empires, like their non-Muslim counterparts elsewhere, became the sole legitimate purveyors of violence. There was never a question of eliminating violence but rather justifying its use for higher ends.

One must instead ask again the question Is warfare, when declared by a Muslim ruler, always and everywhere a reflex of Islamic norms and values? That was the question that occupied Ibn Taymiyya, but its practical consequence was nil, as much of the violence that characterized premodern Islamic polities was intra-Islamic, that is, Muslims were fighting Muslims for imperial gain, better taxation, and public prestige. Consider the case of the Ottomans.

In its origins, the Ottoman Empire goes back to the thirteenth century and the Seljukids. The first of the newly converted Turkish nomads to expand beyond their central Asian homeland, the Seljuks had overrun Buyid Iran in the eleventh century and conquered Baghdad by 1055. The Seljuks created a new empire in the name of Islam, but they also drew on Sasanian traditions still in place with their conquered subjects. They had a graduated taxation system that depended for its efficiency on *iqtas* or land grants. Warriors were supported through *iqtas* in return for their service on behalf of the Seljukid rulers.

The Seljuks were also assisted and tested by Turcomans, nomadic frontiersmen with less interest in settled or city life than the Seljuks. The Turcomans helped the Seljuks by operating as *ghazis*, or warriors for the faith, on the frontiers with the Byzantine Empire. They readily invoked jihad in their cause. After the Battle of Manzikert, where the Seljuks defeated the Byzantines in 1071, the Turcomans helped to Islamize and Turkify the region of Anatolia, still culturally linked to Byzantium.

The Seljuks might have become the masters of Anatolia and survived much longer had they not become victims of the Mongols. The same Mongol invasion that led to the sack of Baghdad in 1258 had earlier led to a Seljuk defeat in 1243. The Seljuks survived as a reduced polity in Asia Minor but as a vassal Mongol state; their last Sultan died in 1306. In the meantime, between 1260 and 1320, the Turcomans, mobilized by their *ghazi* tribal chiefs, and in tandem with the Seljuks, waged jihad against Byzantine forces that still held parts of Anatolia. Their leader was Osman Ghazi, who held the frontier land in western Asia Minor that was farthest north and closest to the Byzantines. He gained immense prestige when he defeated an imperial Byzantine army in 1301 at the Battle of Baphaeon. Many other nomadic Turkish soldiers came to Konya, Osman's capitol. They became known as *beys*, commanders of complements of fighters who were loyal to them, just as they, in turn, were loyal to Osman. At Osman's death, his son, Orhan expanded the empire still further, capturing major strategic and commercial cities in Anatolia. Bursa became the new Osmanli capital after 1326 and remained so until 1402.

At the same time as they were expanding in the east, the Ottomans were also making inroads into the Balkans, and a measure of their success is that one of Orhan's successors, Murad, made Adrianople (also referred to as Edirne) his capital in order to consolidate Ottoman conquests in Rumeli.

The success of the Ottomans invoked Islam and the doctrine of jihad, but it was banked on the logic and limits of conquest. They formed a pyramidal military state, with roots that went deep into local society, and allowed the Ottoman Sultan at the apex to control the beys, who also represented geographical and economic interests crucial to the burgeoning state.

As ideal as the system sounds, it had limits inherent to the very strengths that made the system possible. Ottomans were heirs to the Byzantine as well as the Sasanian empires. Like their Umayyad predecessors, it was the Byzantine model, especially as reflected in Istanbul, which both fueled and restricted their imagination. They expanded by conquest, making the army responsible for two fronts, one in Asia and one in Europe. Yet the army could only fight when the Sultan was on the battlefield to lead his troops in person. The competitive pull of two war zones produced a major donnybrook for the fledgling Ottoman state in 1387. Murad I had to confront an Anatolian resistance movement, the Karmanids, at the same time as the Serbs, joined by dissatisfied Bosnians and Bulgarians, were posing a challenge in the Balkans. Though the Ottomans won the Battle of Kosovo in 1389, Murad was killed in the fray, and in its aftermath his son and successor, Bayazid, executed the Serbian king, Lazar.

More threatening to the state than Anatolian or Balkan rivals, however, was the emergence in the East, in Rum, of a threat from central Asia. It came from the Chagatai Turkish successor to the Mongols: Timur Leng, or Tamerlane. When Ottoman and Timurid forces clashed in Ankara in 1402, the Timurids were victorious. Bayazid, humiliated as well as defeated, died at his own hand a year later in 1403. The Ottoman experiment, like many of its *ghazi* emirate neighbors, might have vanished with Bayazid, but it survived for several reasons. First, it had attained legitimacy as a Muslim polity when Bayazid, anticipating the threat of Timur, had invested himself with recognition as an official Muslim ruler: The Mamluk ruler of Cairo had become the caliph or nominal leader of all Muslims after the Mongol sack of Baghdad in 1256, and in 1394 he made Bayazid the sultan of Rum. Second, he had introduced a system of recruitment and adminis-tration that conjoined the *timar* system with the expansion of territory. Like his Seljukid predecessors, he recruited non-Muslim youth, then, after converting them to Islam, had them trained as slaves, or *ghulams*, for mili-tary and palace duty. In effect, Murad began what became known as the janissary system, a backbone of later Ottoman state policy.

The religious establishment was important as a third element of regime enhancement. Bayazid fostered it as he did the janissary or slave system, extending patronage to its recipients but at a price: preferential deferral or even outright acquiescence in the authority of the state. Muslim scholars and teachers, Sufi masters, and juridical experts came from neighboring Islamic polities to Anatolia and to the Ottoman court. They came because of patronage from the emperor, and they were expected to assist him in his effort to be not just a conquering ghazi but also a Muslim Sultan. In other words, Islam became an explicit ideology, and building block of public prestige, for the newest Turkish Muslim empire.

The defining moment for the new Ottoman polity came in 1453 when Muhammad II, also known as Mehmed the Conqueror, achieved an ambition that had eluded all his Muslim predecessors: the conquest of Constantinople (Istanbul). It was a singular moment that saw not just the collapse of the truncated Byzantine Empire but also the rededication of Constantinople as a Muslim capital city.

Following the conquest of Istanbul, Syria, Egypt, and the Hijaz region of Arabia were conquered in the early sixteenth century. The conquest of

Egypt conferred further Islamic legitimacy, as the caliphate devolved from the defeated Mamluks to the victorious Ottomans. With the possession of Jerusalem, Mecca, and Medina, they controlled the three holiest cities in Islam. Rumeli remained no less important to the imperial ambitions of the Sultans: By the sixteenth century, Belgrade and Hungary, Moldavia, and Wallachia and Transylvania had all become tributary principalities under nominal Christian rulers. But the Ottomans were limited by the need to maintain supply lines to their sources. On the European front, they could not go beyond Vienna, where the time frame for sieges was limited and so never succeeded. On the southern rim of the Mediterranean, they continued to expand beyond Egypt, annexing Algiers, Tripoli, and Tunis and establishing *beys* and *deys* as rulers or surrogates on behalf of the Ottoman sultan, who was now also the commander of the caithful. Thus, at its apogee under Suleiman I in the mid-sixteenth century, the Osmanli realm was the most powerful empire in the world. Overshadowing his nearest European rival, Suleiman I enjoyed revenue twice that of Charles V.

But the state had limits both theoretical and empirical. In theory, it sustained an Islamic empire, with the sultan the uncontested source of religious as well as secular authority. He combined in himself the apogee of *shari'a* (religious) and *qanun* (civil) law. Suleiman was known as Suleiman *qanuni*. The notion of the state as a harmonious structure permeated the state military and civilian bureaucracies. It derived from the classic Perso-Turkish source, Nasir ad-din Tusi (d. 1273). No theory or account of Islam and violence can be complete without reference to Tusi's circle of justice. The circle of justice became the basis for Ottoman consciousness. Since the Sasanian social ethic emphasized order, stability, legality, and harmony among the theoretical four estates of priests, soldiers, officials, and workers, Tusi recycled Sasanian principles within an Islamic program. Tusi projected a dual function: hierarchical duties mirroring a consensual reciprocity between different groups, each aware of its specific role in the hierarchy. While the loyalty structure is a pyramid, its function is projected as a circle, the circle of justice. There can be no royal authority without the military (*askeri*):

> *There can be no military without wealth*
> *The reaya or agriculturalists produce the wealth*
> *The sultan keeps the loyalty of the reaya by ensuring justice*
> *Justice requires harmony in the world*

The world is a garden, its walls are the state
The state's axis is the religious law
There is no support for religious law without royal authority.[4]

The elegance of this formulation belies its inner tension. The accent is on justice rather than right religion as the basis for effective rule, not elimi-nating conflict or violence but redirecting its force to the benefit of the state. While the ruler and the ruled depend on each other, theirs remains an asymmetric relationship, for the circle begins and ends with the state and its supreme subject, the ruler. Only the middle line suggests that har-mony and justice are coterminous one with the other, yet justice is not justice between equals but rather justice as "just" rewards or allotted pay-ments for participation in the system. It never approaches parity much less equality. The religious classes, custodians of religious law, require state support, just as the state, in turn, requires the askeri or military classes who are its foundation. One could either label this system as con-trolled violence or the harmonious balance of competing self-interests, but it projects a consistent stress on justice.

Enlightenment notions of nonreligious loyalty to a state marked by both equality and justice for all are confounded in the Sasanian, then Ottoman notion of justice as a circle with the ruler at its center and also its apex. The pyramidal nature of authority becomes clear when one traces the circle via the four classes or differentiated orders, also derived from Tusi. The men of the sword dominate, with the men of the pen as their closest allies, while all other groups, whether Muslim or non-Muslim, urban or rural, have a lesser stake in the system but cannot escape its influence.

A review of its empirical limits demonstrates the faultlines within the Ottoman Empire. The system could only work as long as the conquests continued. Suleiman's reign may have been the apogee of power, but it also cast a shadow on the subsequent period of Ottoman history. The last significant conquest in the Mediterranean theater was Cyprus in 1570 (soon after his reign), and no other conquest came till Crete in 1664 almost a century later. The battles to the east of Rum, specifically with the Iranian Safavids, did not produce any major territorial gains. Without conquests, the Ottoman state could not claim to be the major Muslim empire of its day. Lack of conquest undermined its own logic, signaling its reduction in status and eventual demise. The empire's ideology was two pronged. It was dominated by and oriented toward the bureaucracy and governing institutions, yet at the same time it was reinforced by the religious schools and courts. The focal point of the ideology was the emperor. The success of the system depended on his personal stature. The emperor was at the same time the supreme religious leader, the owner of all land, and the commander in chief of the armed forces.

So there were indices of autocratic violence—structural, societal, and political—that characterized not only the Ottoman Empire and also its rivals, the Safavids and Mughals, but also its regional subsets, later to become independent polities, from Morocco on the edge of the Atlantic to Egypt at the base of the Mediterranean.

Overshadowing these rivalries, however, was engagement with Europe, above all, a response, sometimes cooperative but more often oppositional to European initiatives to control parts of Africa and Asia. Commercial trade became the Achilles heel for Ottomans as for other Muslim polities. Closely controlled by the state, trade was primarily in luxury items (Ottoman silk and Asian spices). It did not propel the economy out of its sense of self-sufficiency nor did it enable the state to control the number of competing centripetal forces within the empire that put Ottoman officialdom at risk in dealing with external polities, whether European or Muslim. Diplomatic relations with France revealed the strength as well as the weakness of the Ottoman system. A French-Ottoman alliance, forged in order to combat Charles V and the Holy Roman Empire, effectively delayed the Ottoman need to enter into permanent relations with other European powers until 1793, with the result that the Ottomans actually knew little about their future rivals, including the Russians. There were efforts to recuperate lost opportunities in the nineteenth century, but the great chase deprived not just the Ottomans but other Muslim polities from any sense of parity vis-à-vis their European rivals, then rulers.

Comparative Perspectives on Regional Empires

Comparable political economic processes informed the Ottomans along with their neighbors and rivals, the Safavids and Mughals. The rise of each empire involved the imposition of a strong state with tribal origins on a predominantly agrarian economy and society. In all three cases, after a prosperous period of stable reproduction of social relations and expansion of wealth in the sixteenth century, a retreat or decline seems to have been registered in the seventeenth century in the form of agrarian crises with political economic causes and political outcomes.

Several major developments altered the political scene in the seventeenth and eighteenth centuries: the Ottoman Empire became decentralized as Istanbul's hold on the provinces weakened and autonomous authorities sprang up almost everywhere; the Safavid regime collapsed, giving way to several decades of internal fragmentation and turmoil; and Mughal India reached its apogee, only to be sacked by Nadir Shah, an Afghani adventurer, in the early eighteenth century.

Alongside the shifts in the internal power relations came changes in the region's position in regard to Europe. While Safavids, Ottomans, and Mughals remained virtually untouched by European culture, they now fought and traded with Europeans on a more extensive basis than before and on increasingly unfavorable terms. Military conflict with European countries raged along a wide front extending from the Black Sea area and the Balkans to the western Mediterranean and the Indian Ocean. The region's armies were able to hold their own until the second half of the eighteenth century, when disastrous defeats by Russia and the easy fall of Egypt to Napoleon brought home to the Ottoman leaders the recognition that global power had shifted definitely in favor of Europe.

European Colonial Presence and Violent Muslim Responses

There is no generic category of religious protest that applies to the modern period of world history, from 1600 to the present.[5] Instead, there are three distinct phases of Islamicly valorized protest. In each phase, certain Muslim groups revolted against the ascendant, which has become the dominant, world order linked to western Europe. Only the first phase is properly speaking revivalist. It is succeeded by a second that can and should be termed reformist, and it is only after the revivalist and reformist phases and, in large part, due to their failures that there what is now termed Islamic fundamentalism or Islamism emerged.[6]

All three—revivalism, reformism, and fundamentalism—are historically specific socioreligious movements propelling marginalized male leaders into public view as they attempt to reclaim the space challenged and reduced, impoverished and redefined, by the expanding sea powers of western Europe. From the eighteenth century to the present, all the major Muslim polities experienced financial crises, demographic disruption, and agricultural stagnation. If there is a case to be made for structural violence as the backdrop and often the catalyst for physical violence, then the European interlude must be considered when addressing the topic of Islam and violence. Some of the malaise in early modern Muslim polities resulted from indigenous challenges. Provincial Arabs chafed under Ottoman Turkish rule, Afghans protested Qajar control within Iran, and Marattas rebelled against Mughal hegemony in South Asia. In each instance, however, the situation of ruling elites was complicated and worsened by: the external diversion of commodity trade from the Mediterranean and Indian Ocean routes to the Atlantic Ocean following the discovery and exploitation of the New World and the internal infiltration of European trade through a nexus of foreign merchants and local middlemen or *compradores* cooperating to establish new products, new markets, and new communication networks also as new sources of profit and reinvestment. Islam, in effect, became an idiom of protest against the gradual contraction of internal and external trade, brought about by the mercantile activities of European maritime nations, specifically, the Portuguese, Spanish, Dutch, British, and the French. What was contested in the name of Islam by Islamic revivalists was control over vital commodities—slaves, textiles, coffee, tea, and spices—as well as gold, all trafficked along the major trade routes from the Atlantic coast of West Africa to the Indonesian archipelago.

The major Muslim revivalist movements were without exception preindustrial. Their leaders mobilized followers in response to the European redirection of global trade, even when they did not acknowledge the extent to which European advances were reshaping their lives.

One of the earliest instances of European influence concerns the upstart Wahhabis. In western Arabia, the Wahhabis aligned with a Najdi chief named Ibn Sa'ud. That combination in time produced what is now regarded as a legitimate government, though it remains the only Muslim polity named after a tribal group: the present-day Kingdom of Saudi Arabia. Both Ibn Sa'ud and his appointed ideologue, Ibn 'Abd al-Wahhab, benefited from the loss of revenues suffered by their chief rival, the sharif of Mecca, who in the eighteenth century reigned as the legitimate ruler of the Hijaz. Dependent as he was on the lucrative Indian trade, primarily in textiles, indigo, and spices, the sharif could not sustain its diversion away from the Arabian Peninsula by the British. Weakened economically, he also became vulnerable militarily. His Najdi rivals rallied to their side other groups who had been deprived by the British ascendancy in trade, and toward the end of the eighteenth century they were able to dislodge and replace the sharif of Mecca. Although the Wahhabis had other battles to wage, with the Turks and also with Muslim loyalists from rival tribes who did not accept their leadership, their initial success was a by-product of incipient European colonialism.

Unfortunately, the influence of Muhammad ibn 'Abd al-Wahhab on both Muslim and non-Muslim scholarship of Islamic revivalism has led his movement to be overvalued beyond its actual historical achievement. It is often presumed that a literal, text-restricted reading of the Qur'an prevailed from the origins of Islam. It did not, nor has it ever been the practice for most observant Muslims. Ibn 'Abd al-Wahhab had a narrow reform agenda not shared with other eighteenth-century and later Muslim reforms. Even his notion of the boundaries of faith were limited to exploring and explaining the concepts of *tawhid* and *takfir, iman* and *kufr,* that is to say, how you make God exclusively one and declaim all other Muslims who fail to express the same level of creedal commitment. Ibn 'Abd al-Wahhab never claimed to be a reinterpreter of the scholarly legacy of the past. He never concerned himself with the wider Muslim community and its integrity. He never addressed issues of tyranny and social justice.

Yet the Wahhabi paradigm created numerous analogues elsewhere on the seams of commercial activity that became increasingly under British rule. In northwestern India, the Brelvis tried to wage war against indigenous groups the Sikhs and Hindus, but the latter were better positioned than the Brelvis in regard to British commercial interests. The Brelvis were strategically isolated before being defeated on the battlefield by Sikhs. Elsewhere, in northeastern India, the Faraidis perceived the shift to a moneyed, international economy as advantageous to Hindu landlords while impoverishing Muslim peasant laborers. They mobilized resistance, at first in local protests, later in region-wide acts of defiance; neither succeeded in reversing the tides of change.

It was the same story, with different actors but a similar outcome in Africa. The best documented of the revivalist movements, the Fulani-Qadiris in Nigeria, pitted Muslim herdsmen and traders against British markets and middlemen who were often being recruited from rival Muslim tribes. Though the revivalists enjoyed superb Islamic credentials, they were eventually defeated on the battlefield. There were temporary successes: the Sanusis prevailed in the Cyrenaica region near the Ottoman province of Libya, strengthening Islamic identity for more than fifty years until the Italian invasion of 1911. A Somali chieftain, too, was able to mobilize interior tribes against British, Italian, and French forces in the coastal areas near Mogadishu. He won several battles and continued to rule for more than twenty years, only to have the British bomb and machine gun their way to victory in 1920. Finally, on the other side of the Muslim world in Southeast Asia, a puritanical movement known as the Padris galvanized Sumatran Muslims dispossessed by the shift from gold and pepper trade to a new cash crop, coffee. During the course of the nineteenth century, the Padris were harassed and coerced, enduring defeat after defeat in bloody encounters before finally succumbing to the Dutch authorities.

All these revivalist movements were violent, but they followed a pattern of responsive violence. It is not accidental that they all occurred at crucial seams in the expanding imperium of maritime Europe. All were Sunni Muslim movements. The single parallel within Shia Islam were the Bahais, a group still despised by Twelver Shia clergy. The vilification masks a deeper fear: The first Bahais embodied and projected the latent messianic impulse of Twelver Shiism. Yet the Bahais became harbingers of ecumenical pluralism and so represent a graphic example of how Islam and violence cannot be neatly matched.

Apart from the Bahais, Islamic revivalist groups were succeeded by Islamic reformers. Interposed between Islamic revivalism and Islamic fundamentalism, Islamic reformers are closely linked to nationalist movements, and in retrospect it can be seen that, despite their universalist rhetoric, almost all the Islamic reformers were shaped by the influences of the colonial period. Especially keen is the emphasis on science and technology in education, constitution and parliamentary democracy in politics, and the revised role of women in social life. If Muslim nationalism became mimetic, it is due to the fact that movements that claimed a loyalty to Islam were also mimetic, picking up elements of the West that they hoped could be transformed into an Islamic system. Far from reacting with violence to European presence and control, they attempted to accommodate to an emergent, if asymmetric, world system. There is no independent Muslim movement after the colonial period; all are reacting to some force or series of forces that emanate from the Western world, which is to say northern Europe and the United States.

Muslim reformers recognized the power of the institutions that were propelling European maritime nations to a unique position of global prestige. The reformers came from those countries whose Muslim elites were most engaged by the specter of European commercial and military penetration—Egypt and India, Iran and Turkey before World War I, but then, following the war, also Tunisia, Algeria, and Morocco. The North African reformers coalesced into a movement known as Salafiya, or Islamic traditionalism. Criticized for their unwitting promotion of historical retardation, its leaders seemed to hark back to a golden age that never existed or at least could never be reconstructed, and so their passionate pleas merely drained energies away from the task at hand, to accommodate to the new reality of a European world order. Yet most of the reformers acted in good faith, as committed Muslims conflicted by the gap between Europe's pragmatic success and what seemed to be its spiritual vapidity. It was as though they were witnesses to a novel and "unholy" revelation. For them, "the arbiter of truth and knowledge suddenly ceased to be enclosed in the revealed word of God. Another text, with no specific author or format, had made a permanent intrusion. It was the West in its political systems, military presence and economic domination which now appeared in the background as an authoritative code of practice."[7]

But the authoritative code was not uniform. The intervening European powers quarreled with one another. Some Muslim polities, such as the Sharifian kingdom of Morocco, benefited from these quarrels, able to resist direct rule because no Mediterranean power wanted its rivals to control the seat of the Arab/Muslim West. But all polities were affected by the great wars, sometimes known as the Christian wars, which were waged by these self-same powers twice in the twentieth century. It was only due to the enormous expenditures and consequent destruction of these wars that protest movements among Muslims and others were able to mobilize into national liberation movements. Gradually, as the smoke cleared from the second of these horrific Christian wars, most Muslim ruling elites were able to grasp the laurel of independence. Even so, not all were marked by the same political order.

Even countries that were not colonized directly, such as Saudi Arabia and Iran, still experienced the effects of colonial economic penetration into the eastern Mediterranean and Indian Ocean, and the structures that arose after independence reflect this influence, above all in the sphere of politics and law. It was because the nature of self-rule was shaped as much by European as by indigenous models that one must speak of "mimetic nationalism." Though Arab, as also non-Arab, Muslim leaders embraced nationalism to chart the path to independence, the models of governance were derived from the departing colonials. Whether one looks to constitutional charters or to the adoption of separate executive and legislative bodies, the impress of European precedents is evident. At the same time, the boundaries of new nations reflected a patchwork of compromise that was worked out by the European powers not by their Muslim subjects. Saddam Hussein's outburst in fall 1990 over the manipulation of Iraq's borders with Kuwait was at once justified and spurious. It was justified because the borders of all African and Asian countries were set in the colonial period or its immediate aftermath. It was spurious because many countries benefited as well as lost from such manipulation: Without the addition of parts of Kurdistan, especially the oil-rich region around Mosul, Iraq, for instance, would not have had the geopolitical resources that make it potentially the economic giant among all Arab states.

The truth about the process by which postcolonial borders were decided may be simpler, though no prettier, than conspiracy theories allow: Disparate communities of Asia and Africa had been welded together as parts of the British, French, or Dutch empires. They could not be dissolved and reconstituted in their precolonial form with independence. Often the conditions of self-rule had to be set by colonial authorities and imperial administration, because consent could not have been secured on any other basis. Yet the end result was to make the entire process of Arab/ Muslim nationalism seem imitative or mimetic. It appealed only to a limited stratum of elites. The mechanisms to curb military control and to spur the emergence of a middle class were never set in place. Structural violence took on a new face, but it was still violent and its tensions, contradictions, and excesses continue to the present day.

While most Europeans and Americans have lived within "secure" national borders for several generations and see themselves as beneficiaries from the tradition of nation-state loyalty, many third world citizens, and Afro-Asian Muslims, in particular, do not share either their experience or their trust. For most Muslims, it is hard to applaud the random, top-down process by which almost all their polities came to assume their present form.

Not only the external boundaries of territory but also the internal boundaries of identity are open to challenge and reformulation. In thinking about Islamic protest, it is especially important to note how the clash at the core of all other clashes between nationalists and fundamentalists is the totalizing impulse guiding each. In the Muslim world, the state functions as an obedience context, and the rulers of the Muslim state demand total compliance with the state's vision of Islam. Tacitly it recognizes that the norms it imposes are not universally shared by all Muslims, yet publicly it arrogates to itself and to its custodians the right to decide which elements of Islamic belief and practice are to be supported. The memory of other Islams is too strong, however, to be erased. In each instance, Muslims have to decide how to preserve their symbolic identity within a public order that is antireligious at worst, as in the Union of Soviet Socialist Republics, China, Indonesia, and Turkey or pseudoreligious at best, as in most Arab states, Iran, Pakistan, and Bangladesh.

Twentieth- and now twenty-first-century nationalism produced for the entire Muslim world a cleavage of enormous magnitude. The most evident rift was between Muslims and the dominant culture of western Europe. But an equally great divide devloped among Muslim themselves, between those who were attracted to European achievements, seeking to appropriate their benefits, and those others who sought to oppose them.

While the legacy of colonialism reshaped the Muslim world into truncated territories and contested borders, capitalism left it with economies that could only function on the margins, benefiting the major powers of the high-tech era. These powers were the technologically advanced, professionally differentiated, and economically privileged societies of western Europe, North America, and, now, East Asia. Even before the rubric of first, second, and third worlds was invented in the 1950s, a third world existed. It embraced all Muslim societies, even those benefiting from the petrodollar infusion that began in the 1950s and 1960s but did not accelerate until the 1970s and 1980s.

Jihad in Modern Times

Among the ongoing effects of the postcolonial legacy in Muslim polities has been the overwhelming attention to Islam and violence. From medieval to modern to contemporary history, the trope of Islam as violence has focused on jihad, and so it is important to note how those who came to be labeled fundamentalists invoked the early experience of the Prophet Muhammad and the Medinan state on behalf of their own authority to proclaim jihad. None did so more stridently or effectively than Sayyid Qutb, the Muslim brother who opposed Nasser, the Egyptian president from 1954 to 1970. Executed on charges of sedition in 1966, Sayyid Qutb produced a series of writings, some from prison, that exposed modern-day nationalism as itself a form of *jahliyya*. In effect, it was equated with the kind of tribal order that Muhammad had opposed and that he, together with his early followers, had to overcome in order to establish the ummah, or single supratribal Muslim community. In one of his most memorable string of homologies, Qutb reappropriated nationalism for "true" Islam: "[N]ationalism is belief, homeland is Dar al-Islam, the ruler is God, and the constitution is the Qur'an" (quoted in Lawrence 1998: 68).

Qutb's message and his resort to jihad as the just cause for Muslims under threat resonated through Egypt and the Arab world and with the Taliban and the attackers of 9/11. It is impossible to make this temporal transition from the seventh to the twenty-first century without noting how eschatological religion is instrumentalized through modern means, not least martyr operations. The connection has been nimbly charted by Hans Kippenberg:

> When they attacked the United States in September 2001, jihadists were interpreting the Middle East conflict in Islamic concepts, but they did so in a radically different manner from the mainstream of the Muslim Brethren (following the lead of Sayyid Qutb rather than his predecessors). The power of the United States and Israel has made Islam so rotten and corrupt that no external institution is now able to represent it credibly; it is only the pure intentions of the last surviving upright believers that can form the core of a new community of the elect. And this is what they demonstrate by means of martyr operations (carried out by Al-Qaeda and in the name of Osama bin Laden).
>
> (Kippenberg: 201)

The Legacy of Osama Bin Laden: The Cosmic Warrior Mediated

We now come full circle from 611, the beginning of a nonviolent protest movement led by an Arab merchant turned prophet, to 9/11, the day of infamy for twenty-first century Americans. The source of that violence that brackets Islam with the worst forms of violence was Osama bin Laden; but it was Bin Laden, the Islamic apocalypticist as mediated through modern visual and satellite technologies. Now that Osama bin Laden has been killed by a US Navy seal team in Abbotabad, Pakistan, in early May 2011, it is possible to reflect on his impact on Islamic notions of war and violence.[8]

There is probably no aspect of Bin Laden's profile that is more critical nor less understood than his use of the media, especially *al- Quds al-'Arabi* and al-Jazeera. One episode from late 2003 illustrates how intertwined the interests of the Saudi dissident and the major Arabic language media were. On December 10, 2003, the London-based Arabic daily *Al-Quds Al-Arabi* reported that Al-Qa'ida, headed by Osama bin Laden, "is gearing up for a big operation to coincide with Eid Al-Adha [February 2, 2004]...

a new videotape of bin Laden will be circulated shortly before the holiday...it will surface in conjunction with 'a great event that will shake the region,' and it will be broadcast by Al-Jazeera television." The source explained that Al-Qa'ida had an agreement with Al-Jazeera by which it was committed to broadcast any videotape that the Sahab Institute provides about Al-Qa'ida. He pointed out that the institute would sever its relations with the station if it refused to broadcast a videotape, and reiterated that the station is obligated to broadcast any videotape we send to it.[9]

In the several messages included in my collection of Bin Laden's writings, his relationship to Al-Jazeera proves to be almost as important as his decision to wage jihad. Prior to December 1998, when the United States and Britain launched an attack on Iraq, called Operation Desert Fox, Al-Jazeera had been a local satellite news service. Founded in February 1996 by the emir of Qatar, its goal was to promote freedom of information among Arabic-speaking citizens of the Gulf and its neighbors. In 1998, the Baghdad office got the big break when they filmed the missiles launched against Iraq from British and American airplanes. Bin Laden gave an interview that was broadcast on Al-Jazeera in December,[10] and he became an instant international attraction. So significant was the impact of this interview that, nine days after September 11, 2001, it was rerun by Al-Jazeera. Accompanying the ninety-minute video were pictures of Bin Laden firing a gun. The message, in images as well as in words, was that the war is religious, the war is between aggressive crusaders and defensive believers, and Muslims have a stark choice, either to side with the infidel oppressors or to support the beleaguered but pure and resolute Muslim defenders.

The same message was articulated in all of Bin Laden's subsequent epistles that were broadcast via Al-Jazeera. Each was tailored to the audience he addressed. Jason Burke observed that "bin Laden seemed to show an incredible instinctive grasp of modern marketing techniques" (Burke: 175). Flagg Miller goes further, explaining why the genre of epistles may be one of the best marketing techniques for his message:

Epistles became a defining medium of eloquence in the 9th-century Abbasid court of Baghdad. In epistles colorful pleasantries, competitive verbal jousts, and political wrangling are all of a piece. Bin Laden deploys the genre with his own rhetorical flourishes. As pious public lecturer, militant *jihadist*, and now enfranchised literate scribe, Bin Laden excoriates ruling Saudi leaders for corruption, fiscal mismanagement, human rights abuses, and especially for their alliance with 'American Crusader forces' since the Gulf War of 1990. Such accusations gain religious significance for Bin Laden as apostasy (*shirk*) insofar as Saudi leaders are represented as recurring to man-made state law instead of to true Islamic law (*shari`a*), the latter of which remains confidently underspecified. Overall, the pious tenor of Bin Laden's epistle is consistently maintained as an act of remembrance (*dhikr*), so central to Islam's message that mankind is essentially forgetful, and is thus in need of constant reminding.

(Miller)[11]

The epistles functioned as sermons, delivered from on high and projected globally in ways that enhanced Bin Laden's charismatic stature.

His epistles to the Iraqis were elaborated with scriptural and historical citations and also with poetic verses, some from his own pen. His epistle to the Afghans flowed with cascades of Qur'anic citations as he reminded them of his struggle on their behalf against the Soviets. His letter to the Americans and Europeans, by contrast, contained an unadorned accusation: They were blindly following leaders who were dooming them to an endless war of attrition. In every instance, he was an antiimperial polemicist on behalf of global jihad, shaping the message to reach the audience.

In the sermon he delivered in 2003 on the holiest day in the Islamic calendar, Id al-Adha, he combines elements from all his letters and declarations to address Muslims around the world. He talks to individuals directly, commending each one's worthiness to participate in global jihad and accusing their leaders of criminal corruption. Like the first encounters that the seventh-century Arabs had with unbelieving Persians, the current jihad pits absolute good against absolute evil. Psychologically speaking, it is as though Bin Laden is charged with a paranoid certainty about the end time, the apocalyptic moment in which all are living but only he and the guided warriors from Al-Qa'ida understood fully. Numerous Qur'anic citations and prophetic traditions are woven into his fervent appeal to believers to take up arms against the United States, Britain, Israel, and their collaborators in the Arab world. Like the Prophet Muhammad's followers, Bin Laden's Muslim armies will prevail. They have a recent history of victories over the superpowers. Who was it that defeated the Soviet Union in Afghanistan and the Russians in Chechnya if not the Afghan-Arab mujahidin? Was it not they who conquered the Americans in Lebanon,

Somalia, Aden, Riyadh, Khobar, East Africa, at home, and, most recently, in Afghanistan? The myth of American democracy and freedom has been shattered, thanks be to God! And then, remarkably, he concludes with his own poem in which he vows to fight until he becomes:

> a martyr,
> dwelling in a high mountain pass
> among a band of knights who,
> united in devotion to God,
> descend to face armies.

Unfortunately, due to the dizzying shifts of technology in the Information Age, one loses all sense of just how dramatic Bin Laden's moves as a risk taker were. As one analyst explains:

> Bin Laden's bald comparisons between hallowed personages of early Islamic history and contemporary actors and events subject him to decided risks. Not only does he hazard alienating Muslim listeners by compromising the unique role that the Prophet played in Islam; he also risks becoming a poor historian, one whose anti-quarian zeal fails to re-connect narrated events with present concerns. It is precisely here that Bin Laden adopts an entirely new tactic, one that moves him from his role as pious public lecturer to the roles of tribesman, poet, and ultimately cosmic warrior. In the midst of this set of transformations, the temporal distinctions of 'then' and 'now' become entirely blurred, and listeners are invited, through the most sonorous and impassioned portions of the cassette, to mobilize as eternal holy combatants."

> (Miller)

The oracle who speaks has recast himself as a cosmic warrior, auguring both the end time and its "certain" outcome.

While Bin Laden not only mastered modern media and was also its primary beneficiary, no one should assume that Bin Laden benefited from his use of the media, in general, and Al-Jazeera, in particular, without some cost to his project. The channel of influence and of risk taking runs two ways. Bin Laden advocated the maximal response to imperialism. He constantly called on sacrifice, especially of youths through martyrdom for a greater cause, yet he gave no hint of a future frame beyond the shibbo-

leth "Islamic state" or "rule of God on earth." The emptiness of his political vision was made clear in the Taysir Alluni interview in October 2001
(MW # 11), when he declared that jihad will continue until "we meet God
and get His blessing!" Yet earlier, in the Ladenese epistle of August 1996
(MW # 3), he had seemed to call for a deferral of apocalyptic rewards,
insisting on the value of oil revenues for a near term Islamic state: "I would
like here to alert my brothers, the Mujahidin, the sons of the nation, to
protect this (oil) wealth and not to include it in the battle as it is a great
Islamic wealth and a large economical power essential for the soon to be
established Islamic state, by the grace and permission of God."

Still later, in his second letter to the Iraqi people (February 11, 2003;
MW #18), he called again for establishing the rule of God on Earth but
only through incessant warfare against multiple enemies, with no agenda
for structure or network that succeeds the current world system.

While there are many ways to connect Bin Laden to the early generation of Islam, perhaps the crucial move is to see how he contrasted the
perfection of early Islam with the desecration of the twenty-first century.
In the same way that former President George W. Bush saw freedom and
democracy as standards of global virtue, projecting both holistic sound-
ness and indivisible oneness for "the axis of good," so Bin Laden saw sacrifice and war as the dual emblems of early Islam that persist until today
as the axis of hope for all committed Muslims who recognize the serious-
ness of the moment. Yet his was a hope that could never be realized under
the current world order because all its denizens were living in an end time
of total crisis. There was no rush to restore the caliphate nor to remake the
Ottoman Empire in the pre–World War I image of a pan-Islamic Muslim
polity. Instead, the ultimate criterion was "meeting God and getting his blessing." That was a deferred hope, one that could not be achieved in this world
during the lifetime of Muslim martyrs but was deferred for all humankind
to experience in the terrible reckoning that God Almighty has prepared.[12]

The Muslim Legacy Post-Osama Bin Laden

The great unaccounted for in the scenario of Osama Bin Laden are those
Muslims who still consider themselves custodians of the faith and followers of the Prophet yet do not see perpetual warfare in the name of jihad as
the only measure of Islamic loyalty. Instead of opposing perfections, they
try to see the will of God in this age through different instruments, affirming the current world order, at once trying to maximize its benefits while

curbing its excesses. They need more than scriptural dictates, poetic balm, or binary shibboleths to chart their everyday life, whether as individuals or as collective members of local communities, nation-states, and the world at large. For them, Bin Laden's legacy, especially in the aftermath of his death and with seeds of hope sprouting from the Arab Spring (January– June 2011), is one of deviance and damage rather than persistence and profit in the cause of Islam. The world is not coming to an end, and other means have to be found to advance Islamic principles and the well-being of the Muslim community (ummah).

For pragmatists, Muslim as well as non-Muslim, the real work is to prepare for an eventuality beyond the diatribes of apocalyptic doomsayers. It is not easy but it is the only way forward, and if God wills, it may yet augur the next chapter in Islam beyond violence, mirroring the first phase of the life of the Prophet Muhammad as also the consistent intent of the full panoply of divine directives mandated in the Holy Qur'an and pursued through the major epochs of Muslim history.

Notes

1. Unless otherwise noted, all the Qur'anic verses quoted here and subsequently derive from or are adapted from Thomas Cleary, *The Qur'an—A New Translation* (Starlatch, 2004).
2. Suleiman Mourad in an e-mail dated September 23, 2003. Elsewhere in an April 15, 2011, interview (http://www.smith.edu/insight/stories/jihad.php, Professor Mourad, who is co-authoring a book titled *The Radicalization of Sunni Jihad Ideology in the Crusader Period* (to be published by Ashgate Press), observed that: "Jihad is not what the Prophet initiated but what a scholar in 12th-century Damascus (Ibn Asakir)was paid by his political patron to promote and disseminate."
3. In the analysis that follows, I have benefited from the seminal work of Marshall G. S. Hodgson, *The Venture of Islam: Conscience and History in a World Civilization* (Chicago: University of Chicago Press, 1974), volume 3: The Gunpowder Empires and Modern Times, as also the more recent, by Stephen F. Dale, *The Muslim Empires of the Ottomans, Safavids, and Mughals* (Cambridge, UK: Cambridge University Press, 2010), but neither Dale nor Hodgson is responsible for my inferences about the interconnection between Islam and violence during the long span of these premodern Muslim empires.
4. For the elaboration of this concept among Ottoman ruling elites, see Cornell Fleischer, "Royal Authority, Dynastic Cyclism, and 'Ibn Khaldunism'" in Bruce B. Lawrence, ed. *Ibn Khaldun and Islamic Ideology* (Leiden, Netherlands: E. J. Brill, 1984): 48–51.

5. The issue of Muslim responses to European colonial presence in Afro-Eurasia has been explored in Bruce B. Lawrence, *Shattering the Myth: Islam beyond Violence* (Princeton, NJ: Princeton University Press, 1998), and in what follows, I have relied on the analysis provided in chapter 2 "Islamic Revivalism: Anti-Colonial Revolt," especially pp. 41–52.

6. On the debate between Islamic fundamentalism and Islamism as analytical categories, see Richard C. Martin and Abbas Barzegar, eds., *Islamism: Contested Perspectives on Political Islam* (Palo Alto CA: Stanford University Press, 2010). My essay, "Islam at Risk: The Discourse on Islam and Violence" (93–98), challenges assumptions behind the more recent terms, *post-Islamism* and *neofundamentalism*, especially as deployed by Olivier Roy (98).

7. Youssef M. Choueiri, *Islamic Fundamentalism* (Boston: Twayne, 1990): 35. I am indebted to Choueiri for his clear exposition of Islamic fundamentalism, but I demur from his use of "radicalism" to refer to the last or most recent phase of Islamic protest. The term *radical*, unlike *revivalism* and *reformism*, has no positive referent. It presupposes some other norm, and in my view, that norm is a strict religious code or sense of inalterable, all-encompassing fundamentals, thus my use of *fundamentalism* in preference to *radicalism* to denote the last and most significant phase of Islamic protest.

8. Much of the material that follows comes from the final section of my article "Osama bin Laden—The Man and the Myth," in Charles B. Strozier, ed. *The Leader: Psychohistorical Essays*, 2nd edition (New York: Springer, 2011): 119–134.

9. See the (too) brief reference to Al-Sahab in Hugh Miles, *Al-Jazeera: How Arab TV News Challenged the World* (London: Abacus, 2005): 180. Other sources are equally dismissive or neglectful of this crucial conduit to the Osama bin Laden media strategy.

10. Osama Bin Laden, "A Muslim Bomb" in Bruce Lawrence ed. *Messages to the World—The Statements of Osama bin Laden* (London and New York: Verso 2005): 65–94.

11. W. Flagg Miller, "On 'The Summit of the Hindu Kush': Osama Bin Laden's 1996 Declaration of War Reconsidered," unpublished talk delivered at the University of Michigan in March 2005, cited here by permission of the author.

12. The notion that apocalypse as end of the world appeals to other contemporary Muslim audiences is also reflected and documented in Jean-Pierre Filiu, *Apocalypse in Islam* (Berkeley: University of California Press, 2011). His monograph also provides apt and striking parallels to Christian apocalyptic thoughts, movements and leaders.

Bibliography

Burke, Jason. *Al-Qaeda: The True Story of Radical Islam*. London: Penguin, 2004.
Choueiri, Youssef M. *Islamic Fundamentalism*. Boston: Twayne, 1990.

Cleary, Thomas. *The Qur'an—A New Translation*. Burlington, VT: Starlatch, 2004.

Dale, Stephen F. *The Muslim Empires of the Ottomans, Safavids, and Mughals*. Cambridge, UK: Cambridge University Press, 2010.

Donner, Fred McGraw. *The Early Islamic Conquests*. Princeton, NJ: Princeton University Press, 1981.

Filiu, Jean-Pierre. *Apocalypse in Islam*. Berkeley: University of California Press, 2011.

Fleischer, Cornell. "Royal Authority, Dynastic Cyclism, and 'Ibn Khaldunism.'" In *Ibn Khaldun and Islamic Ideology*. Edited by Bruce Lawrence, 198–220. Leiden, Netherlands: E. J. Brill, 1984.

Hillenbrand, Carole. *The Crusades—Islamic Perspectives*. Edinburgh: Edinburgh University Press, 1999.

Hodgson, Marshall G. S. *The Venture of Islam: Conscience and History in a World Civilization*. Chicago: University of Chicago Press, 1974.

Kippenberg, Hans G. *Violence as Worship: Religious Wars in the Age of Globalisation*. Palo Alto, CA: Stanford University Press, 2011.

Lawrence, Bruce. *Shattering the Myth: Islam beyond Violence*. Princeton, NJ: Princeton University Press, 1998.

Lawrence, Bruce. *Messages to the World—The Statements of Osama bin Laden*. London and New York: Verso, 2005.

Lawrence, Bruce. *The Qur'an—A Biography*. New York: Atlantic Books, 2007.

Lawrence, Bruce. "Osama bin Laden—The Man and the Myth." In *The Leader: Psychohistorical Essays*. Edited by Charles B. Strozier, 2nd edition, 119–134. New York: Springer, 2011.

Martin, Richard C. and Abbas Barzegar, eds. *Islamism: Contested Perspectives on Political Islam*. Palo Alto, CA: Stanford University Press, 2010.

Miles, Hugh. *Al-Jazeera: How Arab TV News Challenged the World*. London: Abacus, 2005.

Mourad, Suleiman, with James E. Lindsay. *The Radicalization of Sunni Jihad Ideology in the Crusader Period*. Aldershot, UK: Ashgate, 2011.

Chapter 7

African Traditional Religion and Violence

Nathalie Wlodarczyk

IN AFRICA, THE religious beliefs and practices that predated the arrival of Christianity or Islam existed as oral traditions. When, as a result of the slave trade, some of these beliefs were exported to the Americas, they were equated with the savage traditions of the African slaves—more carnal and bloodied than the sanitized religious beliefs of the slave traders and owners. On the plantations in the Americas, the beliefs became associated with the wild, uncontrollable, and angry African population. On the African continent, Christian and Muslim missionaries also sought to counter the indigenous beliefs of the tribes and communities they came across to bring them what they saw as both salvation and civilization. This view of African traditional religions as something savage and brutal has retained currency and is regularly reflected in writings on Africa. In particular, attempts to explain and understand the brutality of civil wars since the end of colonialism have been peppered with references to traditional practices as an illustration of an apparent return to a savage past.

In reality, African Traditional Religion is no more or less of an ancient or modern tradition than other religions. The cosmologies predate colonialism by centuries, but over the years they have come to incorporate aspects of the various cultures and other religions on the continent. The ability to adapt to changing realities without being subsumed has been the strength of African Traditional Religion, a strength in large part derived from the same lack of central doctrine and hierarchy that has given it an appearance of insignificance. The peoples who subscribe to the traditional religious beliefs find in it not only answers to most practical and esoteric questions but also a means of drawing directly on the spirit world to affect events in the material world. Perhaps unsurprisingly these means have been drawn on repeatedly and regularly, both to promote peace and healing and to provide strength and power to ensure victory in conflict.

What is African Traditional Religion?

The vast majority of people who subscribe to traditional African religious beliefs reside on the African continent. In areas of the world with large African diasporas such as Britain, France, and the United States, some of these beliefs have accompanied the migrant communities. When Africans first began to leave the continent in large numbers, under duress during the slave trade, some of these beliefs were also brought to the Caribbean and South America where they blended with local religions to form the Vodun, Santería, and Obeah of today. Nonetheless, African Traditional Religion remains primarily an African phenomenon, and as a result, it is tightly connected to the cultures and realities of the continent. To talk of African religion is, therefore, to a large extent to talk of religion in Africa.

Common Themes

African Traditional Religion is the set of beliefs that originated on the African continent before the introduction of Christianity, Islam, or other religions from further afield. It is a repository of oral traditions without a single founder or central sacred text but, nonetheless, with a striking number of coherent themes across this vast continent. As opposed to variants of Christianity and Islam, the common themes of African religion are not so much enshrined in doctrine or even narrative but rather in non-text-based, yet shared approaches to the nature of power and to man's and the world's relationship to it. While the many peoples of Africa have their own deities and spirits as well as their own rituals and celebrations, their traditional belief systems share some core features. This means that individual societies and even communities will have their own names for spirits and deities and their own myths recalling the characters and adventures of these beings. It is rare that they translate exactly from one place to another. However, while the Yoruba in Nigeria refer to their spirits as *Orisha* and individual spirits such as Eshu, Yemaya, and Ologun have their own distinct personalities and abilities, they nonetheless share traits with the djinns of East Africa, the spirits of northern Uganda (referred to as *Jok*) and the spirits of Sierra Leone (commonly called "devils").

Some have referred to African traditional religion as simultaneously monotheistic and polytheistic (Lugira 2009). There is almost always a supreme being, usually the creator of the universe and all life, unrivaled by a multitude of nonetheless powerful lesser gods and spirits. However, while the supreme being holds the greatest power, it is also the furthest removed from daily human life. Although creation stories differ across the continent, a large number share the idea that the supreme being retreated from the earth as a result of human action. In some cases it is said that humanity became too demanding of the supreme being and retreat was the only way to find peace and quiet from the incessant demands of humans. In others, the aggressive and disobedient behavior of man is said to have led the supreme being to turn away and deny them his presence (Parinder, 1969). In contrast, the lesser gods and, even lower down the ranks, spirits tend to be both approachable and actively engaged in human affairs. Ancestors also play a significant role in most African religious traditions, usually as mediators who both guide their descendants from their new spiritual state—achieved through death—and intercede with nonhuman spirits and gods on their descendants' behalf.

The spirit world permeates the material world, and culture has become closely entwined with religion. Local cultures in Africa are often defined to a significant degree by the history of its people and heroes, many of whom have assumed places in the spirit world since their passing and whose history while walking the earth was shaped by the intervention of spirits. All events in the material world are assumed to be the cause of dealings in the spirit world, although these dealings could well have been instigated by people rather than the spirits themselves. As a result, everyday life becomes a spiritual affair, in which appeasing or beseeching ancestors, spirits, or deities is the key means of ensuring life progresses as planned. This appeal to the spirits is made more challenging by the fact that spirits and even the gods are assumed to be largely morally neutral. Their power can be used for positive or negative—constructive or destructive—purposes. This places significant onus on adherents to engage proactively with the spirit world to ensure they get the desired result.

The spirit world can be reached through spiritual practitioners, of which there are a number. Each culture has its own names for its spiritual practitioners and their functions vary somewhat, but most of them include versions of priests, spirit mediums, diviners, healers and witch doctors, and witches. Priests, or the acknowledged local authority on religious practice, usually officiate significant rituals and offer guidance on spiritual matters and practice to community members. Priests often double as mediums, healers, or diviners. Spirit mediums can effect possession by one or several spirits and allow people to communicate with "their" spirits in this manner. They also often offer consultations with individuals' spirits when they speak directly to the spirits without possession. Diviners use craft to consult with spirits or to find answers to specific questions, about the past, present, or future. Healers or witch doctors offer a mixture of medical craft and spirit access to heal illness and often also to counter the activities of witches or the destructive practices of spirits or other spiritual practitioners. The witch doctors along with witches also tend to be the ones able to compel spirits to do their bidding through their craft. Often the main distinction made by people between witches and witch doctors is simply the nature of the end to which they are using their craft—constructive use that is deemed good for the community is condoned, whereas destructive use that lets an individual benefit at the expense of another is not. But witches are a more elusive group and one that is defined mostly by their enemies rather than an identity they have claimed for themselves. In most societies, bad things are blamed on the activity of witches who are assumed to be consciously looking to upset the peace in their communities. They are generally thought to be born with their spiritual power, which can put them under the control of spirits with a bent for destruction. For this same reason, they often become the scapegoats for unwanted developments and events, and rarely do the accused witches own up to the activities of which they are accused.

The proactive nature of African traditional religion has allowed it to blend relatively easily with imported religions. Whereas Christianity or Islam are seen as concerned primarily with the afterlife—ensuring one's place in heaven—traditional religion offers a means of affecting life on a daily basis through the local spirits. Even though both Christian and Muslim authorities oppose this syncretism, it nonetheless remains a reality across Africa. In West Africa, the *mori* men and marabouts blend Islamic mysticism with local traditions to offer spiritual services to the local communities. The arrival of marabouts and Islam to an area with predominantly traditional beliefs has not tended to discourage beliefs in the power of charms; rather, the traditional forms of divining were replaced by new ones based on the Quran (Bledsoe and Robey 1986: 209). Similarly, as Christianity spread with missionaries across central and southern Africa, particularly in the nineteenth and twentieth centuries, traditional practice was incorporated in church worship using the same types of songs and dance to offer prayer as had been used to communicate with indigenous gods and ancestors.[1] Spirit possession traditions have since found new expression in Christian movements that emphasize communion with the Holy Spirit and, in the other direction, some traditional cults now use the Bible for divination.

African Traditional Religion is in many ways highly practical. The endgame is more often the immediate impact on daily life than eternal salvation. The relationship between humanity and the supernatural is in some ways more equal than in religions such as Christianity or Islam, in the sense that practitioners do not have to settle for requesting assistance from spirits and gods—if they are good at their craft they have a chance of compelling them to intervene. However in most traditional religion on the continent, this ability to force the spirits' hands also opens up for potential trickery by spirits that resent being used for human purposes. As a result, most rituals are a bargaining process. While practitioners are attempting to convince a spirit to do their will, they offer incentives to do so, usually through sacrifice but also through the maintenance of taboos or prohibited behavior.

Power

The notion of power lies at the heart of the cosmology. In many ways, life is conceived of as a constant struggle for and balancing of power—between good and bad spirits, individuals in a family, community and state. Power is seen as something that is generally ambivalent and ambiguous. The power source and the use to which it is put can therefore be alternately positive or negative depending on the intent of the practitioner. The same power that can be used to inflict harm on an opponent can also be used to heal an ailment. This ambiguity extends further to turn what appears to be straightforward dichotomies of outcomes on their head. For example, the use of spirit power (*ashe*) to help an ambitious person enhance his or her position can be seen by the wider community as constructive if the person is thought to benefit the community, while the same power can also be used to curb people who are thought to be overly ambitious and disruptive to community good (Geschiere 1997). In a similar manner, the healing provided by spirits in northern Uganda included an act of retaliation against the aggressor that had caused the suffering in the first place, which could lead to his or her death (Behrend 1999). This ambiguity makes the use of spirit power a malleable tool for addressing personal and communal concerns, although it also creates ample room for challenges by people with a different view of what constitutes a destructive or constructive agenda.

Power is both spiritual and material and often explicitly so. Spiritual power is assumed to lead to material power—political influence and wealth. In some cultures, this link is made even more explicit in that the spiritually powerful are assumed to have a physical substance in their body that houses the spiritual power.[2] This has led to idioms of "power being eaten" across the continent. It is also reflected in the many rituals that involve the ingestion of herbs and potions or carrying them in pouches and amulets. In wartime, this same imagery has been taken to an extreme in human sacrifice and cannibalism. Overall, spirit power is assumed to permeate the material world, which makes this world both something to be wary of and something that can be used in interactions with the spirits.

The intimate connection between material and spiritual power has meant that those in positions of power are assumed to have gained these positions at least in part through spiritual prowess—whether traditional, Christian, or Muslim. Poor leadership and good leadership alike are explained with reference to the way the leaders have used their spiritual power. This does not mean that natural explanations—whether scientific or social—are discarded altogether, but they are placed in the context of the invisible world of spiritual power. Spirit power is assumed to give the impetus for worldly activity. For example, many would recognize that HIV/AIDS is caused by a virus but would point to the spirit world to explain why a certain person was infected at a certain time (Stadler, 2003). This understanding of causation also opens up for redress—if the underlying cause can be identified it can be addressed to revert the outcome.

Most societies in African use rituals to mark significant transitions in life as well as to effect change. For the former, rituals tend to accompany the transition from childhood to adulthood, marriage, births, and death. For the latter, rituals offer a means of inciting change of a particular kind, for example, to heal ailment or to ensure prosperity or wealth. Almost all rituals are physically tangible and involve the administering of potions, herbal remedies, or amulets alongside incantations, dancing, and prayers in various combinations. Some of these involve a sacrifice to thank, reward, or entreat the invisible world of spirits to intervene in the desired manner.

African Traditional Religion as a Driver of Violence

When looking at the role of religion in violence there are two main dimensions—the role of religion in inciting violence and its role in carrying out the violence.

Witchcraft and Witchcraft Accusations

Witchcraft is at the heart of most violence that can be said to be incited by African Traditional Religion. Accusations of witchcraft have become more common in conflict or postconflict countries in Africa where the strain of poverty and rebuilding lives and livelihoods shattered by war is most pronounced. Children, elderly people, and widows and widowers with no family left to protect them are often the most vulnerable to accusations of witchcraft. To the communities that accuse them, they offer an answer to why life is not improving despite the end of war. Although the accusations in recent years have tended to be led by revivalist Christian churches, for example, in the Democratic Republic of Congo and Angola, the belief and concept of a witch that they use is firmly traditional. Accusations leveled at children have attracted particular attention because of the often violent implications. The children are accused of knowingly and maliciously bringing harm to the community. But while the accusation is no dramatic departure from other settings, the means of redress through the new churches has tended to be much more violent than in most traditional religious contexts. In the new churches, exorcisms of the child witches often involve severe beatings and starvation and sometimes lead to the death of the child. Although adults are often more able to defend themselves, the administering of mob justice often involved in witchcraft cases can leave them equally vulnerable. In some instances, witches are simply executed by their accusers. An older woman in Tema, Ghana, was set on fire by a group of people accusing her of witchcraft, one of which was a pastor (BBC 2010). Incidents like this are becoming increasingly commonplace across sub-Saharan Africa. In contrast, "exorcisms" by traditional witch doctors or priests are often focused on ritual cleansing with a view to reintegrate the witch into the community. Of course, in many cases accused witches face mob justice when neither traditional nor church approaches to dealing with witchcraft are necessarily adhered to, often with even graver implications for the accused.

Whereas witch accusations are ultimately aimed at undoing the destructive magic caused by the suspected witchcraft, the power of witch doctors that is intended to provide this service sometimes requires destruction as well. Some of the medications and potions witch doctors provide require human body parts—some of which leave the donor dead. In smaller villages and communities, this type of magic and medicine has generally been tightly controlled but in the growing urban sprawls of many African countries today the relative ease of abducting victims for this purpose has led to an upswing in both supply and demand for this powerful magic. Although it is far from condoned by most practitioners of African Traditional Religion, most would nonetheless acknowledge the power of such medicines. This power, as much as the required death, is the reason these medicines are taboo, as their use is assumed to upset power balances dramatically.

War

Unlike some of the other world religions, however, African Traditional Religion has rarely been the cause (real or proclaimed) of wars. Because of the lack of central doctrine and, therefore, hierarchy and institutions, it has never become the powerful tool for state conquest that Christianity or Islam have become. Although traditional religious explanations for misfortune have helped legitimize the cause of many insurgent groups and aided their recruitment, this has tended to be on a smaller scale than state-sponsored warfare. In part, this is because of the cultural disconnect between most African states at a central level and the local authority structures within them—both during and after colonialism. The powerful African empires that reigned in East and West Africa prior to the arrival of colonizers from outside of course faced a different reality. Interestingly, however, the greatest of these empires (in reach and power) built their successes partly on their adoption of Christianity or Islam. In Ethiopia, the Aksumite Empire, while polytheistic, shared more religious traits with its neighbors on the Arabian Peninsula than those farther west and south, and its early adoption of Christianity became a core component of the identity of the empire as it spread across the Horn. The Malian Empire spread Islam through the Sahel region from the thirteenth through sixteenth centuries as rulers and traders gained access to the privileges associated with sharing the quickly spreading religion. Later, the Songhai Empire continued this tradition, also firmly grounded in Islam. Their wars of conquest were a combination of holy war to spread the faith and the extension of geographical power to support trade and the generation of wealth.

However, among the smaller empires and kingdoms, war was not imperial in outlook and rulers rarely sought to spread their power and influence far across the continent. Most wars were to settle grudges and disputes with neighboring kingdoms, to secure wealth through loot, or to avert threats from neighbors with similar ambitions. In the postcolonial period, these kingdoms had lost their power almost all across the continent, and the power to wage war had been limited to central governments or insurgent opposition. The secular ideologies that accompanied postcolonial governments made religious beliefs—whether traditional or otherwise—an awkward reference point, even for those that launched wars. However, in many cases, the reality beneath the secular surface was filled with traditional religious belief and practice. This can be seen most clearly in the civil wars that have afflicted the continent since colonialism but is also reflected in the approach taken for protection from crime in many African cities or even in domestic disputes.

Explaining misfortune is a key function served by African Traditional Religion. It is therefore only natural that political, economic, or social grievances will be related back to the spiritual world and that redress will be sought in part from it. In Zimbabwe, during the civil war in the 1970s, the rebel Zimbabwe African National Liberation Army (ZANLA) quickly learned that the way to gain the support of local populations was not to reference a secular socialist agenda but to present the group's cause with reference to local cosmology. When members entered Zimbabwe and sought to recruit from local communities, they were told to consult with the spirit mediums who would guide their strategy and whose blessing would give them access to prospective fighters (Lan 1985). The mediums accepted the insurgents, in part, because their struggle against the Rhodesian government resonated with local resentment of the collapse of traditional land rights and hierarchies but also because they fit within the local spiritual order: Some of the most prominent local ancestral spirits were warriors, and the newly arrived rebels could be given the authority of these spirits. This authority had previously been held by traditional chiefs, but as the chiefs became increasingly entangled with the Rhodesian state, the spirit mediums took over their authority in the eyes of many. As a result, when the war came, they were the ones able to bestow legitimacy on a cause. The mediums that represented the spirits of deceased chiefs (*mhondoro*) represented the authority and legitimacy of the respected chiefs of the past. This legitimacy they passed on to ZANLA guerrillas by naming them the successors of the mhondoro. With the aid of the mediums, the ZANLA fighters were therefore able to hold recruitment rallies at which they could explain their ideology and cause to local youth and bring them within their ranks.

By the time the insurgency of the Resistëncia Nacional Moçambicana (Renamo) was launched in Mozambique in the early 1990s, the traditional religions were the most potent in the country. Like ZANLA in Zimbabwe, Renamo therefore appealed to potential recruits on the basis of traditional religious beliefs. They denounced the government for suppressing traditional practitioners such as the *feiticeiros* (spirit mediums) and *curandeiros* (traditional healers) and blamed the drought of the early 1980s on the government's alienation of the ancestors. They explicitly said their struggle was "of the spirits" and "for the ancestors" (Weigert, 1995).

Similarly, in Uganda, the brief insurgency launched against the government of Yoweri Museveni in 1986 drew support from the Acholi population in northern Uganda by pointing to the need for a spiritual cleansing of the land to restore local peace and prosperity. The Holy Spirit Movement (HSM) and its armed wing the Holy Spirit Mobile Force (HSMF) blamed the social upheaval in the north on the sins committed by Acholi soldiers during the previous civil war (between the National Resistance Movement [NRA] and the Uganda National Liberation Army [UNLA] in 1981–1986), when they had been involved in killing civilians in the Luwero area farther south. When the soldiers returned home they failed to respect local traditions of cleansing following war, and as a result, the community was thought to be haunted by the vengeful spirits of the dead.[3] Alice Auma, a local Acholi spirit medium who channelled the spirit Lakwena (more commonly known as Alice Lakwena), organized the HSMF to wage war against the government and witches to redress the misfortunes brought on by this sin. Her rhetoric built on the spiritual tradition in northern Uganda that recognized spirits as responsible for misfortune and catastrophe but also as a power against disaster—a tradition echoed across the continent. It was a spiritual matter in need of spiritual remedy. For a population that had interpreted its misfortunes as a manifestation of witchcraft and mischievous spirits for some time, this rallying call engendered significant support (Behrend 1999).[4] However, while the HSMF came a long way on the power of their rhetoric alone (they marched almost all the way to the capital, Kampala, before being defeated), they had failed to combine their powerful cause with sufficient military capability—something subsequent rebel groups in northern Uganda tried hard to remedy. The most recent, the Lord's Resistance Army (LRA), that also claims spiritual legitimacy, has been the most long lived after more than twenty years of fighting. The LRA have shown that a spiritual agenda and rhetoric are not enough to win the support of a people. Their inability to win the support of key local leaders forced them to adopt a recruitment strategy reliant on abduction, which further alienated them from the community they claimed to be fighting for. As a result, they have come to be seen as using spiritual power for destructive rather than constructive purposes, just like the shunned but feared witches of most African societies.

African Traditional Religion as a Component of Violence

The proactive nature of access to spirit power in African Traditional Religion makes it eminently suitable for people looking to enhance their ability to compel others forcefully, whether in outright warfare or other types of violence. It offers a resource that can enhance power and strength with some immediacy. In contrast to religions that require long periods of prayer or even a lifetime of service to achieve rewards, African Traditional Religion generally offer the option of turning to a spiritual practitioner to gain access to spirit power, often as part of a simple financial transaction. This option has been exercised in almost all wars the continent has seen, and transactions to gain spiritual power regularly turn up also in smaller-scale violence, whether as part of criminal activity or political confrontations. The at times violent nature of rituals also means violence is visited on victims who fall prey to some spiritual practitioners. This has perhaps been most visibly illustrated by the high-profile cases of ritual killings of children in southern Africa but also beyond African shores in the United Kingdom.

As in any transaction, the more valuable the service or commodity is, the higher the price. Higher stakes, for example, amassing great wealth or winning political office, require more difficult and expensive rituals but often also costlier sacrifice. This has fueled trade in parts of rare animals as well as humans. While some animal and human body parts are widely acknowledged as being powerful ingredients for magic—notably hearts and livers but also bones and reproductive organs—others become sought after as a result of more short-lived trends. For example, in recent years, albinos in Tanzania and Kenya have been targeted for their body parts, especially their pale skin, believed to bring luck and offer potent ingredients for healers and witch doctors.

Yet while the powerful nature of human sacrifice is hardly ever in doubt in African Traditional Religion, it is equally widely acknowledged as a destructive form of spiritual practice and rarely condoned. Nonetheless, the market exists and especially in urban sprawls where the poor and vulnerable often go missing, the trade in human body parts is a reality. Some of these practices have been exported along with diaspora communities—initially with the slave trade to the Caribbean and more recently to Europe and North America. In Europe, the discovery of the torso of a young boy in London in 2001 shocked a community that believed ritual sacrifice had not been exported out of Africa.

The vast majority of sacrificial rituals, however, do not require human or even blood sacrifice. Nonetheless, the idea of the potency of blood rituals has fueled violent manifestations of traditional belief in conflict situations. Particularly during war when social control is loosened, the stakes are high and then the pursuit of power unchecked. But blood ritual also emerges in times of acute community distress or in the pursuit of great power and wealth.

In warfare, traditional religious practice offers a means of enhancing powers to fight, survive, and win. The practical nature of the belief system allows fighting parties to request specific types of power and protection from their priests and other spiritual practitioners, not unlike the requirements for designing offensive and defensive weapons.

Most commonly, fighters are offered protection from enemy fire and attack. This protection usually comes in the form of charms, amulets, and potions alongside behavioral rules and taboos that must be upheld. What has been given can therefore be taken away, which provides a strong incentive for fighters to uphold rules and maintain discipline.

Images of fighters covered in amulets and charms became prolific with the African civil wars of the 1980s and 1990s but are a reflection of a much longer tradition. It draws on a long tradition of warrior heroes and sacred warriors, which is part of the oral mythology of most African peoples and therefore a given point of reference for fighters. For example, the Malian warrior king Sundiata Keita (alternatively known as Sunjata) who founded the Malian Empire in the thirteenth century is also the central character of an epic that describes his rise to power through the assistance of spiritual power and objects, including a staff made from a sacred tree that allows the hunchbacked child Sundiata to stand up straight and walk (Janson 2001). Among the Dinka in southern Sudan, Aiwel Longar was the son of a water spirit and a human woman and through his power protected his warriors and founded the spear master tradition that still lives among the Dinka. In West Africa, the tradition of hunting societies in which the hunters drew on spiritual power to trap and kill animals in peacetime and enemies in times of war have become prototypes for more recent fighting groups. The Civil Defence Forces that emerged to counter the threat from rebels during the Sierra Leone civil war drew their imagery, identity, and practices from their traditional hunting societies. The traditional image of the hunter was of a man imbued with magic that allowed him to track and kill animals in the wild while surviving the tribulations of the forest. Because of their powers, these hunters were also the guardians of their communities who would return to protect their villages when external threats arose, cementing their identity as a hunter-warrior. When war broke out in 1991 and the government proved unable to counter the threat of the rebels, this tradition was reinvented to create a fighting force whose main purpose was to protect communities. Although these civil defence forces were a far cry from the hunter-warriors of local mythology they drew on the same spiritual traditions, albeit adapted to fit the challenges of the contemporary war (Wlodarczyk 2009). In a similar manner, LRA rebels in northern Uganda also drew on old traditions of ritualistic protection against death and injury to form part of their armor. The idea that warriors can be protected from death and injury through rituals and the application or ingestion of magical substances surfaces again throughout the continent, both in historical accounts of war and in contemporary conflicts.

The ways in which protective magic has been used in the wars of the last twenty years is not necessarily the same as they would have been a century ago. As political and traditional power structures have been renegotiated—some violently and some not—first in the colonial and then the postcolonial period, traditions have also changed. In wars in which the challenge of traditional authority lay at the heart of the conflict, this meant the rituals and spiritual means employed to fight the war also had to be reinvented to fit the agenda of the fighters. For example, in Sierra Leone, the Revolutionary United Front (RUF) rebels that took on the government in 1991 in what would be a decade long war explicitly opposed the power hierarchies of the existing elites as well as the traditional deference to elders. The youth that made up the bulk of the rebel force sought to overturn this order and therefore would have struggled to rely on the very beliefs and practices that represented that order. Nonetheless, whereas they may not have believed in the political system or even some of the rituals and practices of their communities, they believed in the power of the invisible spirit world. The result was a syncretic blend of new, secular rituals that echoed the old spiritual ones and an ambivalent attitude toward the potency of spirit power. In most Sierra Leonean communities outside the capital, initiation into traditional secret societies provides the transition from childhood to adulthood, usually through a time of seclusion in the forest along with other initiates and shared trials—physical and psychological—alongside teachings about the responsibilities and realities of being an adult. Initiation is steeped in ritual and presided over by those with spiritual power. The RUF, opposed to the hierarchies of the secret societies, nonetheless ended up closely mimicking the process of initiation for their own recruits to mark the transition from civilian to fighter. They secluded new recruits from the group and made them go through ritualistic trials and hardship as well as listen to preaching on the rebel cause (Richards 2006). Similarly, they derided the power of priests and witch doctors while at the same time claiming that their own leader possessed the ability to fly and to gather intelligence through the air across vast distances. This reflects the deeply engrained belief in an invisible and powerful spirit world, even among those who look to counter or reject parts of it.

In the same way, the Frelimo government forces in Mozambique ridiculed the Renamo reliance on witch doctors to enhance the power of their fighters but ended up employing the same tactics as the war dragged on and Renamo proved both persistent and powerful. In one instance, Frelimo managed to capture an important pro-Renamo medium and displayed him around a government-held town as a morale booster. They also described the capture of the medium as the result of spiritual might— a Frelimo soldier had supposedly gone into a Renamo camp protected by magic that allowed him to abduct the medium unseen (Wilson 1992; West 1997).

The attraction of incorporating spiritual practice in warfare is twofold. In a context in which belief in the existence of supernatural power is almost always a given, attempting to access that power in times of need is a logical choice. The fact that this belief is shared, usually across enemy lines, also makes it a powerful signal to the enemy, especially through the visible display of amulets and charms but also through the spreading of rumors. For example, Renamo would tell battle stories that interpreted the group's successes through a spiritual lens, which both raised the spirits of their own troops and intimidated Frelimo fighters.

Conclusion

African traditional religious practice is as much a reflection of the social dynamics in a given country or community as it is a frame of reference and source of power for the members of that community. The beliefs offer a means of engaging with the world that has the added edge of spirit power. But the ends to which it is directed is usually dictated by the concerns of the material world. This has made it at times a violent practice and at others a promoter of peace. Perhaps more so than other religions, African traditional beliefs put the onus of morality primarily on the practitioner. It provides the tools for shaping the world without clear moral guidelines for their appropriate use. Of course as in most communities, these guidelines have also emerged but not always as a direct result of religious authority.

A proliferation of news stories and images from across Africa of persecuted albino communities, victims of ritual sacrifice, or magically empowered rebels might give the impression that traditional religion and violence are more intertwined than ever. While the religion has not become more violent or changed in scope, social pressures and circumstances have pushed forward the more extreme features of the belief system. As the challenges become greater—whether as a result of political upheaval, poverty, or disease—the means for overcoming them also become more severe.

Notes

1. This is still the case with many "Zionist" churches in southern Africa, for example, the Marange church in Zimbabwe or the Harris churches in Côte d'Ivoire.
2. This belief exists in communities across the continent and has been documented by Peter Geschiere in Cameroon, Evans-Pritchard among the Azande in Ghana, Joseph Tonda in Gabon and the Republic of Congo among many others. In each setting, this "witch substance" is referred to by a different name—*djambe* among the Maka in Cameroon, *mangu* among the Azande, and *ikundu* among the Mbochi in Congo—but is always understood as a physical substance that gives its host power.
3. Luwero is the area in the south where some of the worst atrocities were committed during the war between the UNLA that dislodged Idi Amin in 1979 and the NRA of Yoweri Museveni that took power in 1985, the perpetration of which was associated with the Acholi because of their prominent presence in the UNLA.
4. In this case, witchcraft was seen as the destructive practices inspired by bad spirits, and increasingly polarized by the Christian framework that was used by the HSM.

Bibliography

Behrend, Heike. "Power to Heal, Power to Kill, Spirit Possession and War in Northern Uganda." In H. Behrend and U. Luig (eds.), *Spirit Possession: Modernity and Power in Africa*, 20–33. Oxford, UK: James Currey, 1999.

Bledsoe, C. H. and K. M. Robey. "Arabic Literacy and Secrecy among the Mende of Sierra Leone." *Man*, new series, 21.2 (June 1986): 202–226.

Geschiere, Peter. *The Modernity of Witchcraft: Politics and the Occult in Postcolonial Africa*. Charlottesville: University Press of Virginia, 1997.

Janson, Jan. "The Sunjata Epic—The Ultimate Version." *Research in African Literatures*, 32.1 (Spring 2001): 14–46.

Lan, David. *Guns and Rain: Guerillas and Spirit Mediums in Zimbabwe*. London: James Currey, 1985.

Lugira, Aloysius. *African Traditional Religion*. New York: Chelsea House, 2009.

Parinder, Geoffrey. *African Mythology*. London: Paul Hamlyn, 1969.

Richards, Paul. "The Emotions at War: Atrocity as Piacular Rite in Sierra Leone." In A. Treacher, et al. (eds.), *Public Emotions*, 62–84. London: Palgrave Macmillan, 2006.

"Shock in Ghana over Gruesome Death of 'Witch.'" *BBC News*, 26 November 2010 (http://www.bbc.co.uk/news/world-africa-11848536).

Stadler, Jonathan. "Rumor, Gossip and Blame: Implications for HIV/AIDS Prevention in the South African Lowveld." *AIDS Education and Prevention*, 15.4 (2003): 357–368.

Tonda, Joseph. *Le Souverain moderne. Le corps du pouvoir en Afrique Centrale (Congo, Gabon)*. Paris: Karthala, 2005.

Weigert, Stephen. *Traditional Religion and Guerrilla Warfare in Modern Africa*. London: Macmillan, 1995.

West, Harry G. "Creative Destruction and Sorcery of Construction: Power, Hope and Suspicion in Post-War Mozambique." *Cahiers d'études Africaines*, XXXVIII, 147.3 (1997): 675–698.

Wilson, K. B. "Cults of Violence and Counter-Violence in Mozambique." *Journal of Southern African Studies*, 18.3 (1992): 527–582.

Wlodarczyk, Nathalie. *Magic and Warfare: Appearance and Reality in Contemporary African Conflict and Beyond*. New York: Palgrave, 2009.

Chapter 8

Religion and Violence in
Pacific Island Societies

Andrew Strathern and Pamela J. Stewart

THE PACIFIC OVERALL is a broad region, encompassing many historical and cultural variations, reflecting waves of prehistoric migrations and vicissitudes of colonial and postcolonial experience. Polynesia, Micronesia, and many parts of what has conventionally been called Melanesia (i.e., the southwest Pacific, see Strathern and Stewart 2002) were colonized by speakers of the vast Austronesian set of languages (see Blust 2009) and tend to be characterized by systems of rank and chiefship. Much greater cultural and linguistic diversity is found among older strata of populations, in which forms of nonchiefly leadership predominate. Where there is rank, there tend also to be gradations of ranked deity figures; where rank is absent or weakly developed, rituals center on ancestral spirits and spirits of the landscape with power over fertility. In all of these regions, deities and spirits are traditionally invoked in major concerns of social life, both integrative within the group and involving hostility toward others or in the mediation of intergroup relations. (For detailed accounts, see A. Strathern, Pamela J. Stewart, et al. 2002.)

The title of this chapter juxtaposes religion and violence, suggesting an exploration of relationships between these two categories. Our major purpose is to illustrate some of the complexities of these relationships in regard to materials from Pacific Islands ethnographies. Our perspective on these materials is holistic: If violence seems at times to be supported by religion, at other times religion is equally involved in supporting nonviolence or the production of peace. Ritual action is also frequently called into play in Pacific Island cultures to produce mock forms of violence, symbolic displays of strength that may lead to outright conflict but may equally lead to the avoidance of physical harm while expressing the ambivalence of social relations or a potential threat (epideictic displays as Rappaport 1967 put it). Sorcery, however, should be interpreted somewhat differently. If people suffer misfortunes, become ill, or die, this may be attributed to sorcery, which can be interpreted as a deflection of immediate physical violence into mediated forms of aggression utilizing symbolic projections of hostility and harm. The hermeneutics of sorcery and sorcery accusations, thus, are different from those surrounding immediate acts of physical harm. With sorcery, people's aims may be to trace back from the misfortune to its possible cause in hostile sorcery; with physically observed harm, this process is unnecessary, because the cause is generally known (other than in cases in which wounded bodies are discovered after their death and the killers are not known). Sorcery has to be considered as a part of the whole complex of ritual activities and their place in the control of social relations. For example, killings in physical conflict may provoke demands for compensation, may issue in revenge killings, or the protagonists may turn to secret forms of sorcery to pursue vengeance in a way that is less risky than open combat; and the "ghosts" of the dead may be brought into play in any of these contexts. Hostility can also be deflected into rhetorical speeches, in which issues are discussed in a coded way so as to avoid inciting further physical violence. Or, equally, language may be used as a venue for escalating conflict (Brenneis and Myers 1991, originally published 1984; see also, for subtle extensions of this perspective, Kitts 2010 and Noegel 2010). In general, in a processual analysis, violence and peacemaking may alternate over time, and religious and ritual practices can be called into play at specific moments of transformations in relationships between networks of groups.

We further recognize that violent acts can occur in many contexts, for example, in networks of kin or spousal relations. In these, religion as such may initially play no special part. However, in processes of reparation or in the "mystical" understandings of the disruption caused by such events, religious notions certainly may enter in. A central cultural concept for the Mount Hagen people of Papua New Guinea is the notion of *popokl* or "anger" (see Strathern and Stewart 2010) that can lead people to commit violent acts, either legitimately or otherwise, depending on the perspective adopted. It can also be a mark of a person's dissatisfaction with a current state of affairs and can make persons ill, so that their grievances must be attended to if they are to recover their health. Where popokl drives people to take revenge, it is said to be accompanied by the popokl of the ghost of the kinsperson who was killed by enemies. Within the domestic group, the illness that a person experiences may be interpreted by kin as a result of their popokl, which must then be revealed and steps taken to deal with its causes: In this case, also, the ghosts are thought traditionally to be involved, because it is they who may be implicated in causing sickness to afflict their living relatives. In a third scenario, the person may have done wrong, perhaps simply the wrong of not sacrificing to the ancestral ghosts of the dead. In this instance, the ghosts/ancestors are traditionally said to withdraw their protection and to allow wild spirits of the bush (*tipu rōmi*) to break through the fence of that protection and make the victim ill. In all of these instances, it is evident that religion is centrally involved. (These scenarios have changed with the advent of Christianity from the 1930s onward, but the basic ideas remain relevant.)

Because our aim is to illustrate and explore processes to show the intertwining of religion, violence, and other social practices, we do not aim at any kind of encyclopedic coverage of Pacific societies. The cases we examine can, however, be considered as more or less paradigmatic, using this term in the sense introduced by Meyer Fortes in his work on the comparative study of kinship systems (Fortes 1969). Our plan in the chapter, then, is to examine a few cases in some detail, while giving an idea of parallels and variant complexities in other ethnographic contexts.

Another analytical point needs to be made at the outset. All Pacific societies depended on some kind of social context in which peaceful relations were maintained. The elementary form of this context was expressed by Peter Lawrence with his reference to the "security circle" among the Garia people of Madang Province in Papua New Guinea (Lawrence 1971). Within the security circle, ritual practices are likely to be supportive of the maintenance of co-operation and reciprocity between people. Outside this circle, not only may hostile relations enter or prevail, but the same religious forces that help to maintain peace inside the circle may be brought into play in the production of violent action. When this is so, the violence involved is no longer of contested legitimacy among the people but is regarded as legitimate. War is the context in which violence is redefined in this way, by those involved, and is then said to legitimize violence, perhaps even as a way subsequently to produce peace through domination, incorporation, or grudging coexistence.

There is a considerable difference in this regard between societies without a centralized chiefship and those in which chiefs and kings or queens emerged at the centers of protostates, often with specialized warriors or armies. Somewhat paradoxically, it may be that the chiefless societies, conventionally portrayed as "without rulers" or even "anarchic," have historically equipped themselves better for peacemaking, largely because they are not geared to the achievement of long-term domination over one another. Centralization of power may bring peace at the center and strife at the peripheries (see Ferguson and Whitehead 1992): strife that over time may reach back into the centers themselves. These considerations are pertinent to the cases we will examine, especially with regard to the Fijian polity of Bau. Finally, here, within the security circle, however it is defined, in structural or situational ways, there is an ethic of settling disputes primarily by elaborate sessions of talk rather than by hasty recourse to physical violence. This is the arena pinpointed by the editors of and numerous contributors to the volume *Disentangling: Conflict Discourse in Pacific Societies* (Watson-Gegeo and White eds. 1990). The term *disentangling* aptly points to the complex unravellings of causes of a dispute and possible ways to settle it. Ritual practices and religious notions may be involved, and it is perhaps particularly here that Christianity has been able to slot into the roles of previous indigenous customs. Thus Boggs and Chun, in their discussion of contemporary Hawaiian disentangling, note that the leader, in handling a dispute, conducts opening prayers and lessons read from the Bible. Boggs and Chun suggest that the leader's role is reminiscent of the *mana* or ritual power of persons to whom suppliants could appeal as refugees (Boggs and Chun 1990: 128). At the same time, Boggs and Chun make it clear that, at the level of practice, a great deal of careful management and assessment has to be conducted by leaders, if disentangling is to be successful. While *mana* is conceptualized as an external and spiritual force, practical abilities feed into it.

Fiji: Hegemony and Its Limits

Marshall Sahlins (2004), basing his analyses partly on the extensive earlier work of A. M. Hocart (e.g., 1927, 1952), has produced an interpretation of the rise and fall of the influence of different rulers in the tiny island of Bau in Fiji. The Bau chiefs extended their hegemony over a wide area through maritime activity, both by trade (or tribute) and warfare culminating in struggles with Rewa during the 1840s (Sahlins 2004: 27). A complex cosmological history underlay the rise of Bau. Common to all chiefly systems in Fiji, there is a division between war chiefs and sacred rulers of the land (the Roko Tui). Usually, the Roko Tui was considered superior to the war chief, but in Bau this situation was reversed (Sahlins 2004: 27).

The rulers had also moved to Bau from the mainland of Viti Levu nearby, creating it as an offshore fortress, after one sacred Roko Tui was assassinated. In Fiji, also, the sacred rulers of the land are usually thought of as autochthons, but in Bau the tradition was that it was the sea people (*kai wai* in Fijian) who first settled it and remained its "owners" (Sahlins, 33). Many of these original sea people had also been subsequently sent out to colonize other areas of eastern Fiji and they retained their allegiance to Bau, bringing in tribute. One of the valued items brought in such tribute was sperm whale teeth (*tabua*), which Sahlins characterized as "the most valuable of all valuables" (34).

Tabua were sacred. Sahlins goes on: "Presented as binding proposals of marriage and assassination, as offerings to gods and chiefs, or in return for providing cannibal victims, the whale tooth" (34) was the equivalent of a human life. It was thus used in the same way pearl shells and pigs were in the Papua New Guinea highlands: They were also the equivalents of a human life. The implications of such a cultural feature are twofold. These kinds of valuables, at the apex of a hierarchy of values, could be used equally as instruments of destruction or as the means of making peace. In the case of Bau, its history took a turn to warfare (in the 1840s), partly because of Bau's control over colonial trade and the introduction of guns (Sahlins, 35). Tabua and other goods could be used to recruit allies. The Bau warriors were contracted to aid their allies among the Cakaudrove people by attacking the people of Natewa. They did so but took great tribute from the Cakaudrove people in the course of this process. Sahlins comments further that Bau's domination of the sea brought them into a politics of wealth and enabled them to bring down Rewa, a "traditional" polity based on the superiority of the land chiefs. The rulers in Bau were the Vunivalu, a name that translates as "the roots of war" (Sahlins, 60), and the war chiefs were seen as active in outside activities, while the sacred land chiefs or Roko Tui were portrayed as "sitting" and receiving wealth from outside. Both war chief and land chief had aspects of divinity. Of the Vunivalu, Sahlins notes that "as the procurer of human sacrifices by acts of transcendent violence, this 'God of War' was in some respects the more terrible of the two" (60). The land chief, on the other hand, was the one who was seen as "the ritual fount of its well-being" (61). It would be the land chief who made peace in internal conflicts, no doubt (compare Sahlins 1962: 289–362).

Over time and perhaps influenced by the British colonial policy of identifying a single chief rather than a complex diarchy such as existed in

Bau, the position of the Roko Tui became further sacralized into that of a "sacred king," served by his subjects with his seat of power seen as the center of the kingdom, surrounded by a series of concentric circles marking greater or lesser proximity to the ritual center. This concentric empire was sustained not by the land people of the king but by the sea people of the Vunivalu, or war chief (Sahlins, 2004: 64), who were accepted as the "owners" of Bau Island, and were fierce warriors and procurers of victims (ibid.). Sahlins comments that Bauan power "depended not a little on a reputation for terror" (ibid.). Over time the Roko Tui of Bau was driven out by the Vunivalu, who installed one of their own as the new king (65) and ushered in the time of Cakobau, a noted military leader, whom Sahlins describes as "the master of the extensive Bauan imperial order" (Sahlins 2004: 269).

The longer-term history of Bau, which Sahlins delves into in great detail, involves fratricidal conflicts between older and younger brothers; the interstitial roles of the *vasu*, or sister's sons, within intermarrying dynasties; and a violent, protracted conflict between Bau and the kingdom of Rewa. This conflict ended with Cakobau's victory over his enemies, and his proclamation as Tui Viti, king of all Fiji, by the British in 1844, combined with his extraordinary conversion to Christianity that entailed the conversion of his followers as well, and the later cession of Fiji to British power in 1874 (Sahlins 2004: 289). It might seem that this conversion marked a new way of establishing peace under a Pax Britannica; but in some ways, it also ushered in a new arena of ritual conflict, because the defeated kingdom of Rewa espoused Catholicism, whereas Cakobau converted to Methodism (Sahlins 2004: 290).

It is clear, at any rate, from this brief account, that both war chiefs and land chiefs were considered legitimate because of the ritual and cosmological underpinnings that supported their power. The values of peace and war were ideally held in balance in the divisions of power, but this ideal balance could easily be subverted by specialisms of imperial-style trade and warmaking. Bau reached the apex of its imperialism in the persona of Cakobau, but the arenas of power were further transformed by Cakobau's conversion to Methodism and the entry of British sovereign power and the plantation economy the British brought with them. In theoretical terms, we see here that religion, violence, and peacemaking are all bound together. But, while tabua (whale's teeth) were supreme valuables like the pearl shells of the Papua New Guinea highlands, it is less clear that they were used for compensation payments to make peace as pearl shells and pigs were in Papua New Guinea: The cultural register may be the same, but social practices may differ.

Bellona: The Dominance and Demise of Revenge

Another domain in which this observation applies is the ideology and practice of revenge (see, e.g., Stewart and Strathern 2002a: 108–136). An ideology or a requirement of revenge is built into the expectations of many peoples with autonomous kin groups that enter into violent conflict with one another. Unchecked, such an ideology can lead to unending chains of killings and counterkillings, and these are prototypically underpinned by the notion that it is the spirits of the dead kinsfolk who look to their living kin to avenge their deaths, on pain of their suffering the effects of ghostly displeasure. Obviously, such a process of ongoing violence is at least partly based in religious and ritual ideas. However, in practice, limitations are usually placed on killings, either by peaceful compensation payments or at least by a recognition that the scores are, for the time being, equal between the opposed groups. In the Papua New Guinea highlands, arrangements for compensation are highly elaborate and, historically, have led to extended sequences of exchanges that replace overt hostilities with ostensibly friendly competitive displays and disbursements of wealth. This microevolution from enchained killings to competitive exchange is most clearly exhibited among groups with strong clans, aspiring leaders known in the literature as "big-men," and intensive systems of agricultural production that enable the multiplication of pig populations that enter the arenas of exchange as prime forms of wealth along with shell valuables and, subsequently, state monetary forms (e.g., Strathern and Stewart 1999, 2000; Stewart and Strathern 2002b). Such an evolution is strongly marked in these highlands societies. A contrasting case from Bellona Island, an outlying Polynesian-settled area belonging politically to the Solomon Islands in the southwestern Pacific, provides a different picture (Kuschel 1988). Kuschel's analysis begins with the imputed first arrival of immigrants on this small island and ends in oral histories up to the year 1938, when Christian missionaries brought about the demise of much Bellonese indigenous culture and, with it, a considerable decrease in revenge homicides.

Bellonese genealogies of settlement apparently reached twenty-four generations (approx. five hundred years), in some cases, by 1938 (Kuschel 1988: 15, 40), although knowledge was lacking in detail about the first eight to ten generations (ibid.). Oral traditions suggest that the people arrived from Uvea in the Loyalty Islands and found an earlier people, the *hiti*, living on Bellona. Later, the immigrants exterminated the hiti in revenge for the killing of a relative (47). Slash-and-burn horticulture was practiced, with yams, taro, and bananas, and later sweet potato (54). Fishing was also important. The island was affected regularly by hurricanes. Land was held by a small number of patrilineal clans, reduced at the time of Kuschel's fieldwork (1968 onward) to only two clan groups (56). Separate subclans of an original clan could intermarry (60), and this fact seems to be connected with hostilities between groups that emerged in this way (ibid.).

One subclan was forced to become largely endogamous as a result of hostilities with others over revenge killings (61). Lineages were recognized subgroups within the subclan, controlling land and inheritance among males.

A review of kinship relations and social organization offers some clues as to why revenge killings were an endemic feature of life on Bellona. Affinal relations, especially between brothers-in-law, were polite but prickly. Marriages were entered into in a relatively simple way, and divorces were common, although mostly in earlier years of a marriage. Affines were expected to present each other with gifts and hold feasts in honor of each other. However, in one instance, a man killed his sister's husband over a slight: When he arrived at the husband's settlement, he had not been properly greeted. On the other hand, in a manner classic for many patrilineal systems, the exclusiveness of lineage ties was broken by the importance of warm and supportive ties between mother's brothers and sister's sons. Kinship ties were cross-cut by status differences, but social stratification was not elaborate. There was a distinction between persons of high status, ordinary status ("commoners" in Kuschels's usage), and low status. Kuschel seems to apply these terms largely but not exclusively to classify men. High-status men were called *hakahua*, and their position was gained by a combination of advantages of birth, such as descent from a line of original immigrants (i.e., rights of precedence), and personal achievements of character and generosity in giving feasts. The latter criterion aligns the hakahua as much with the New Guinea "big-man" type of leaders as with the ideal-typical Polynesian chief. Low-status men (76) were also like their counterparts in the Papua New Guinea highlands: They were dependants who could be ordered to do things, as others could not, and were thus the equivalent of those called *kintmant* ("workers/servants") in Mount Hagen (see numerous references in A. J. Strathern 1972 to "rubbish-men"). Status rivalry between brothers was frequent, leading to endless quarrels and, even if rarely, it could result in homicide.

All activities were considered to be dependent on the deities and ancestors. There were minor rituals to deal with the spirits of the original hiti inhabitants of Bellona (79). Bush spirits, *'apai*, were blamed for otherwise unaccountable misfortunes. The sky gods and goddesses were the most powerful and were held "to assist the fighters, to localize, and kill their enemies" (82) and to protect them against harm. District gods, on the other hand, had more peaceful functions, helping people to gain children and to intercede with the sky gods (ibid.). The multiplication of district gods, Kuschel suggests, reflects the fragmentation of political identities over time as the population on Bellona increased after the arrival of the first immigrants (ibid.). However, district gods could not be mobilized for hostile purposes. Living men, on the other hand, sometimes predicted what they planned to do as ancestors, including taking vengeance for killings. High-status men and also women acted as mediums, interpreting putative statements from the district gods or ancestors. The rituals of great feasts brought together the deities, spirits, and living kin and affines (84). Ignoring kinsfolk at such a distribution was a cause of trouble and could lead to killings (84).

Physical acts of violence were not the only means by which vengeance killings could take place. *Kuba* sorcery rituals could be conducted against the *ma'ungi* or spirit of a victim (life force, comparable to the Duna tini in the Southern Highlands Province of Papua New Guinea; see Stewart and Strathern 2005: 35–47). This sorcery ritual requested a sky god to take the person's ma'ungi away and hide it in a sacred (*tapu*) place (84). An object or a small canoe replica with a figure inside could stand for the intended victim (86), and a formula was pronounced, addressing the deity whose assistance was solicited. The sorcerous act is really, therefore, a request to a powerful deity rather than a straightforward magical act; but it is not clear under what political circumstances redress via kuba, rather than a direct killing, might be chosen. In one case given, the intended victim had gone away elsewhere, to Rennell Island, and her offence was simply to have rejected the man making kuba against her for marriage. She might be hard to kill, then, and the grievance would not have been one that would justify vengeance between lineages. (See further below, on kuba.)

What this and other details make clear is the immense importance of senses of honor, shame, rivalry, and envy that are cited as motivations for

action on Bellona. Such an ethos fits well with a stress on revenge killing. Kuschel begins his chapter 4, on disputes, with the statement that
"Bellonese society has been in a constant state of strife and controversy"
(102). Offenses are not forgotten and are made worse by verbal invective.
Kuschel refers appositely to a Samoan proverb that makes the same point:
"stones decay, but words last" (104). Cutting down valued coconut trees
or destroying a canoe could end in retaliatory killings because these acts
were symbolic equivalents of killing a man's sons. Atonement gifts could
be made to halt escalation. Verbal abuse would heighten conflict and
could be followed by threats of killing (104). Physical fighting could be
accompanied by kuba rituals, Kuschel notes, so this negates the idea that
kuba was only used as a safety device against physical violence. Disputes
often occurred over the use of land. In marital disputes, a woman could
insult or curse her husband, in some cases inducing suicide. A lineage
could split over quarrels, making it vulnerable to enemies (109). People
might try to move to a new settlement or go to nearby Rennell for a while,
to let things cool down. Conflicts were inhibited generally by close kin ties;
but Kuschel notes that every "conflict contained the germ of protracted
disputes which could eventually mean the end of an individual, a family, a
lineage or a clan" (110).

Revenge killings had to be open and carried out by raiding parties,
mostly agnatic male kin, under leaders, for the occasion. They were accompanied by rituals (including kuba ritual) with appeals to the sky gods to
weaken the ma'ungi of the intended victim. The raid was carried out in
stealth but was followed by the overt performance of victory songs at the
leader's settlement. Weapons used were dedicated to the sky gods. A man's
district gods or ancestors might warn him of danger by means of omens
(118). When the killing was carried out, the killer was supposed to tell the
victim the reason for it, and these performative statements passed into
oral traditions (120). Secret killings were despised. Killing, therefore, was
a matter of honor. Sometimes a dead body was mutilated as a mark of
dishonoring it; but skulls were not taken as trophies (121).

The victors in a raid retired to a hillock where they continued to sing
their songs of the killing for a few days. Hillocks were considered sacro-
sanct. Presumably intended victims could take temporary safe refuge
there too. The raiders later destroyed their victim's settlement and ritual
possessions. Women kinsfolk of the victim then began mourning, and
the body was given burial according to status: For example, a high-status
man's corpse was rubbed with turmeric (132). Some mourners maintained

prohibitions on eating any favorite food of the deceased for some months after the funeral. (The same practice held in Hagen: Such customs are the obverse of those emotions of hatred that informed killings.) Memories were held onto; vengeance might be delayed, but it would usually be attempted, sooner or later.

There were peacemaking rituals (144). These were stimulated by a kind of necessity. Both the raiders and the kin of the victims would live in isolation in bush areas until peacemaking was instituted. Women, or men related to both sides, could be the messengers for peace. Women were never killed in feuds, an important fact surely (144). If a peace proposal was accepted, the surviving kin of the victim went to the raiders' settlement, and later the visit was reciprocated. Preparations were then made for a feast. For the occasion, the victim's close male kin rubbed charcoal on their skin, and their leader put special gifts on his head (a special paddle, mat, and flying fox teeth), carrying these to the event. The leader made an opening speech and abased himself before the raid leader, who then wiped charcoal off the other's eyes and declared that he embraced the backside of his former enemies to finish their conflict (147). A speech maker then sprinkled coconut water sacred to the sky god and made a reconciliation speech, citing the coconut as a marker of peace. The raid leader responded, suggesting that in the past the groups had been friendly. A feast and dancing followed, and a few days later the sequence was repeated at the settlement of the victim's kin.

Peacemaking rituals, therefore, were practiced, and the same sky gods appealed to for assistance in killing presided over the rituals that brought about peace. Case histories show, nevertheless, that killings could start up again later between the same groups (Kuschel, chapter 7). Further, vengeance raids also took place between Bellona and Rennell Island (170). One of the factors that both perpetuated and to some extent contained these blood feuds was that strong rules governed who could legitimately be killed. For instance, retribution was limited to the members of the original raiding group and its lineage agnates. One's own close kin should not be killed, nor should any women (223, cf. 61). The range of killing and, therefore, the potential for feud to escalate into warfare was thus restricted. But it was difficult to preempt or circumvent a feuding process once it was set in hand, because there were no overarching authorities and no mediating roles between groups outside the periodic peace rituals. Marital alliances that linked high-status men together could eventuate in peacemaking between them; but high-status men were also involved in the protection of honor though killings. Only Christian mission teachings and the fear of government punishment eventually brought the feuding to a close in 1938. Reliance on government could come to replace self-reliance, the only principle on which agnatic groups had previously been able to operate. The injunction of the Christian God, "Thou shalt not kill," was able perhaps to supersede the earlier sky god's double favoring of both vengeance and peacemaking, because government and mission were seen as working together; and, Kuschel adds, punishment for killers involved exile in distant Honiara, the capital of the Solomons—something more terrifying, it seems, than living a life at home faced by the risk of being killed by those one knew quite well.

The conclusion from this Bellonese case is that the ideology of honor drove the pattern of vengeance killings; that this ideology primarily pertained to men and their agnatic kin; that it was supported by appeals to gods and ancestors, although some of these figures could equally be appealed to for protection from harm; that peace rituals were also presided over by the deities and eventually replaced after 1938 by the injunctions of the Christian God and the British district commissioner; and, finally, that peace rituals did not produce permanent effects nor did they involve any clear element of compensation payments such as are found in the New Guinea cases to be considered next. Instead, in keeping with the intensely emotional small-scale and intimate social relations involved, they involved the ritual reversal of the emotional markers of hatred and disrespect into marks of reconciliation and amity. Without this, nothing could have stopped the Bellonese men from simply annihilating one another to the point of extinction, as happened to some kin groups. Nothing could better demonstrate the importance of religion and its ritual enactments for preserving a see-saw balance between violence and peaceful co-existence. We see here also the "capstone" effect that British colonial control brought with it, just as we saw earlier for the case of Fiji, where the predatory and religiously sanctioned preeminence of Bau was brought both to its culmination and its end by the agency of Cakobau and his final conversion to Methodism.

Mount Hagen, Papua New Guinea: Cycles of Exchange

Materials on exchange and sacrifice in the Mount Hagen area of the Western Highlands Province in Papua New Guinea clearly fit our general argument in this essay, that religion is brought into play both in the cause of violent actions and in peacemaking activities, in each case because it provides an overarching and taken-for-granted legitimacy and motivation for actions. In the Fijian case, we have seen that there was an assumed balance between the powers of war and peace, a balance that was sub-verted in the case of Bau. We have seen also that valuables were used to pay allies in war but without, apparently, a complementary context of peacemaking. Finally, British centralized control and Cakobau's conver-sion to Methodism superseded the terms of the older political structures. In Bellona, feuds between small lineages were endemic, fueled by an ethos of honor, shame and revenge that impinged differently on men since women were not killed in feuds. Peace ceremonies were held in which there was a ritual rebalancing of relations, but wealth items, again, were not directly employed to make compensations for deaths. When we come to the context of the New Guinea highlands, however, we find that the life-giving and life-replacing power of valuables, given in compensa-tion payments, is clearly and forcefully brought into play. This power was embedded in sequential processes of exchanges that implicated genera-tive acts of killings as well as regenerative acts of compensation and the re-creation of positive ties.

The argument can be presented here in a relatively brief form because we have written about these themes extensively in earlier publications. The ethnographic focus is on Mount Hagen, in the western highlands of Papua New Guinea.

Australian explorers first entered these highlands areas in the early 1930s, followed closely by Catholic and Lutheran missionaries. Admin-istrative control and "pacification" proceeded through the 1950s, and national political independence was granted in 1975. Exchange practices of the kind we discuss here date back to precolonial times, with a complex history of expansion in the 1960s and turbulent experiences of change since the 1970s. Our account picks out important enduring features.

For the overall analysis, it is important to highlight the relationship between exchange and sacrifice (see Stewart and Strathern eds. 2008, especially our introduction and chapter 9). If we take a processual look at how acts of killing in Hagen could gradually be transformed into acts of positive alliance, we will see how sacrifice enters at different moments of the process involved.

In precolonial times, a death of a man caused by physical violence in combat between groups would call for revenge, either through renewed collective fighting or by ambush. Similarly, a death attributed to hostile

sorcery and traced to a particular person or their group would call for retaliation, either by countersorcery or by holding a divination test and executing the one held responsible. In either case two interlinked concerns
were at work: the maintenance of group strength and prestige, and duty to
the ghost of the person originally killed or thought to have been killed.
Whether in practice revenge would be sought might depend on the relative power and numbers of those involved by their status in implicitly
agnatic groups of kin. A death set up a potentiality for vengeance, whether
it was immediately carried out or not, and the potentiality would continue
indefinitely until some resolution of it was reached. If vengeance was
sought in war, a sacrifice of a pig or pigs would be made to the aggrieved
ghost as well as to a collectivity of ancestral spirits.

The potentiality for vengeance did not have to result in an actual
revenge killing. Actions taken were contingent on relationships between
the parties of the victims and the killers, and on group alliances and enmi-
ties. Between major, traditional enemies there was little chance of a peaceful resolution, but starting a war was also hazardous. In that case, concealed
countersorcery might be tried, utilizing marginal, interstitial persons with
ambiguous loyalties, either male or female. In all other circumstances,
matters were negotiable, and the likelihood of peacemaking by compensation was enhanced by the density of affinal ties between the groups of
those principally responsible for taking action. Allies in warfare who lost
men in battle would need to be compensated to avoid shifts of allegiance.
These same allies might be, at times, minor enemies in restricted warfare,
and again compensation could be arranged between them by their leaders, "big-men" who could influence others by their deployment of pigs
and shell valuables and who encouraged the transformation of enmity
into friendship by converting compensation payments into two-way competitive exchanges of wealth known as *moka* (see, e.g., Strathern and
Stewart 2000, Strathern 1971 [2007]), especially following "pacification"
in the 1950s. So well-known did the Hagen moka and the use of pearl
shells in it become in the highlands region that government patrol officers
such as James Sinclair, working later to bring about peace settlements in
a distant and remote area of the highlands (Lake Kopiago among the Duna
people), applied the term, with the spelling *moga*, far beyond the Hagen
area as a general expression for effective peacemaking (Sinclair 1966: 207).

Since revenge was sanctioned by the putative and implied wishes of a
victim's ghost and the ancestral dead kin, in general, and was sealed as an
intention by the killing of pigs in sacrifice, the option to make and accept

compensation instead had also to be made acceptable to the dead. Meat sacrifices, in which the pork was steamed or roasted in earth ovens, sent up a smell that was considered appealing to the dead kin, and this was therefore the way of getting the dead on the side of compensation.

Beyond this sacrificial act of soliciting support of the dead, an important and delicate process of diplomacy, negotiation, and making commitments was set in hand, ultimately involving more and more persons (both male and female) as potential exchange partners across the divide created by violent acts. In this process, leaders played a crucial role in raising wealth goods, marshaling support, sorting out conflicts, and making diplomatic and aesthetically powerful speeches to bring about peace. The more they succeeded with their efforts, the more they would be able to instigate the development of wide-ranging exchange relations that would become the vehicle for the expansion of their own careers as leaders. An initial motivation to pay for deaths and halt overt conflicts was thus transmuted over time into a powerful machine for the replication and multiplication of exchange ties founded on complicated "financing" ties masterminded by the big-men.

The religious and ritual background to this expansion remained, underpinning the economic activities. No moka ceremony, it was thought, could succeed without the assistance of the ancestors, whose displeasure might be shown by the decorations of the moka givers failing to appear bright and shining when they danced for the occasion or by a sudden unfavorable onset of rain that would curtail the dancing, singing, and drumming intended to establish the harmony, well-being, and prestige of the group under its ancestors' protection.

From the 1970s onward this expansion of peaceful exchanges was halted by a series of recessive outbreaks of violence between groups. These were caused by a number of influences: the advent of roads and vehicles, disputes over land for growing coffee, conflicts over national politics and electorates, the overall increase in the scale of social relations bringing into contention categories of people not related by language or "ethnicity," and the introduction of guns into warfare, increasing the numbers of deaths and making it harder to pay for them. These conditions continue today (up to the publication of this volume).

It is interesting that, *pari passu* with these changes, people began to turn more to various denominations of Christian churches, especially those with an urban base and new transactional connections with the outside world. It might be expected that because of the formal emphasis in these churches on peaceful relations, the rituals and rhetorics of the churches would be brought into play to transcend the dilemmas of scale brought about by economic and political change. Formidable obstacles stood in the way of this pathway, not least the complex segmented histories of conflict in local areas. There have been clear signs, however, that Christian ideology lends itself to the extension of peacemaking across group boundaries, with prayers and communal feasting and that none of this works without compensation payments.

Conclusion

The three case studies in this chapter have been intended to stand in partial counterpoint to one another. In all three cases, it is obvious that religion and violence were mutually implicated, but the terms of that implication were different.

In the Fijian case, with a chiefly society and centralization of power, we saw that war chief and land chief, both sacralized, were ideally balanced with each other, the one standing for external violence, the other for internal peace. In Bau, this balance was upset and inverted, because the seagoing war chiefs came to occupy a preeminent position by displacing the land chiefs. Bau's empire was established by conquest and by the use of wealth to pay allies in war.

Bellona is an example in which, on a small island occupied by Polynesian seafarers, a kind of hierarchy was established but without governmentality. Instead, relations between lineages were egalitarian and marked by competitive killings. Religion was implicated in these conflicts because the superior sky gods were thought of as supporting raids, while the less powerful district gods were seen as helping to protect people. As with Bau, the balance was tipped toward violence, here in the proliferation of vengeance killings. But there were also rituals for peacemaking, with apologies and acts of reconciliation. Wealth goods were employed at feasts held for peace but not as a prime means as bringing the peace about. Sky gods presided over rituals for peace as for war, bringing ritual closure to vengeance killings.

In the New Guinea highlands societies, we find a higher development of an ideology of wealth used as a life-giving replacement for persons, whether for bridewealth payments, payments to allies, or compensation to enemies. The big-men type of leadership, founded both on a ritual relationship with ancestors and on the deployment of wealth as an integrating medium of defining sociality, ensured that life was encompassed by wealth, and wealth could therefore be used to define both interpersonal and political relations. Sacralization of wealth ensured the possibility of peacemaking. At the same time, as with the other cases, violence could also by underpinned by values held to be sacred. Christianity impacted all three cases (Bau, Bellona, and Hagen) by providing a link with powers that cross-cut the previous structures of relations and made a rationale for creating peace on a different ritual basis, without necessarily removing the causes that could lead to conflicts.

Religion and violence in these societies are perhaps best seen as in a kind of see-saw dialectic. Where violence was practiced, religion might support it; but religion was also brought into play to halt violence and make peace. The broader background that explains how both of these processes could occur lies in the transformative framing powers of ritual and its underlying cosmological perceptions of order, producing self-justifying bases for the legitimization of actions. (See also Schirch 2005 and Strathern and Stewart 2011, ch. 7, on rituals and peacebuilding.)

Over all, religion and violence do not have to be seen as privileged or exclusive arenas of inquiry. One arena of discussion can be whether violent actions are sometimes required or incited by religious notions and ritual actions. Even if this is the case, violence may have other, independent causes and correlates, and religion may equally be founded on and foster other values. A holistic analysis is likely to show that, while religion and violence may intersect in various ways, peacemaking or the avoidance of conflict may equally involve religious ideas. In a processual analysis, cycles of political activity may alternate between violent conflict and quiet peacemaking, so the cycles need to be understood as a whole and not just in part. The definition of *violence* must give the analyst pause before deploying it as a counter in the investigation. For example, what the observer evaluates as violence may not be categorized in that way by the actors, if by the term *violence* we mean a transgressive or disruptive act that is antinormative—murder rather than an execution, for example. We have investigated questions of violence and its definitions, drawing on the work of David Riches and others (Riches 1986), in previous publications (e.g., Stewart and Strathern 2002a). We refer in that publication to the theme of contested legitimacy in relation to violent acts, because the evaluation (or even the classification) of an act as violent can vary between the performers, victims, and witnesses of the act (op. cit.: 25–51). In the English language, violence also tends to carry the sense of inflicting immediate physical harm on persons, but the term can also readily be extended in two further ways: one, to contexts in which people's emotional or social status is harmed or violated in ways they experience as hurtful and, the other, in terms of so-called mystical notions of attack or harm inflicted on others by means of sorcery, magic in general, cursing, and the like—all categories that bring us back into the domains of ritual and religion (see Stewart and Strathern 2004).

Bibliography

Blust, Robert. *The Austronesian Languages*. Canberra: Australian National University, 2009.

Boggs, Stephen T. and Malcolm Naen Chun. "*Ho'oponopono*: A Hawaiian Method of Solving Interpersonal Problems." In Karen Ann Watson-Gegeo and Geoffrey M. White eds. *Disentangling: Conflict Discourse in Pacific Societies*, pp. 122–160. Palo Alto, CA: Stanford University Press, 1990.

Brenneis, Donald and Fred R. Myers eds. *Dangerous Words: Language and Politics in the Pacific*. Prospect Heights, IL: Waveland Press, 1991 [1984].

Ferguson, R. Brian and Neil L. Whitehead eds. *War in the Tribal Zone. Expanding States and Indigenous Warfare*. Santa Fe, NM: School of American Research Series, 1992.

Fortes, Meyer. *Kinship and the Social Order: The Legacy of Lewis Henry Morgan*. Chicago: Aldine, 1969.

Hocart, Arthur Maurice. *Kingship*. Oxford, UK: Oxford University Press, 1927.

Hocart, Arthur Maurice. "*The Life-Giving Myth, and Other Essays*." London: Methuen and Co. Ltd, 1970 [1952].

Kitts, Margo. "*Poinē* as a Ritual Leitmotif in the Iliad." In M. Kitts ed. (Section I: Ritual and Violence), pp. 7–32, vol. III of *Ritual Dynamics and the Science of Ritual*. M. Kitts et al. eds. Wiesbaden, Germany: Harrassowitz Verlag, 2010.

Kuschel, Rolf. *Vengeance Is Their Reply. Blood Feuds and Homicides on Bellona Island*. Copenhagen: Dansk Psykologisk Forlag, 1988.

Lawrence, Peter. "The Garia of the Madang District." In Ronald M. Berndt and Peter Lawrence eds. *Politics in New Guinea, Traditional and in the Context of Change: Some Anthropological Perspectives*, pp. 74–93. Nedlands: University of Western Australia Press, 1971.

Noegel, Scott. "The Ritual Use of Linguistic and Textual Violence in the Hebrew Bible and Ancient Near East." In M. Kitts ed. (Section I: Ritual and Violence), pp. 33–46, vol. III of *Ritual Dynamics and the Science of Ritual*. M. Kitts et al. eds. Wiesbaden, Germany: Harrassowitz Verlag, 2010.

Rappaport, Roy A. *Pigs for the Ancestors: Ritual in the Ecology of a New Guinea People*. New Haven, CT: Yale University Press, 1967.

Riches, David. *The Anthropology of Violence.* Oxford, UK, and New York: Basil Blackwell, 1986.

Sahlins, Marshall D. *Moala: Culture and Nature on a Fijian Island.* Ann Arbor: University of Michigan Press, 1962.

Sahlins, Marshall D. *Culture in Practice: Selected Essays.* New York: Zone Books, 2000.

Sahlins, Marshall D. *Apologies to Thucydides: Understanding History as Culture and Vice-Versa.* Chicago: University of Chicago Press, 2004.

Schirch, Lisa. *Ritual and Symbol in Peacebuilding.* Bloomfield, CT: Kumarian Press, 2005.

Sinclair, James P. *Behind the Ranges: Patrolling in New Guinea.* Melbourne: Melbourne University Press, 1966.

Stewart, Pamela J. and Andrew Strathern. *Violence: Theory and Ethnography.* London and New York: Continuum Publishing, 2002a.

Stewart, Pamela J. and Andrew Strathern. "Transformations of Monetary Symbols in the Highlands of Papua New Guinea." For a special issue of the journal *L'Homme* on money (*Questions de Monnaie*) 162 (April/June 2002): 137–156, (2002b).

Stewart, Pamela J. and Andrew Strathern. *Witchcraft, Sorcery, Rumors, and Gossip.* New Departures in Anthropology series. Cambridge, UK: Cambridge University Press, 2004.

Stewart, Pamela J. and Andrew Strathern. "Cosmology, Resources, and Landscape: Agencies of the Dead and the Living in Duna, Papua New Guinea." *Ethnology* 44 (2005): 35–47.

Stewart, Pamela J. and Andrew Strathern eds. *Exchange and Sacrifice.* Durham, NC: Carolina Academic Press, 2008.

Strathern, Andrew. *The Rope of Moka.* Cambridge, UK: Cambridge University Press, 2000 [1971].

Strathern, Andrew. *One Father, One Blood.* Canberra: Australian National University Press, 1972.

Strathern, Andrew and Pamela J. Stewart. "Objects, Relationships, and Meanings: Historical Switches in Currencies in Mount Hagen, Papua New Guinea." In *Money and Modernity: State and Local Currencies in Melanesia,* 164–191. David Akin and Joel Robbins eds. ASAO (Association for Social Anthropology in Oceania) Monograph Series No. 17. Pittsburgh: University of Pittsburgh Press, 1999.

Strathern, Andrew and Pamela J. Stewart. *Arrow Talk: Transaction, Transition, and Contradiction in New Guinea Highlands History.* Kent, OH, and London: Kent State University Press, 2000.

Strathern, Andrew and Pamela J. Stewart. "The South-West Pacific." In *Oceania: An Introduction to the Cultures and Identities of Pacific Islanders,* pp. 10–98. Andrew Strathern, Pamela J. Stewart, Laurence M. Carucci, Lin Poyer, Richard Feinberg, and Cluny Macpherson. Durham, NC: Carolina Academic Press, 2002.

Strathern, Andrew, Pamela J. Stewart, Laurence M. Carucci, Lin Poyer, Richard Feinberg, and Cluny Macpherson. *Oceania: An Introduction to the Cultures and Identities of Pacific Islanders.* Durham, NC: Carolina Academic Press, 2002.

Strathern, Andrew and Pamela J. Stewart. *Curing and Healing: Medical Anthropology in Global Perspective.* Second edition, updated and revised. Durham NC: Carolina Academic Press, 2010.

Strathern, Andrew and Pamela J. Stewart. *Peace-making and the Imagination:Papua New Guinea Perspective.* St. Lucia, AU: University of Queensland Press, 2011.

Watson-Gegeo Karen Ann and Geoffrey M. White eds. *Disentangling: Conflict Discourse in Pacific Societies.* Palo Alto, CA: Stanford University Press, 1990.

Chapter 9

Violence in Chinese Religious Traditions

Meir Shahar

ALTHOUGH THE HISTORY of the Western monotheistic faiths is replete with inter-religious conflict, it is fair to ask whether China ever experienced inter-religious conflict. Did Chinese of one religious persuasion try to subdue or forcibly convert others, or was war waged in China for control of sacred places? The amorphous religious identity characteristic of China offers a convenient starting point for examining these questions.

Inclusive Religiosity and the Absence of Holy Wars

For the most part, Chinese people find it hard to define their religious identity. When asked about their faith, they might answer vaguely that one or another family member is a Buddhist or a Daoist, or they might reject the question, asserting that they succumb to no one label. Such answers should not be taken to mean that Chinese lives are devoid of a spiritual dimension or of cultic activities. The Chinese landscape is dotted with temples and monasteries, and the Chinese people worship a wide assortment of divinities, even as they consult with numerous clerics: Buddhist monks, Daoist priests, and the spirit mediums of the popular religion, to name just a few. Rather than the absence of religion, the difficulty to define it suggests an inherent difference between the Chinese faiths and the Western monotheistic ones. Before we probe it, a brief survey of the principal Chinese religions is in order.

Scholars usually distinguish between at least three Chinese religious traditions: Buddhism, which arrived to China from the Indian subcontinent in the first century CE; Daoism, which emerged as an organized religion with its own clergy and canonical scriptures during the same period; and the amorphous popular religion, which is also variously referred to as the village religion, the local religion, or as Chinese popular cults. To these three, some scholars add a fourth, Confucianism. The writings of Confucius (551–479 BCE) and his followers have served as the official ideology of the imperial Chinese regimes, providing the foundation for the Chinese educational system for more than two millenniums. Some Chinese literati have found in Confucian philosophy a spiritual dimension, in which sense it could be termed a religion. However, as theological questions occupy a minor place in it, many authors (including this one) prefer to describe Confucianism as an ethical and a political philosophy rather than as a religion. (Though largely in response to Buddhism, the neo-Confucian movement of the eleventh century onward is concerned with metaphysical questions).

Even as they significantly differ, the three (or four) Chinese religions share the important mark of inclusiveness. Neither one requires its followers to declare an exclusive adherence to it. Whereas the monotheistic faiths have forbidden their flocks following more than one—a Jew has not been able to become simultaneously Christian, for example—it is permissible for the Chinese laity to seek solace in diverse religions, alternately or concurrently. Rituals of conversion—which are of paramount significance in the monotheistic tradition—do not exist in China, where the laity freely shops in divergent religious establishments. Rather than committing herself or himself to a given faith by such rites as baptism or circumcision, a Chinese person may pray one day in a Buddhist temple and the next in a Daoist one, all the while seeking ethical guidance in the Confucian classics. Professing that they have no religion, the Chinese do not mean that they believe neither in gods nor in the efficacy of ritual. They assert, rather, that they do not adhere to the kind of exclusive religion that is familiar in the West. The word for religion, *zongjiao*, is a neologism that has been introduced to China—via Japan—following the encounter with the colonial powers. Exclusive as it is, the newly coined term is inapplicable to the native Chinese faiths.

The medical metaphor might illuminate the relative freedom that characterizes the Chinese religious market. Much as we might turn to several physicians—and diverse healing methods—until we find the proper one, a Chinese might seek spiritual help from various religious specialists, consulting one day with a Buddhist priest and hiring the services or a Daoist priest or a village spirit medium the following one. In cases of emergency, the Chinese might convene a consultation with several clerics simultaneously, just as an American hospital might summon a multidisciplinary medical conference. It has been customary in China to hire, concurrently, religious specialists of several faiths for important ritual passages, such as the one separating the living from the dead. If its financial resources permit, the family will commission for one and the same funeral an assortment of clerics: Confucian literati, Buddhist monks, and Daoist priests, no less than the geomancers and astrologers who are associated with the popular religion. Each one will employ his disciplinary tools—whether the reading of the Daoist scriptures or the intonation of the Buddhist sutras, for instance—for the salvation of the deceased, whose soul will be spiritually committed to neither.

Their religious identity unclear, the Chinese have been less prone than their Western counterparts to religious warfare. Where the population cannot be divided into identifiable communities of faith, conflict between them is unlikely. (The statistical attempts to differentiate between Chinese Buddhists, Daoists, or Confucians are artificial at best.) It probably would not be too much of an exaggeration to claim that traditional China never witnessed a holy war. To the best of my knowledge, prior to the encounter with the modern West, no Chinese religious community ever tried to gain military supremacy over—not to mention forcibly convert—another. There has never been an armed conflict between Chinese of diverse religious persuasions (such as Buddhists against Daoists). Significantly, the first Chinese war that has been colored by a proselytizing zeal occurred under Western influence. In 1850, the messianic leader Hong Xiuquan (1814–1864) led his followers into one of the deadliest crusades in history. Declaring himself the younger brother of Jesus Christ, Hong established the Taiping Heavenly Kingdom (1850–1864), in which a modified Christianity was to replace the native Chinese faiths. Hong's ideology combined ideas of social equality and women's liberation with a Christian vision in which he himself figured as a savior. Some twenty million people died before his messianic utopia was crushed by the reigning Qing Dynasty (Shih, 1972).

Whereas the Chinese laity has lacked a clear religious identity (and its concomitant hostility toward the religious other), its clergy has developed identifiable spiritual profiles. Unlike their lay followers, religious specialists have been required to undergo such initiation rites as the Buddhist tonsure and the Daoist ordination ceremony. Following their gradual immersion in a given scriptural tradition and its liturgies, Chinese clerics developed a quintessential ecclesial identity as Buddhist monks, Daoist priests, or ritual masters (*fashi*) of one or another ceremonial lineage. Whether or not Confucianism is considered a religion, its bearers—the male literati elite—likewise cherished a distinct identity. As they gradually climbed through the examination ladder that qualified them for government office, the literati acquired a sense of pride in the Confucian heritage that distinguished them from the ignorant masses. They were likely as conscious of their educational mission as Buddhist monks and Daoist priests were of their respective spiritual vocations. China's clerics have kept distinct identities, even as the religion of the laity has remained obscure.

Possessed of a quintessential religious identity, clerics (unlike their lay followers) vied with one another. The competition extended from the spiritual realm to the economic sphere. Buddhist monks, Daoist priests, ritual masters, and spirit mediums relied for their living on the same lay clientele. Lacking a following, however, their rivalry was rarely translated into physical violence. Religious specialists led no congregations that they could muster for a holy war. The only avenue possible for religious persecution extended through the imperial regime. Those clerics who wished to eliminate their rivals could try to convert the ruler for their cause. The Daoist Kou Qianzhi (365–448 CE) had been exceptionally successful in this regard. Under his spell, the Northern Wei emperor Taiwu (408–452 CE) proscribed the Buddhist faith, going as far as executing monks who were accused of sedition. Taiwu's successor, however, was quick to rescind his anti-Buddhist policies (Mather, 1979). Much like their subjects, most emperors were comfortable sponsoring diverse religious experts, rather than relying on some to the exclusion of others.

Chinese clerics—unlike the laity they minister to—have been conscious of their religious distinction to the extent of competing with others. The rivalry, however, has rarely been as acrimonious—not to mention as violent—as in Western monotheism. Well-known as early as the medieval period, the slogan of "the three teachings unite into one" (*sanjiao heyi*) gained special currency during the sixteenth and seventeenth centuries, when leading thinkers argued that Confucianism, Buddhism, and Daoism led to the same ultimate truth. The neo-Confucian philosopher Jiao Hong (1540–1620) advocated the study of Daoist and Buddhist scriptures, for they could elucidate the meaning of the Confucian classics, and Lin Zhaoen (1517–1598) advanced one step further, arguing that the three faiths were equivalent and hence interchangeable. Beginning in the late Ming period (1368–1644) and continuing to the present, numerous theologians have used interchangeably the Confucian vocabulary of sageness, the Buddhist terminology of enlightenment, and the Daoist parlance of immortality. Rather than quarreling over doctrinal differences, leading thinkers have conceived of their respective religions as diverse avenues to the same goal. Even as they reserve pride of place for their own, clerics have been mindful of the other faiths' spiritual merits (Berling 1980; Brook, 1993).

Sacred geography illustrates the relative tolerance that characterizes Chinese religions. Much like the Western monotheistic faiths, Chinese religions tend to adopt one another's holy places. But whereas in Jerusalem and in Constantinople (Istanbul) this has led to warfare, in China, divergent religious establishments often coexist harmoniously. Holy places are usually located atop sacred mountains, and it is not uncommon for Buddhist monasteries and Daoist temples to share them (Naquin and Yü, 1992). The renowned Buddhist Shaolin Monastery and Daoist Temple of the Central Holy Peak (Zhongyue miao), for instance, are situated on the same sacred Mount Song (in Henan Province). When several years ago I visited the former, a Buddhist monk drew on the Daoist experience to explain his choice of a retreat. "Mount Song is sacred," he told me. "That is why there is a Daoist Temple here." Rather than driving them out, the Shaolin monks cherish their Daoist neighbors for proving the sanctity of the Buddhist monastery's location.

Why have Chinese religions been relatively tolerant of one another? The question might be addressed from a theological angle no less than from an institutional perspective. We may want to consider the polytheistic worldview that has characterized the Chinese faiths, as well as their institutional weakness, which reflected the tremendous power of the Chinese state.

Polytheism, Tolerance, and State Persecution

The Chinese religious tradition has, by and large, been polytheistic. Even though on the doctrinal level Buddhism does not recognize any god, in practice the religion arrived in China equipped with a substantial pantheon of heavenly beings. The Buddhist divinities have been ordered into an elaborate hierarchy of (in descending order) Buddhas, bodhisattvas, *arhats*, guardian deities, and other divine (or demonic) beings ranging from sexual harpies to cannibalistic ghouls. Daoism, likewise, celebrates a vast hierarchy of supernatural beings, ranging from carefree immortals to divine bureaucrats each appointed to a specific post in a heavenly government, which has been fashioned after the traditional Chinese state. As for the popular religion, the number of its gods has been greater still. Drawing on Buddhism and Daoism, it includes in addition to their divinities an endless array of historical figures who have been elevated to divine standing. Ranging from chaste maidens and lively clowns to fearless warriors and upright officials, some have been worshiped in a given locality only, whereas the cults of others have spread throughout the Chinese cultural sphere. Finally, to the degree that it sanctions ancestor worship even Confucianism might be described as polytheistic.

It might perhaps be argued that polytheism tends to be more receptive of other faiths than monotheism. The Hebrew Bible's dictum "you shall have no other gods before me" (Exodus 20:3) might have signaled the emergence of religious zealotry, as the "jealous lord" forbade the chosen people worshiping divinities other than him. Whereas the belief in one god implies one truth, polytheism tolerates many. Unlike monotheism, which by definition precludes other faiths, polytheistic religions have been inclined to adopt one another's gods. This has been the case in China, where divinities have been mutually borrowed by Buddhism, Daoism, and the popular religions. To give a minor example, a well-known figure in the Chinese popular religion is the child god Nezha whose cult was brought to China from India by Tantric (Esoteric) Buddhism during the Tang period (618–907). Originally a minor *yaksa* spirit named Nalakubara, the divine youth had been harnessed by Tantric ritual masters into their elaborate rituals. Summoned to China for the protection of the imperial court, his cult was quickly adopted by Daoist priests, no less than by village spirit mediums. The (originally Hindu) Buddhist god became a major figure in Daoism and the popular religion. Rather than proscribing them, the Chinese religions have been inclined to absorb one another's mythologies.

If polytheism might have contributed to the mutual tolerance of the Chinese faiths, their institutional weakness has precluded violence. No Chinese religion has ever been strong enough to wage war on another. Neither Buddhism, nor Daoism, nor the popular religion, have been able to establish churches of lasting political, economic, or military influence. The institutional impotence of the Chinese faiths has been due to the tremendous power of the Chinese state. Their weakness has mirrored the enormous clout of the imperial—or, recently, communist—regimes. The ineffectiveness of the Chinese faiths alerts us to a prominent aspect of the Chinese experience of violence: Whereas China's diverse religions never fought among themselves, in varying degrees they have all been subject to state oppression. If China never experienced inter-religious warfare, it has witnessed a heavy dose of religious persecution by the state.

During the cold winter season of 1077, a barefoot European emperor was doing penance in the snow in front of the northern Italian castle of Canossa. Pope Gregory VII (1028–1085) was staying at the castle, and the Holy Roman emperor Henry IV (1050–1106) begged his clemency for the sin of intervention in the affairs of the church. The emperor was repenting, in particular, for the liberty he had taken in appointing bishops (in what came to be known as the Investiture Controversy). Such a scene could not have been imagined in China, where the "Son of Heaven" had always ruled supreme. By way of hyperbole, we might say that whereas God has been central to European history, in China he has always been overshadowed by the emperor. Chinese political thought has required that religion be subordinate to the state, and the bureaucracy has been careful to control all faiths. No Chinese religion has ever been permitted to create independent institutions, especially those that might coordinate activities across regional boundaries. In this respect, the Communist Party has inherited its predecessors' policies: Neither imperial China nor the People's Republic would tolerate a religious establishment threatening its absolute authority. Religions that challenged the state would be crushed.

The Tang period (618–907) persecution of Buddhism illustrates the Chinese state's abhorrence of religion. In the course of the first millennium, the Indian-born faith had become a powerful presence in Chinese society. Buddhist temples amassed great wealth in landed property (that for the most part was tax free), employing on their estates hundreds of thousands of peasants. The state eyed with envy the accumulated Buddhist wealth, irritated with the huge numbers of monks (and their serfs) who were exempt from corvée labor no less than from military service. In 845 Emperor Wuzong decided to put an end to the Buddhist church: Thousands of temples were destroyed and their lands confiscated. Hundreds of thousands of monks (and nuns) were forcibly laicized, sent back to their families and brought under the control of regional officials. Even though Buddhism was to have a lasting impact on Chinese religion and society, as an institution it never recovered. Buddhist monasteries of later periods could regain neither the wealth, prestige. or freedom that they had enjoyed prior to the Tang purge (Weinstein 1987; Ch'en 1964).

During the Qing period (1644–1911), the government's wrath was directed less toward Buddhism and Daoism (both of which have been brought under firm government control) than independent religious movements that were labeled heterodox (*xiejiao*). The late imperial period witnessed the spread of millenarian sects, which mushroomed outside of the government-supervised Buddhist and Daoist temples. Commonly referred to as the White Lotus Religion (*Bailian jiao*), these sectarian movements were transmitted by lay masters and disciples. In their heightened sense of (often secretive) religious identity, no less than their strict cultic regimen, they somewhat resembled the exclusive and demanding religiosity familiar in Western monotheism (at least more so than Chinese Buddhism, Chinese Daoism, and the Chinese popular religion did). Furthermore, characterized by a strong millenarian zeal, at least some of these sects posed a threat to the existing political powers. Some White Lotus believers expected the imminent collapse of the imperial regime and its replacement by a messianic leadership establishing heaven on earth.

White Lotus religiosity focused on the cult of a female deity, whose sex made her suspect in the eyes of the bureaucratic elite. Whereas the state typically promoted the veneration of male scholars and generals, sectarian religion placed a goddess at the apex of the divine pantheon. Worship centered on the Eternal Mother (*Wusheng laomu*), from whose womb humankind had been banished and to which it would ultimately return. The cult of the supreme goddess was carried out by the recital of scriptures and magic spells (mantras), often coupled with a vegetarian diet (which had been borrowed from Buddhism), breathing exercises and calisthenics (drawing on the Daoist immortality techniques), and martial arts practice. Whereas the sects were commonly diffused, in times of heightened messianic expectations—or when pushed to it by state persecution—they could unite, mobilizing tens of thousands (Groot [1903–1904] 1970; Naquin 1976; Naquin 1981; Liu and Sheck 2004; ter Haar 1992).

Many White Lotus sects were likely peaceful, centering on personal salvation rather than political redemption. (Scholars have noted that the term *White Lotus* has been loosely used by state officials against all sects they wished to annihilate.) Such sects might have been driven to rebellion by their very oppression. Others, however, had been marked by a heightened messianic expectation, overtly expressed in rebellion. In 1813, White Lotus sectarians known as the Eight Trigrams coordinated an uprising in several cities, including the capital, Beijing. Approximately 80,000 people perished in the unsuccessful attempt to replace the existing sociopolitical system with a divine order, ushering eternal blessing. The messianic hopes of redemption—no less than their violent suppression by the state—have remained alive to this day. Active since the 1990s, the politically sensitive Falungong movement is a direct descendent of the White Lotus sects, combining their odd mixture of Buddhist eschatology with breathing exercises and calisthenics (that are referred to by sect members as *Qigong*). The panicked and brutal reaction on the part of the communist government likewise mirrors the violent suppression of sectarian religiosity by the Qing Dynasty. Dreams of salvation—and their ruthless repression—are as evident in today's China as they have been for centuries.

The state's control of religion has been achieved by the appointment of leading clerics, among other measures. As early as the medieval period, the state had established offices for the control of religious affairs, staffed by Buddhist monks and Daoist priests to its liking. The policy has remained in effect to this day, the ordination of leading abbots and head priests requiring the state's approval. Whereas government officials would not necessarily intervene in the selection of a head monk for a village hermitage, they would be careful to choose themselves the abbots of large temples (especially thoses that function as tourist and pilgrimage attractions and, thus, as sources of potential revenue). The policy has been a major source of friction between the People's Republic of China and the Catholic Church, whose bishops are universally appointed by the Vatican. Refusing to accept the Holy See's intervention in what it considers as its internal affairs, the Chinese government has established the Chinese Patriotic Catholic Association, for the purpose of nominating its bishops. The bitter argument over the clerical ordination—whether it should be decided by the Chinese government or by the Vatican—has been a principal reason for their ongoing breach of diplomatic relations.

Martial Gods and Bloody Sacrifices

Even though no war had been fought in traditional China on behalf of the gods (that is by the devotees of one, against the adherents of another), the gods regularly participated in warfare. Just as in Homer's *Iliad* the Greek divinities join the Trojan campaign, the Chinese gods have been regularly drafted to their believers' wars. Gods of Buddhist and Daoist descent no less than the martial divinities of the amorphous popular religion have assisted in armed conflicts that ranged from the defense of the Chinese state to the conquest of neighboring kingdoms, from struggles of dynastic succession to peasant rebellions. The earliest extant Chinese-language documents record divine participation in warfare. Dating from the second millennium BCE, the oracle bone inscriptions attest that the Shang kings consulted with their deified ancestors before heading for battle. Military campaigns would be undertaken only when sponsored by the gods.

Chinese emperors hired a wide assortment of ritual specialists, assuring their military victories. During the Tang period (618–907) these were often priests of the Tantric (also known as Esoteric) Buddhist tradition. Indian-born ritual masters such as Amoghavajra (705–774) conjured a panoply of Tantric martial divinities for the protection of the Chinese state. Many of these guardian divinities originated in Indian religion, before being drafted into the Buddhist pantheon. The Heavenly King of the North Vaishravana, (in Chinese, Pishamen), illustrates the long journey of the Hindu gods from the Sanskrit epics, through Tantric Buddhist mythology, into the martial pantheon of medieval China. Originally named Kubera, he had been celebrated as early as the second century BCE *Ramayana* as the king of the semidivine semidemonic *yakṣa* troops. Later known primarily as Vaishravana, he was incorporated as the Heavenly King of the North into the Buddhist pantheon. Occupying a central place in the Esoteric rituals for state protection, he was brought to China, where he became the tutelary divinity of the Tang armies. Significantly, the Indian-born Vaiśravaṇa had protected not only the Chinese state as a whole but also its individual warriors. In order to be empowered by his superhuman strength, medieval wrestlers (and criminals) tattooed their bodies with the martial god's image (Demiéville 2010, 38–39; Strickmann 1996, 41; Chou Yi-Liang 1945, 305–306; Hansen 1993, 80–83; Zheng Acai 1997, 432).

The very names of some Chinese deities attest their military function. The "Perfect Warrior" (Zhenwu) also known as the Emperor of the Dark Heavens (Xuantian shangdi) has lent his martial prowess to rebels and emperors alike. In 1774 he was called on by the White Lotus leader Wang Lun to join his (ultimately failed) uprising, just as centuries earlier he had supported Emperor Chengzu's (r. 1403–1424) usurpation of the imperial throne. Posthumously known as the Yongle Emperor, Chengzu had attributed his military victories over his nephew, Emperor Huidi (r. 1399–1402), to the divine warrior's assistance. There is some evidence to suggest that he had participated himself in spirit medium seances in which, possessed by the martial god, he was taught his superhuman fighting skills. Once he became emperor, Chengzu (Yongle) embarked on a massive building campaign on his divine patron's behalf. Three hundred thousand corvée laborers built an enormous temple complex dedicated to the "Perfect Warrior" atop Mount Wudang (in Hubei Province). The martial god who had helped the reigning emperor was honored by seven large monastic complexes and numerous additional shrines, all staffed by government-sponsored Daoist priests (Naquin 1981, 39, 165; Seaman 1987, 23–27; Lagerwey 1992).

Martial gods have helped those who fought against the political order, no less than those who supported it. Throughout the late imperial period—and into modern times—rebels and revolutionaries headed to battle convinced of divine protection. The valiant gods they worshiped were, for the most part, the deified protagonists of such popular novels as the *Three Kingdoms* (*Sanguo yanyi*), the *Journey to the West* (*Xiyou ji*), and the *Water Margin* (*Shuihu zhuan*, also known in English as *The Outlaws of the Marsh*). The epic novels of either historical or mythological warfare have served as a source for oral literature and drama, reaching every segment of society, literate and illiterate. Familiar to every peasant, their heroic protagonists such as the *Three Kingdom's* Guan'gong (Guandi) have been venerated as guardian divinities. The martial pantheon invoked in popular uprisings demonstrated, therefore, the inseparability of Chinese religion and popular culture. The divine warriors who empowered the rebels were those whose exploits were celebrated by itinerant storytellers and actors. Rebel armies such as the 1990s Boxers headed to battle possessed by the gods whose adventures were enacted on the village stage (Esherick 1987, 38–67).

The military gods protecting the peasant-rebel often share his mutinous ideology. Possessed of outstanding fighting skills, many are equally remarkable for their opposition to the existing order. Worshiped as tutelary divinities, the martial protagonists of late imperial fiction are often marginal figures who question accepted social norms, challenging the powers that be. The *Water Margin's* heroes are Robin Hood–type bandits, distributing to the poor the spoils of the rich, and the *Journey to the West's* Sun Wukong challenges divine, no less than earthly, authority. Rising in arms against the entire heavenly bureaucracy, the fearless Monkey aims to usurp its highest post. The Great Sage Equal to Heaven, as the defiant Monkey calls himself, struggles to occupy the Jade Emperor's throne. No wonder that he has been chosen as a rallying symbol by rebels ranging from the 1900 Boxers to the 1960s' Red Guards. Such unruly gods as Monkey illustrate the potential for resistance that is inherent in many Chinese martial divinities (Shahar and Weller 1996). Providing symbolic resources for insubordination, they have been cherished by all those who strayed from or challenged the existing order from late imperial insurgents and outlaws to contemporary gangsters. It might further be argued that military gods have contributed to the shaping of masculinity at large. Chinese men, especially but not only of the lower classes, often emulate the enticing combination of generosity and violence, loyalty and defiance that is characteristic of the deified warrior in popular culture (Boretz 2011).

Martial gods have conferred invulnerability on their warrior devotees. During the nineteenth and twentieth centuries, peasant armies headed to battle tragically convinced that divine protection would make them immune to swords, spears, and even firearms. The search for battle invulnerability has ancient origins. As early as the medieval period, Chinese masters of Tantric Buddhism conjured a magic shield around their bodies that protected them from the demons of disease no less than from enemy weapons. Called "Diamond Armor" (*Jin'gang jiazhou*), it reflected the centrality of the adamantine vocabulary in the Tantric movement, which had been known by the alternate name of the "Diamond Vehicle" or *Vajrayana* (Shahar 2012). By late imperial times, Chinese invulnerability techniques were commonly known by the generic names Golden Bell Armor (*Jinzhong zhao*) and Iron-Cloth Shirt (*Tiebu shan*). The impenetrable body was achieved by a combination of physiological and ritual practice. Adepts circulated their internal energy (*qi*) pounding the flesh with bricks and sandbags, even as they swallowed charms (burnt and mixed with water), making offerings to valiant deities. In some cases, magic immunity was obtained by rituals of possession, the martial divinities descending into the warrior's body as he headed to the battlefield. In others, the polluting, yet magically potent, power of women was put into use, as prostitutes were instructed to urinate from city walls so as to defend it against the enemy's artillery (Naquin 1976, 30–31; 37, 320 note 125; Naquin 1981, 100–101; Esherick 1987, 96–98, 104–109, 216–222; Perry 1980, 186–205; Shahar 2012).

Martial gods require meat-based offerings. In order for them to accomplish their heroic feats they have to be nourished by animal flesh. This leads us to another aspect of religion and violence—the aggression toward the sacrificial victim. In ancient China, human sacrifices were not uncommon. During the second millennium BCE, the Shang kings ritually slaughtered war prisoners as offerings to deified ancestors (Shelach 1996;). Slaves were similarly killed to accompany their deceased lord in his journey to the netherworld. By the middle of the first millennium BCE, such human sacrifices largely disappeared, being replaced by the offering of animals or, in the case of funerary ceremonies, by effigies (instead of real persons). To this day, animal sacrifices have remained widespread in the popular religion. Most gods are offered the flesh of slaughtered animals (most commonly pigs). Even though Buddhist monks and Daoist priests refrain from animal sacrifices (the former maintaining vegetarian offerings, the latter specializing in the oblation of written scriptures), their lay clientele have adhered to the offerings of the flesh. Daoist priests often participate in religious festivals that feature animal sacrifice, even though they do not take part in it. In the temple's inner shrine the priest performs the Daoist rites (that do not involve meat offerings), even as in the adjacent courtyard animals are slaughtered for the same religious occasion.

Even though human sacrifices no longer figure in China, human blood is still drawn in religious ceremonies. On major occasions such as a deity's birthday, spirit mediums and ritual specialists (*fashi*) mortify the flesh. The self-torture is a public spectacle in which the performer may stab his flesh with a spear, slash it with a sword, or hit it with a ball of nails. Mediums often go as far as piercing their cheeks with metal skewers, which are carried for hours, sometimes with weights attached. In one sense, the medium functions in the ritual as the community's sacrificial scapegoat, his streaming blood an offering to the gods (Dean 1993, 181–182; Elliott 1984 [1955]). From another angle, his sacrifice provides the village with magic protection. Ritual masters of the Lushan lineage, for example, smear their blood on the flags of the Five Armies (*Wuying*) that are stationed in the Five Directions: north, south, east, west, and center. Made of divine troops, the Five Armies protect the village against demonic influences. In medieval times, the mortification of the flesh figured also in Buddhist circles, even though its purpose differed. Hoping for salvation or divine epiphany as depicted in the Lotus Sutra, monks and lay persons would burn body parts, experiencing liberation in a moment of excruciating physical pain (Benn 2007; Michael Jerryson's "Buddhist Traditions and Violence," chapter 2 in this volume).

Martial Arts and Spiritual Practice

The Chinese martial arts are a multifaceted system of physical and mental self-cultivation that combines military, therapeutic, and religious goals within the same training routine. Even though it sometimes makes use of weapons (including staffs, swords, and spears among others), practice is usually done barehanded, for which reason the Chinese fighting techniques are known by the generic term *quan* ("fist"). Gymnastic exercises that combined limb movements, breathing, and meditation had been practiced in China as early as the first centuries BCE. Intended for health and spiritual cultivation, they were integrated during the first centuries CE into the emerging Daoist religion, becoming an integral aspect of its immortality practice. During the late Ming and early Qing periods (the sixteenth and seventeenth centuries) the ancient Daoist gymnastic techniques (which originally were not intended for fighting) were integrated with the barehanded martial arts, creating the unique synthesis of martial, remedial, and spiritual aspects that, by the twenty-first century, has made the martial arts popular the world over (Shahar 2008; Wile 1996; Wile 1999).

The names of prominent martial styles attest their self-conscious spiritual goals: Taiji Quan ("Supreme-Ultimate Fist"), Xingyi Quan ("Form and Intent Fist"), Bagua Zhang ("Eight Trigrams Palm," so called after the *Classic of Changes'* eight primary configurations of the *yin* and the *yang*), and Shaolin Quan ("Shaolin Fist," named after the renowned Shaolin Buddhist Temple, which monks have been practicing fighting for more than a millennium). These diverse fighting techniques lead the practitioner into a mystical experience of liberation—or union with the divine—that is obtained in the body, by a combination of physiological practice and mental concentration. The sixteenth- and seventeenth-century creators of these martial arts drew on diverse sources: Daoist manuals of gymnastics, medical treatises of acupuncture, cosmological interpretations of the *Classic of Changes*, and Buddhist scriptures. The result was a unique amalgamation of physiological and spiritual vocabularies, as fighting manuals simultaneously employed diverse religious terminologies to articulate their spiritual goals. The imagination of Daoist immortality, the cosmology of the Supreme Ultimate, and the vocabulary of Buddhist enlightenment were equally harnessed to describe the practitioner's mystical experience.

We may want to conclude this chapter by quoting a brief passage from an influential martial arts manual. The early seventeenth-century *Sinews-Transformation Classic* or *Yijin jing* (which carries a forged preface attributing it to the semilegendary fifth-century Buddhist saint Bodhidharma) has played a major role in the emergence of the late imperial and contemporary martial arts. The treatise's combination of military, therapeutic, and religious goals is articulated by both Daoist and Buddhist vocabularies. Its postscript assures of not only the practitioner's physical health and mental well-being but also that he becomes an immortal and a Buddha:

> I have been studying the *Sinews-Transformation Classic* because I realize that in the two schools of Buddhism and Daoism those who seek the Way are as numerous as cattle's hair, but those who obtain it are as few as the unicorn's horn. This is due not to the Way being hard to achieve, but to the adepts not recognizing its gate. Due to the lack of a foundation, in Chan meditation there is the danger of insanity; in gymnastics there is the fear of exhaustion; in sexual practices there is the specter of premature death; and in drug-taking there is the anxiety of being parched—all because people have not read the *Sinews-Transformation Classic*. If they obtain it and practice it—if they take it and expand upon it—then on a large scale they will render the state meritorious service, and on a small scale they will protect self and family. The farmer will by it diligently till the land, and through its practice the merchant will carry heavy loads on long journeys. The sick will regain his health, and the weak will be strengthened. The childless will abundantly reproduce, and the old will revert to his youth. The human will progress into a Buddha, and the mortal will be transformed into an immortal. Little practice will bring modest results; thorough practice will lead to great accomplishments. The *Sinews-Transformation Classic* is indeed the world's ultimate treasure.
>
> *(Shahar 2008, 174)*

Bibliography

Benn, James A. *Burning for the Buddha: Self-Immolation in Chinese Buddhism*. Honolulu: University of Hawaii Press, 2007.

Berling, Judith A. *The Syncretic Religion of Li Chao-en*. New York: Columbia University Press, 1980.

Boretz, Avron. *Gods, Ghosts, and Gangsters: Ritual Violence, Martial Arts, and Masculinity on the Margins of Chinese Society*. Honolulu: University of Hawaii Press, 2011.

Brook, Timothy. "Rethinking Syncretism: The Unity of the Three Teachings and their Joint Worship in Late-Imperial China." *Journal of Chinese Religions* 21 (1993): 13–44.

Ch'en, Kenneth K. S. *Buddhism in China: A Historical Survey*. Princeton, NJ: Princeton University Press, 1964.

Chou Yi-Liang. "Tantrism in China." *Harvard Journal of Asiatic Studies* 8.3/4 (1945): 241–332.

Dean, Kenneth. *Taoist Ritual and Popular Cults of South-East China*. Princeton, NJ: Princeton University Press, 1993.

Demiéville, Paul. "Buddhism and War." Translated by Michelle Kendall. In *Buddhist Warfare*. Edited by Michael Jerryson and Mark Juergensmeyer, 17–58. Oxford, UK: Oxford University Press, 2010.

Elliott, Allan J. A. *Chinese Spirit Medium Cults in Singapore*. Taipei: Southern Materials Center, 1984 [1955].

Esherick, Joseph W. *The Origins of the Boxer Uprising*. Berkeley: University of California Press, 1987.

Groot, J. J. M. de. *Sectarianism and Religious Persecution in China*. Taipei: Ch'eng Wen, 1970 [1903–1904].

Hansen, Valerie. "Gods on Walls: A Case of Indian Influence on Chinese Lay Religion?" *Religion and Society in T'ang and Sung China*. Eds. Patricia Buckley Ebrey and Peter N. Gregory, 75–113. Honolulu: University of Hawaii Press, 1993.

Lagerwey, John. "The Pilgrimage to Wu-tang Shan." In *Pilgrims and Sacred Sites in China*. Edited by Susan Naquin and Chun-fang Yu. Berkeley: University of California Press, 1992.

Liu Kwang-Ching, and Richard Sheck, eds. *Heterodoxy in Late Imperial China*. Honolulu: University of Hawaii Press, 2004.

Mather, Richard B. "K'ou Ch'ien-chih and the Taoist Theocracy at the Northern Wei Court, 421–451." *Facets of Taoism*. Eds. Holmes Welch and Anna Seidel, 103–122. New Haven, CT: Yale University Press, 1979.

Naquin, Susan. *Millenarian Rebellion in China: The Eight Trigrams Uprising of 1813*. New Haven, CT: Yale University Press, 1976.

Naquin, Susan. *Shantung Rebellion: The Wang Lun Uprising of 1774*. New Haven, CT: Yale University Press, 1981.

Naquin, Susan, and Chün-fang Yü. *Pilgrims and Sacred Sites in China*. Berkeley: University of California Press, 1992.

Perry, Elizabeth J. *Rebels and Revolutionaries in North China, 1845–1945*. Palo Alto, CA: Stanford University Press, 1980.

Seaman, Gary. *Journey to the North: An Ethnohistorical Analysis and Annotated Translation of the Chinese Folk Novel Pei-yu-chi*. Berkeley: University of California Press, 1987.

Shahar Meir, and Robert Weller, eds. *Unruly Gods: Divinity and Society in China*. Honolulu: University of Hawaii Press, 1996.

Shahar Meir. *The Shaolin Monastery: History, Religion, and the Chinese Martial Arts*. Honolulu: University of Hawaii Press, 2008.

Shahar Meir. "Diamond Body: The Origins of Invulnerability in the Chinese Martial Arts." *Perfect Bodies: Sports, Medicine and Immortality.* Ed. Vivienne Lo. London: British Museum, 2012.

Shelach, G. "The Qiang and the Question of Human Sacrifice in the Late Shang Period," *Asian Perspectives.* 35.1 (1996): 1–26.

Shih, Vincent Y. C. (Shi Youzhong). *The Taiping Ideology: Its Sources, Interpretations, and Influences.* Seattle: University of Washington Press, 1972.

Strickmann, Michel. *Mantras et mandarins: le Buddhism Tantrique en Chine.* Paris: Gallimard, 1996.

ter Haar, Barend J. *The White Lotus Teachings in Chinese Religious History.* Leiden, Netherlands: Brill, 1992.

Weinstein, Stanley. *Buddhism under the T'ang.* Cambridge, UK: Cambridge University Press, 1987.

Wile, Douglas. *Lost T'ai-chi Classics from the Late Ch'ing Dynasty.* Albany: State University of New York Press, 1996.

Wile, Douglas. *T'ai-chi's Ancestors: The Making of an Internal Art.* New City, NY: Sweet Ch'i Press, 1999.

Zheng Acai. "Lun Dunhuang xieben 'Longxing si Pishamen Tianwang lingyan ji' yu Tang Wudai de Pishamen xinyang" ("On the Dunhuang Manuscript 'The Divine Efficacy of the Longxing Temple's Heavenly King Vaiśravaṇa' and the Vaiśravaṇa Cult of the Tang and Five Dynasties Period"). *Zhong'guo Tang dai wenhua xueshu yantaohui lunwen ji, di san jie.* Taipei: Zhong'guo Tang dai xuehui, 1997.

Contributors

Gideon Aran is professor of sociology and anthropology at the Hebrew University, Jerusalem, specializing in religious and political extremism. His forthcoming book is *The Cult of Dismembered Limbs: Suicide Terrorism, Radical Religion, Contemporary Judaism, Body, Death and the Middle East Conflict.*

Veena Das is Krieger-Eisenhower Professor of Anthropology and professor of humanities at the Johns Hopkins University. She is the author of *Structure and Cognition: Aspects of Hindu Caste and Ritual; Critical Events: An Anthropological Perspective on Contemporary India; Life and Words: Violence and the Descent into the Ordinary;* and *Affliction: Health, Disease, Poverty.* She is coauthor of *Four Lectures on Ethics* and is editor and coeditor of several books on themes of social suffering, violence, and the relation between philosophy and anthropology.

Ron E. Hassner is an associate professor of political science at the University of California, Berkeley. He is the author of *War on Sacred Grounds* (2009) and *Religion on the Battlefield* (2016), editor of *Religion in the Military Worldwide* (2013), and coeditor of *International Relations and Religion* (2016), as well as the author of multiple articles on religion and conflict.

Michael Jerryson is associate professor of religious studies at Youngstown State University. He is the author of *Mongolian Buddhism: The Rise and Fall of the Sangha* (2008), *Buddhist Fury: Religion and Violence in Southern Thailand* (2011), coeditor with Mark Juergensmeyer of *Buddhist Warfare* (2010), and editor of *The Oxford Handbook of Contemporary Buddhism* (2016). He also co-edits the *Journal of Religion and Violence.*

Mark Juergensmeyer is professor of sociology and global studies, Kundan Kaur Kapany Chair of Global and Sikh Studies, and fellow and founding director of the Orfalea Center for Global and International Studies at the University of California, Santa Barbara. He is author or editor of over twenty books, including *Terror in the Mind of God: The Global Rise of Religious Violence* and *God in the Tumult of the Global Square*.

Margo Kitts is professor of humanities and coordinator of religious studies and east-west classical studies at Hawai'i Pacific University in Honolulu. She is the author of *Sanctified Violence in Homeric Society* (2005, 2011) and over thirty articles on Homer, the ancient Near East, ritual, and violence. She is coeditor of *State, Power, and Violence* (vol. 3 of *Ritual Dynamics and the Science of Ritual*, 2010) and, with Mark Juergensmeyer, *Princeton Readings in Religion and Violence* (2011). She co-edits the *Journal of Religion and Violence*.

Bruce B. Lawrence is Marcus Family Professor of the Humanities Emeritus, professor of Islamic studies, and inaugural director of the Duke Islamic Studies Center. On the faculty at Duke University since 1971, he has won several fellowships and authored or coauthored, edited or coedited, and translated or cotranslated eighteen books, including *Messages to the World: The Statements of Osama bin Laden* (2005) and *The Qur'an: A Biography* (2007).

Cynthia Keppley Mahmood is Frank Moore Chair of Anthropology and professor of anthropology at Central College in Iowa. She is the author of *Fighting for Faith and Nation: Dialogues with Sikh Militants* (1996), *The Guru's Gift: Exploring Gender Equality with Sikh Women in North America* (2000, with Stacy Brady), *A Sea of Orange: Writings on the Sikhs and India* (2002), *One More Voice: Perspectives on South Asia* (2012), and many academic articles on the anthropology of religion and conflict in South Asia.

Meir Shahar is professor of Chinese studies at Tel Aviv University. He is the author and editor of several books, including *The Shaolin Monastery: History, Religion, and the Chinese Martial Arts*; *Crazy Ji: Chinese Religion and Popular Literature*; and *Oedipal God: The Chinese Nezha and His Indian Origins*.

Lloyd Steffen is professor of religious studies, university chaplain and director of both the Lehigh Prison Project and the Center for Dialogue, Ethics and Spirituality at Lehigh University in Bethlehem, Pennsylvania. He is a religion and ethics scholar whose books include *Ethics and Experience: Moral Theory from Just War to Abortion*; *Holy War, Just War:*

Exploring the Moral Meaning of Religious Violence; and, with Dennis Cooley, *The Ethics of Death: Religious and Philosophical Perspectives in Dialogue.*

Andrew J. Strathern and Pamela J. Stewart (Strathern) are a husband-and-wife research team at the Department of Anthropology at the University of Pittsburgh, as Andrew W. Mellon Professor and senior research associate, respectively. They are coauthors and coeditors of over forty-five books and more than two hundred articles, including their coauthored books *Violence* (2002), *Witchcraft, Sorcery, Rumors and Gossip* (2004), and *Peace-making and the Imagination* (2011).

Nathalie Wlodarczyk is vice president and a research scholar for Information Handling Services (IHS), a global economics organization. She has taught contemporary security issues at both King's College London and the School of Oriental and African Studies. Nathalie has a PhD in war studies from Kings College London and a BSc and MSc from the London School of Economics in international relations. She is the author of *Magic and Warfare: Appearance and Reality in Contemporary African Conflict and Beyond.*

Index